CCAR Journal
The Reform Jewish Quarterly

Sacred Teaching and Spiritual Learning

Contents

FROM THE EDITOR
At the Gates — בשערים 1

ARTICLES
Introduction to This Issue by the Guest Editors 3
Sandy Eisenberg Sasso and Michael Shire

SECTION ONE: THE STATE OF JEWISH SPIRITUAL EDUCATION
Beyond Romanticism: Having Something Spiritual
    to Say 9
Lawrence A. Hoffman

The Middle Realm, the Creative Process, and
    the Creator in Religious Education 21
Jerome W. Berryman

A Transformational Model for Jewish Education 41
Rami Shapiro

SECTION TWO: CHILDREN'S JEWISH SPIRITUAL EDUCATION
Avirah Ruchanit—Creating a "Spiritual Atmosphere"
    for Jewish Teens 57
Moshe Ben-Lev

Good Grief: Helping Jewish Children Live with Death 74
Jennifer Gubitz

Choose Life: Identifying and Addressing the Spiritual
    Needs of B'nei Mitzvah Students and Families 89
Goldie Milgram

An Experiment in Spiritual Education: Teacher as
Researcher, Student as Theologian 104
Joel Mosbacher and Wendy Grinberg

Practices that Nurture Young Jewish Children's
Spiritual Development 116
Deborah Schein

"I Knew That Within Me There Was God"—Teaching
Spiritual Awareness to Children 134
Amy Scheinerman

SECTION THREE: JEWISH SPIRITUAL GUIDANCE AND FORMATION
The Quest for Meaning: Insights on Nurturing Adult
Spiritual Development 150
Roberta Louis Goodman

Jewish Spiritual Direction: Developing a Vocabulary
for the Experiences of Our Inner Lives. 164
Jacob J. Staub

The Practice of Teaching Jewish Spirituality: Some
Lessons I Have Learned 176
Sheila Peltz Weinberg

SECTION FOUR: THE ARTS AND JEWISH SPIRITUALITY
(Re)Learning L'Hitpaleil: The Performance of Prayer as
Spiritual Education. 190
Tamar Heather Havilio

Jewish Early Adolescent Spirituality 207
Micah Lapidus

Storytelling and Spirituality: Sacred and Shared
between Generations 220
Peninnah Schram

POETRY ON THE THEME OF THE SYMPOSIUM
She Said Yes. 235
Barbara AB Symons

Akiva 236
Joseph Black

Hide and Seek 238
Brad L. Bloom

CONTENTS

Morning Prayer **239**
Tamara Cohen

Astronauts. **241**
Judy Katz

At the Gates — בשׁערים

Many rabbis have influenced and helped me, both before and after ordination. But three men (as it turns out) were indispensible to my becoming a rabbi, each in his own specific way: Norman Hirsch, Richard Levy, and Lennard Thal. Along with Laura Geller, Lisa Edwards, the late Carole Meyers, and others, they taught me, directly and indirectly, that being a rabbi is holy work in which spiritual awareness plays an important role.

Thus I responded with enthusiasm when Michael Shire proposed to the *Journal* editorial board the topic of this symposium issue. With Marcus Burstein, two years ago Michael guest-edited "Finding our Path: Becoming a Rabbi After Ordination," and colleagues continue to refer back to that issue. A teacher of rabbis and scholar of Jewish Education, Michael invited Sandy Eisenberg Sasso, a pioneer in the field of children's spirituality, to join him in conceptualizing and actualizing what became "Sacred Teaching and Spiritual Learning."

Working with Michael and Sandy on this issue has special resonance because it's my final one as *Journal* editor. When it arrives in my mailbox months hence, I will open it as one among other CCAR members. The past five years have gone by in a flash, even while being filled with new learning and relationships. I am grateful to Jonathan Stein and Steve Fox for their confidence, as well as their help during the early and some later periods of my tenure.

I am also grateful to Hara Person, whom we are most fortunate to have as director of the CCAR Press, and whom I have sometimes referred to as my "boss." Hara's ability to see the large and small pictures simultaneously, to know when to be honest and when diplomatic, complement her skill and good taste in rabbinic as well as publishing matters. I could not have gotten through the steep learning curve period without her, and she has continued to advise me all along. My thanks also go to Debbie Smilow and Ortal Bensky of the CCAR office.

Further gratitude goes out to our partners in the publication process that brings the *CCAR Journal* to its readers: our typesetter Publishing Synthesis and our copy editor Mike Isralewitz.

Deborah Constantine and Otto Barz of PS and Mike stand at the top of my list of cyberspace good friends. While they are professionals compensated for their work, Deborah and Mike go well beyond contractual terms to make our publication look good and read well. Mike has become my model of what it means to avoid a *rosh katan*: he feels responsible to the overall project and the people involved, and so continually goes beyond the call of duty.

And finally, I am grateful to those colleagues who've served as guest editors of symposium issues and on the editorial board during my tenure. Book Review Editor Larry Edwards and Poetry Editor Adam Fisher have been pleasures to work with, full of energetic responsiveness and creativity. To their ranks as section editors was added Dan Polish, who helped conceptualize the new *Maayanot* (Primary Sources) rubric and continues to develop it. I will restrain myself from listing the twenty-five current and past board members, who have given of themselves as reviewers and collaborators in deliberation. I believe deeply in rotating leadership, a lesson learned years ago from Richard Levy in the context of a faculty discussion group. In the context of the CCAR and the *Journal,* such leadership means that editorial board members rotate off after one or two terms—and that one editor is succeeded by the next to produce a strong, multi-link chain.

Providing the next link in this *shalshelet* is our colleague, the new editor, Paul Golomb. Paul continued on the editorial board when I took the reins, and he rejoined the board recently. He's published in the *Journal* and elsewhere while serving in a range of rabbinic settings. It's been a pleasure implementing an orderly transition with Paul, ensuring that planned issues move along and authors don't fall through the cracks. Because of the long lead-time for each issue, by the time you read these words, Paul will have been functioning as editor for some months. Hopefully he's enjoying the wide range of responsibilities; I'm sure he's enjoying the opportunity to connect with colleagues and serve the Reform Movement.

I would be remiss to conclude without thanking my supportive, loving family. Most affected and supportive of all has been my beloved husband, John Antignas. May he and I share God's bounty, for which we are most grateful, well into the future. And may the *Reform Jewish Quarterly* be there with, and even beyond us, flourishing and contributing.

Susan Laemmle, Outgoing Editor

Introduction to This Issue by the Guest Editors

Sandy Eisenberg Sasso and Michael Shire

This issue of the *CCAR Journal*, entitled "Sacred Teaching and Spiritual Learning," and part of the Spring 2014 issue are devoted to examining ways in which Jewish educators and clergy see their teaching role as holy work and encourage spiritual awareness among young people and adults. This symposium responds to the following questions:

1. In what ways can we provide Jewish spiritual education to children and adults?
2. What is the impact of teaching for spiritual awareness? Why is it important?
3. How can we prepare educators to view Jewish education as holy work?
4. What do we know about children's spirituality? What does Jewish tradition have to teach? What can we learn from other spiritual traditions about transmitting spiritual practice in an authentically Jewish mode?

RABBI SANDY EISENBERG SASSO (RRC74) holds an MA from Temple University, a D.Min. from Christian Theological Seminary (CTS), and honorary doctorates from a number of institutions including RRC in 1999 and HUC in 2013. She has Emerita status at Congregation Beth-El Zedeck in Indianapolis, where she was senior rabbi from1977-2013. Sandy is director of the Religion, Spirituality and the Arts Initiative at Butler University and CTS. She has written award-winning children's books and essays on nurturing the spiritual imagination of children, as well a book for adults, *Midrash: Reading the Bible with Questions Marks*. She is among the editors of *Nurturing Child and Adolescent Spirituality: Perspectives from the World's Religious Traditions*.

RABBI DR. MICHAEL J. SHIRE (LBC96) holds an MARE from HUC-NY and a Ph.D. from HUC-LA96, and was awarded an honorary doctorate from HUC in 2008. He is dean and professor of Jewish Education at the Shoolman Graduate School of Jewish Education at Hebrew College in Newton Centre, Massachusetts. Michael has written widely on Nuturing the Spirit of the Child in Jewish Education, including "Spirituality: The Spiritual Child and Jewish Childhood" in the *International Handbook of Jewish Education,* Springer 2011.

5. What are the different ways of introducing children or adults to traditional and nontraditional modes of spiritual practice in ritual, prayer, or the performance of mitzvot?
6. How can Jewish spiritual practice be an integral component of the goals for Jewish education?

Along with our contributors, we as guest editors ask the question what would Jewish education look like if it had at its heart a Jewish spiritual pedagogy, if it cared as much for enriching souls as it did for expanding knowledge, if it offered not only ritual practices but purpose to our hands, feet, and speech? What is it we are seeking to achieve in Jewish education? Do we believe that spirituality is innate and needs to be nurtured or that it is something that must be explicitly taught? Do we currently look for ways to deepen Jewish practice, to go beyond performance to the experience and meaning underlying it? Do we seek to create religious individuals, open Jewish minds, touch Jewish souls, and foster communities of holiness?

Many Jewish religious educators are not just looking for new programming but a transformation of Jewish education. We want to explicitly address sacred teaching and spiritual learning as an integral part of our vocation. We want a new generation to have deep religious experiences, to struggle with life's essential and enduring questions of meaning and purpose, to recognize what it might mean to encounter the presence of the Divine. How do we educate for this religious awareness?

Jewish education in the post–enlightenment age has been mainly about constructing the "Educated Jew." In the nineteenth century, that meant a Jew tutored in Western Civilization in order to become integrated into modern society, to be enlightened.

In the last generation, constructing the "Educated Jew" has come to mean something else: a Jew educated in his/her own forgotten heritage, reaffirming or discovering his/her Jewish identity among a series of postmodern identities and engaging with a tradition and text and community that has been neglected.[1]

Is Jewish education now ready to make another paradigm shift? As we struggle with a sense of the purposes of teaching Torah in its widest sense, we may ask: What is the ideal outcome of attending Jewish schools and synagogues, camps and youth programming, early childhood and adult classes? Is it to solely affirm an identity, develop cultural literacy, construct lenses to view the outside world, develop skills for Jewish living, build pride and joy in being part of Israel—people, land, and destiny?

Something is missing here. For years, books about God were put aside for fear there was not enough time to transmit the vast body of Jewish knowledge. The larger questions about our purpose in life, what happens when we die, and why life is unfair were postponed until a child could demonstrate proficiency in Hebrew, rituals, and liturgy. Yet research shows that we are all born with an innate spirituality; what we lack is a language to express it. Jewish education needs to discover how to provide that language and to honor the spiritual yearnings of the soul. How can we be sensitive and aware of our spiritual searching? How do we understand the process of our religious growth? How do we educate for spirituality and religiosity, and find approaches to learning that foster the qualities of being *tamim* (wholehearted) that integrates explicit and implicit connections to God,[2] the sacred, personal faith, and community holiness?

In his article in this issue, Larry Hoffman diagnoses the problem: "The underlying cause of this conversational lacuna is our Jewish prejudice against 'God-talk.' Single-mindedly committed to the world of science, Jews feel self-conscious discussing matters of the spirit. Believing that linguistic statements must correspond to empirical reality, we balk at theological conversation that operates according to other criteria of meaningfulness."

A new paradigm of Jewish education needs to address questions of meaning and probes these issues of the spirit. Bahya Ibn Pakuda (eleventh century) was open to understanding his quest for a wholehearted Judaism when he described the *Duties of the Heart*[3] as the primacy of Jewish growing and learning. At its core, learning about and from a religious tradition is for all who seek a way to be more fully human, more fully faithful to a vision of the good life. As Professor Art Green has written, "It is striving for the presence of God and fashioning a life of holiness appropriate to such striving"[4] that defines a spirituality in Judaism. Knowledge of Torah and the performance of mitzvot may bring a sense of accomplishment, but it cannot refresh the soul, deepen sensitivity to life, or help us see reverence in our daily life.

Professor Eugene Borowitz, in a seminal article published in *Religious Education* in 1980, writes that we need to find a way to take people "Beyond Immanence" to balance their religious devotion with a sense of the transcendence in their lives.[5] As an early advocate of a pietistic Reform Judaism, he proposes three ways that educators might foster this spiritual quest: through the tradition of marking moments in time with the recitation of *b'rachot*, through the powerful meanings expressed in Psalms, and through verbal and nonverbal expressions of our spiritual and religious yearnings. A quarter of a century later, we have yet to find compelling ways to use these rich traditional tools in Jewish education to inculcate spiritual awakening and build a Jewish spiritual practice for our young.

In regard to the fourth child at the seder who does not know how to ask, Mordecai Kaplan reminds us that it is the parents' responsibility to teach the child to ask: "That is the sum and substance of education. Its main purpose would be to educate people to ask the right questions about the world and themselves."[6] He writes how even some higher education provides a "kind of intellectual suntan," when what is needed is the kind of education that gives birth to wonder.

Jewish education needs to grapple with what it means not only to teach the mind but to nurture the soul, to help us grow as human beings and to understand the nature of the holiness in childhood. What does the very nature of childhood have to say about the seemingly natural and quintessential human-Divine encounter— the nature of play, laughter, spontaneity, and wonderment that is so richly a part of childhood? Even as Jewish education began to recognize the spiritual needs of adults, it ignored children, falsely believing that God and the sacred could only be encountered at an age where abstract language was fully formed. Without providing stories, experiences, and conversations about the holy, individuals came to assume that Jewish learning was only about facts, information, and skills.

In *The Chosen*, Chaim Potok highlights one of the major purposes of a Jewish education when he laments the sole brilliance of his son: "I went away and cried to the Master of the Universe, 'What have you done to me? A mind like this I need for a son? A heart I need for a son, a soul I need for a son, compassion I want from my son, righteousness, mercy, strength to suffer, not a mind without a soul!'"[7]

The articles in this symposium encompass a wide variety of attempts to grapple with these crucial questions for Jewish education.

Our call for papers elicited twenty-two strong and substantial submissions, which turned out to be too much material for one issue. Thus we have divided the articles into five sections, with the fifth section slated to appear in the Spring 2014 issue.

This issue contains:

Section 1: The State of Jewish Spiritual Education
The authors in this section help define Jewish spiritual education and discuss its possibilities for transforming Jewish life and learning. (Lawrence Hoffman, Jerome Berryman, Rami Shapiro)

Section 2: Children's Jewish Spiritual Education
These articles uniquely demonstrate innovative practice in the work of Jewish spiritual education with children. (Moshe Ben-Lev, Jennifer Gubitz, Goldie Milgram, Joel Mosbacher and Wendy Grinberg, Deborah Schein, Amy Scheinerman)

Section 3: Jewish Spiritual Guidance and Formation
In this section, practitioners and educators describe the work of Jewish spiritual guidance and formation across the Jewish community. (Roberta Goodman, Jacob Staub, Sheila Peltz Weinberg)

Section 4: The Arts and Jewish Spirituality
This section explores the use of the expressive arts as ways to open up new dimensions of a spiritually motivated Jewish education. (Tamar Havillo, Micah Lapidus, Peninnah Schram)

The Spring 2014 issue will contain Section 5: Nurturing the Sacred in Individuals and Community: Engaging Prayer and Theology
Its articles focus on engaging and teaching prayer and theology as a means to form and nurture God's presence in the lives of individuals and communities. Those articles are by Mike Comins, Jeffrey Goldwasser, Arthur Green, Saul Kaiserman (with Daniel Reiser, Lisa Kingston, and Hannah Goldstein), Rex Perlmeter, Marcia Plumb, and Seymour Rossel.

We have been blessed by the wonderful and creative contributions of our fellow educators and clergy, including the Rev. Jerome Berryman, whose pioneering work in spirituality and children and the theology of childhood has influenced our thinking about Jewish spiritual pedagogy. We hope that this symposium represents the beginning of sustained and deliberative development of a religious and spiritual Jewish education.

Notes

1. Michael A. Meyer, "Reflections on the Educated Jew from the Perspective of Reform Judaism," in *Visions of Jewish Education*, ed. Seymour Fox, Israel Scheffler, and Daniel Marom (Cambridge: Cambridge University Press, 2003), 149–61.
2. Bahya Ibn Pakuda (eleventh century) calls for a spiritual integration of the duties of the limbs and duties of the heart to a state termed *tamim*. Michael Rosenak, *z"l* in his *Commandments and Concerns* (JPS, 1980) also refers to an explicit and implicit religion to which religious education needs to integrate.
3. Bahya Ibn Pakuda, *Duties of the Heart* (Jerusalem and New York: Feldheim Publishers, 1978).
4. Arthur Green, ed., *Jewish Spirituality* (New York: Crossroad Books, 1987), intro.
5. Eugene B. Borowitz, "Beyond Immanence," *Religious Education* 75, no. 4 (1980): 387–408.
6. Mordecai Kaplan, *Not So Random Thoughts* (New York: Reconstructionist Press, 1966), 53.
7. Chaim Potok, *The Chosen* (New York: Simon and Schuster, 1967), 264.

Section One: The State of Jewish Spiritual Education

Beyond Romanticism: Having Something Spiritual to Say

Lawrence A. Hoffman

Education for spirituality depends on what we mean by spirituality, a relatively new word in the Jewish pantheon of worries. What
exactly is it, or, better put (for my purposes here), what sort of thing
are we looking for? By and large, we treat spirituality as something
that is experiential, rather than cognitive. But experience is transi-
tory, hard to guarantee, and apt to seem chimerical if we have no
conceptual way to frame the experience after the fact. This essay is
a contribution to the cognitive framework within which we think
about and discuss the spiritual experiences we have.

Whether great movies, rewarding books, street demonstrations,
or beautiful sunrises, it is human nature to want to discuss what
we experience. Our models of conversation come from elsewhere,
however—not from the experiences themselves, which are mute,
and even (we say) apt to leave us speechless. So we borrow ways of
talking about them from the education we have received at home,
from friends, and from the schools we attend. Jews, however, are
apt to report, that to the extent their parents and synagogue school
have discussed Judaism , they have left spirituality out.

As adults, we further our conversational capacity with friendship circles, but Jewish conversations are usually about Israel, current events, or synagogue politics, not spirituality, and whatever
non-Jewish friends have to say on the subject probably comes
clothed in equally non-Jewish language. A further resource is

RABBI LAWRENCE A. HOFFMAN, Ph.D. (NY69), author or editor of some three
dozen books and a two-time winner of the National Jewish Book Award, serves
on the faculty of HUC-JIR and is cofounder of Synagogue 3000—Next *Dor*. He
consults with synagogues and lectures widely across North America.

op-ed columns, entertainment critics, book reviews, and so on, but the sources Jews read rarely traffic in spirituality. Of late, the Institute for Jewish Spirituality has experimented with appropriate language, but its model is just one of many, and, in any event, as a community, we have a very long way to go before we internalize that (or any other) spiritual vocabulary into the repertoire of things we easily talk about.

Several decades ago Roman Catholic liturgical experimenters went from parish to parish asking people if they could name instances of God's presence in their lives. They pretty much all could. When I try the same experiment in congregations, I discover that Jews pretty much all can't. When I change the request to ask for instances of the profound in people's lives, Jews have no trouble responding positively. And when I ask them to delineate their instances of the profound, they replicate almost precisely what Roman Catholics call God's presence. It is not the experience but the language of God that eludes them.

Pause for a moment to consider the irony here. Jews are nothing if not longtime masters of the word. How often have we reveled in the notion that God created the world through speech and that we who are made in God's image are masters of speech as well? Didn't our medieval philosophers label us *m'daber*, the species that speaks? Don't we begin and end the *Amidah* with petitions to "open our lips that we may speak God's praise," and to "guard our tongues against speaking evil"? What other culture thinks that slanderous speech is a capital offense? How many Jews are novelists, playwrights, screenwriters, marketers, executives, and speech writers; yet when it comes to matters of the sacred, we lapse into silence.

Alternatively, we reduce the sacred to something less than what it is. Take creation, revelation, and redemption—the usual triad of concepts that we have inherited from the nineteenth century and that we sometimes call the key theological determinants of Judaism. For most Jews, "Creation" becomes science without the awe of the scientist. "Revelation" elicits critical judgments upon texts that have political origins but no spiritual consequences. "Redemption" is the historical accident of Jewish continuity but purely a naturalistic phenomenon, devoid of the wonderment that Martin Buber attributed to the Israelites who saw the Red Sea as a miracle.

The underlying cause of this conversational lacuna is our Jewish prejudice against "God talk." Single-mindedly committed to the world of science, Jews feel self-conscious discussing matters of the spirit. Believing that linguistic statements must correspond to empirical reality, we balk at theological conversation that operates according to other criteria of meaningfulness.

But surely the task of education is precisely to teach us how to talk about things. Theological discourse need not contradict science and reason. When it comes to spirituality, we can do more than just have it, encounter it, feel it, or smile knowingly about it; we can further it and deepen it, by having something to say about it.

Our underlying metaphor of "spirituality as experience," can be identified as part and parcel of our current fling with romanticism, a point of view that emphasizes "the individual, the subjective, the irrational, the imaginative, the personal, the spontaneous, the emotional, the visionary, and the transcendental"[1]—which is to say, feeling rather than thinking. This romanticism is a convenient justification for our ongoing critique of classical Reform, which is perceived as hierarchical and male-dominated: hence, overly intellectual, judgmental, preachy, and stern. So, down with the mind and up with the heart! Hurray for the boy with the whistle, the oxcart driver who recites the alphabet because he doesn't know the prayers, and all the other revisionist readings of Jewish culture that characterized the Chasidic critique of Lithuanian yeshivot—and that we have accepted as a model for our own rebellion against *Wissenschaft* and the knowledge-based Judaism of our German Reform forebears.

Those forebears were not as bad as we make them out to be, however. To be sure, they strode onto a pulpit in robes, orated from a distance, and trafficked in ideas that had been penned in the solitude of their studies. But they were hardly heartless: Lots of them knew how to pray with the sick, hold the hand of mourners, and speak tenderly not bombastically. Our romantic reaction to those days has led us to throw out the baby with the bath water. Rabbis today give few sermons, spend little time thinking, and risk having little of substance to say.

This anti-intellectual approach draws sustenance from its own implicit metaphor of contemporary life as essentially unhealthy. We work too hard (so we must take care of ourselves); the world is too much with us (so we need retreats into quietude and internality); we all are secretly hurting (so we need wellness for an ailing self); we are lonely (so we need community). Spirituality becomes a set of alternative experiences to our increasingly demented world. Synagogues become therapeutic places of healing, of relationship, and of affirmation, through such offerings as a pastoral presence, yoga, sing-through services, text study in the round, silence retreats, and meditation.

I am in favor of them all, but modernity need not mean deprivation; it can equally be described as giving healthy people the liberty to think big thoughts and design ever more expansive lives. Give up the paradigm of sickness and great ideas become part of the solution, not the problem. Spirituality becomes more than experience. It encompasses also the ideas we empower people to have.

We love Jewish culture and history, ethnic ties of peoplehood, and calls for Jewish continuity. But Jews these days seek justification for Jewish survival, a compelling claim to matter in the world, a convincing set of ideas as to Judaism's profundity. Why indeed should we care about Judaism in the twenty-first century, not to mention the centuries after? These are spiritual matters, which Jews are largely unable to discuss because they transcend empirical demonstration, and we remain fixated on the empirical.

Empirical data are not irrelevant; they are just not the entire story. Spirituality should be likened to metaphysics, but for our time—as described in a classic article by philosopher J. J. C. Smart:

> Examples of metaphysical questions are: How do mind and matter interact? Is the will free? What would it be like if time went backward? Do we see things as they really are or do we only see appearances? . . . I shall make it a definition of a metaphysical question that (1) it has at any rate the appearance of being factual; (2) it is in some way puzzling—we don't quite know how to get clear about the question, how even to set about answering it . . . Perhaps I should add a third criterion for calling a question metaphysical, for normally we are inclined to call a question metaphysical only if it is ideologically significant, that is, that we feel that it matters what the answer is.[2]

Self-evidently, these are examples of questions that plague thoughtful people today as they have for centuries. We Jews, who have overwhelmingly gone to college and who read widely about almost anything and everything, are perfectly capable of experiencing the intellectual thrill of speculating on them. But consider, now, the subclass of metaphysical questions that involve religion in general and Judaism in particular: the nature of God, the justification for Jewish particularism; what Reform Jews have called "the mission of Israel"; life after death; the nature of injustice; the purpose of life. To judge by the reticence we Jews feel about speaking up on such issues, it would seem that when metaphysics becomes religion, we very quickly resign from the conversation.

Two years ago, Steven Cohen and I undertook a survey of Jewish spirituality. We asked people if they thought much about God, whether they wished they had mentors with whom to discuss spiritual matters, if they liked thinking about life after death, and so forth—all matters that figured prominently in established scales of spirituality in sociological literature. As we expected, Jewish respondents scored significantly lower than Christians, but largely because the language of God and of spirituality was foreign to them.

There was a differential, however, between generational responses. On all five scales, Jews of lower age scored higher than their elders.[3] More significantly we subdivided these younger Jewish respondents into three categories; Orthodox, children of two born-Jewish parents, and children of fewer than two born-Jewish parents (one or both were not born as Jews). The second category (having two born-Jewish parents) scored low, akin to their elders. The third category (just one born-Jewish parent—or none at all) scored higher, as did Orthodox respondents, who scored the highest.

The failure of non-Orthodox older Jews to score higher is directly related to the discomfort they feel with conversation on spiritual yearnings. The same is true of children with two born-Jewish parents. By contrast, younger Jews who have not been cloistered in ghettoized situations, who opt for intermarriage with little hesitation, and who see the world in universal terms, are more likely to be at home in the general culture's use of language. They are more open to questions of spiritual experience and the possibility of God in their lives. This is not to say that they have any kind of sophisticated Jewish notion of what that God might be—indeed, Jewish society and culture are unlikely to have given them any adult discussion on the subject at all.

Can Jewish education engage inquiring adult minds in responsible metaphysical inquiry from the Jewish point of view? Can we supplement our usual hand-holding and healing with the excitement of thinking differently about "God, the universe, and all that?" Think of religion as the meeting point of three grand ideas about the universe: theology (the doctrine of God), anthropology (the doctrine of human nature), and cosmology (the doctrine of what's out there altogether). Is God real? Is there some kind of "moreness" to the world, a guiding spirit of some sort, or at least, an abiding presence? Are people trustworthy? Is life worth living? Is the world perfectible? Is it even good to have been born into it? These are metaphysical questions that have too long been missing from the Jewish conversation. And they are spiritual to their core.

Suppose we define Judaism as a conversation—a rolling conversation through the centuries about itself, ever willing to discuss the evolving nature of reality in all its fullness rather than to shrink it to the arbitrary boundaries of the safe and sure. The world is what it is: We cannot change that. But we can decide how we approach it. Consider, for example, these two conflicting interpretations of what is worth talking about, both of them by Jews, and by very smart Jews at that: in one case, philosopher A. J. Ayer; in the other, Rabbi Joseph B. Soloveitchik (the Rov).

Alfred Jules Ayer (1910–1989) was the son of a Dutch Jewish mother and a Swiss Calvinist father who had been secretary to one of the British Rothschilds—a man who became Ayer's godfather. The family lived for a time in St. John's Woods, an area in London known by the old-moneyed establishment as being somewhat undesirable, principally because it was "fairly popular with wealthy Jews."[4] Ayer was thoroughly assimilated.

At age eighteen, the young Freddie (as he was known) came across Bertrand Russell's *Skeptical Essays* and was taken by the claim that "it is undesirable to believe a proposition when there is no ground whatever for supposing it true."[5] In short order, Ayer's devotion to philosophy made him a primary advocate for the British school of logical positivism, a position represented originally in Europe by a coterie of philosophers who held science to be the sole arbiter of truth. In 1919, a pamphlet had announced the formation of a "Vienna Circle" composed of thinkers dedicated to the logical positivist program. Of the fourteen original names associated with the Circle it is significant that eight were Jewish or of Jewish descent.[6] Ayer's voice joined theirs from across the Channel, reaching international prominence after 1936 with his *Language, Truth and Logic*, which argued the proposition that the only statements that can be true or false are those that appeal to empirical evidence. It followed that statements regarding ethics, aesthetics, and theology are meaningless. To declare something morally right or artistically excellent is simply "to express feeling about certain objects, but not to make any assertion about them."[7] The same is true of theology: "To say that God exists is to make a metaphysical utterance which cannot be either true or false."[8]

Ayer and his fellow positivists were in revolt against the confusion of metaphysics with science—which really is a dubious procedure. But as I have said, metaphysics unconfused with science need not be bad. If spirituality is metaphysics, it need not, on that account, be science; but even if it is not science, it need not, on that account, be less than real.

More on that later, but for now, we should return to the curious fact that the Vienna Circle with which Ayer was in such sympathy was so largely Jewish. There were other Jewish fellow travelers as well: Karl Popper for example (1902–1994), who reformulated the criterion of verifiability that grounded logical positivism's definition of meaning. My point is simply that a goodly number of Jews, then and now, approach the world with the a priori assumption that since science cannot verify the Divine, there can be no Divine; as if the necessary absence of the spiritual were hardwired into reality as part of the very nature of things.

The philosophers of Jewish extraction I cite here as part of the Vienna Circle were quite assimilated, but their default position of seeing the world in starkly empirical terms was typical also of Jews who still identified Jewishly. The same has remained true of America, especially among Jews who hail from Eastern Europe, where Judaism was an ethnicity more than a religion, and where little modern religious sensitivity crept into the Jewish religious establishment. If Eastern European Jews built synagogues in this new world, it was not necessarily because they had a deep religious sensibility that they wanted to express. They were simply responding to America's demand that everyone be religious in some form or other—a sentiment that dominated post–World War II America during Eisenhower's Cold War years. Two or three generations later, we still face the problem of addressing spirituality in intellectually sophisticated terms with Jews who may never have read A. J. Ayer or heard of the Vienna Circle and Karl Popper, but who, nonetheless, have trouble wrapping their heads around the possibility of a reality that cannot be captured in the scientific method and temperament.

A helpful foil for Ayer's logical positivism is Joseph Soloveit-chik's Halachic Man. My interest is less his justification for halachah, than it is his a priori insistence on seeing the world with a whole lot more in it than what science recognizes as real. It is not that Soloveitchik denies science; indeed, he depends on it. But he brings a nonscientific judgment to bear upon it, the same way, he says, that the mathematician does.

> [Halachic man is like a mathematician] who fashions an ideal world and then uses it for the purpose of establishing a relationship between it and the real world . . . When halachic man comes across a spring bubbling quietly, he already possesses a fixed a priori relationship with this real phenomenon: the complex of laws guarding the halachic construct of a spring: it is fit for the immersion of a zav (a man with a discharge); it may serve as mei chatat (waters of expiation); it purifies with flowing water; it does not require a fixed quantity of forty se'ahs . . . When halachic man chances upon mighty mountains he utilizes the measurements which determine a private domain (reshut hayachid): a sloping mound that attains a height of ten handbreadths within a distance of four cubits. When he sees trees, plants, and animals, he classifies them according to their species and genera . . . He investigates the matter of the nurturing of trees and plants: the relative importance of the branches vis-à-vis the roots. He approaches existential space with an a priori yardstick, with fixed laws and principles.[9]

What differentiates Ayer and Soloveitchik is not their respective scientific judgment of the world that they encounter but what they wish to do with that world upon encountering it. It is what we do with reality that matters, says John Dewey, who defines a "concept" as "nothing more than a set of operations; the concepts are synonymous with the corresponding set of operations."[10] We should ask, then, what Ayer and Soloveitchik wished to do with reality, and how their respective concepts served their respective ends.

It is not that Ayer had no judgments of ethics and aesthetics, and even of religion. He denied God, admired Dutch art, and applauded Andre Malraux for the role he played in liberating Toulouse from Nazi occupation. But these were matters of personal predilection. He was also a notorious womanizer, of whom one of his girlfriends, Dee Wells, said, "Some men played golf; Freddie played women."[11] He was, by all observers, something of a hedonist, dedicated to his work, however, and to his country during World War II. His philosophy allows for ethical and aesthetic judgments but only as personal matters of preference. Soloveitchik arrives at the world already committed to the proposition that a commanding force lies behind it. He is unable to encounter the world without the brand of divine mathematics that he calls halachah.

Spirituality is like halachah, in that (following Dewey) it is a conceptual framework that permits us to perform certain operations upon the world. It is not any single thing, then, so much as it is the name we give to a set of life-enhancing judgments we wish to make and the ideas we might apply to reality in order to arrive at those judgments. Insofar as spiritual education is conceptual rather than experiential, it is the evocation of categories of thought with which to encounter bubbly springs, mountains, plants and trees, and so on. It is an extra-empirical system that permits the imagination needed (as William Blake so memorably put it), "To see a World in a Grain of Sand / And a Heaven in a Wild Flower / Hold Infinity in the palm of your hand / And Eternity in an hour."

My point so far is that Jews seem almost congenitally unable to do all of this, the reason being that they are still enthralled by the philosophy of A. J. Ayer and the Vienna Circle—even though they may never have encountered that philosophy directly and despite the fact that, in any event, its extreme empiricism has been discredited for some time now.

The major force for discrediting it was yet another sometime Jew, Ludwig Wittgenstein. His grandfather had not just been baptized, but had also taken on the middle name "Christian," and instructed his children that they were never to marry other Jews. Grandson Ludwig had been born in Germany but through a tortuous route ended up in Cambridge as a younger contemporary of Bertrand Russell. His earliest work (*Tractatus Logico-Philosophicus*), written in the trenches of World War I (while fighting on the German side of things), made him a celebrated proponent of logical positivism, in that, following positivist principles, he undertook to determine the nature of everything that might legitimately be said about reality. Anticipating Ayer's *Language, Truth and Logic* by fifteen years (the *Tractatus* was published in 1921, and translated into English the year after), he claimed, "It is impossible for there to be propositions about ethics. Propositions can express nothing that is higher."[12] The same could be said of aesthetics and religion.

But even as he was concluding his masterpiece, judged as one of the classics of the twentieth century, he was having misgivings—not about the veracity of his analysis but about its ultimate value. He remained convinced that "the correct method of philosophy would really be to say . . . nothing except what can be said, i.e., propositions of natural science."[13] But he concluded with the now-famous observation:

My propositions serve as elucidations in the following way: anyone who understands me eventually recognizes them as nonsensical, when he has used them—as steps—to climb up beyond them. (He must, so to speak, throw away the ladder after he has climbed up it.) He must transcend these propositions, and then he will see the world aright.[14]

Wittgenstein was himself in search of the spiritual. Despite his recognition that technically one could say nothing nonscientific about reality, he judged the sum total of those statements to fall seriously short of the things that make life worthwhile in the long run. "There are indeed things that cannot be put into words," he averred. "They make themselves manifest. They are what is mystical."[15] In his later philosophy, Wittgenstein returned to an exploration of the things that technically could not be said, but that people say anyway, wondering how it is that people do, in fact, make judgments of ethics, aesthetics, and religion—which is to say, how they reasonably and properly discuss the mystical.

The details need not consume us but the principle should. Dewey had seen concepts as operational means to achieve ends; now Wittgenstein concluded that language is a set of tools from which we select certain kinds of utterances depending on what we want to achieve. Spiritual statements, then, do not so much describe scientific reality as they perform operations upon that reality in much the same way that halachah does. A statement like, "God is present" has validity, although not quite the same way as the similar statement, "my neighbor is present." The latter is scientifically demonstrable while the former is not. But for millions of people whose lives are enriched by descriptions of God, it is surely absurd to describe their conversations, as Ayer would have it, as meaningless.

Franz Rosenzweig is famous for labeling his theology "the new thinking."[16] What I have in mind is similar, but better described as "new talking." The question is not simply what and how we think, but how we get to thinking properly in the first place. Rosenzweig was getting at it himself, when he defined the new thinking as relational—the act of thinking out loud, so to speak, with someone else in the conversation. It is what happens in dialogue with someone else.[17] More recently, Richard Rorty has contended that we make progress in thinking not by arguing better but by talking differently. It all comes down to conversation: the willingness to try out new sentences by talking differently, which, I maintain, is exactly what Jews are unwilling to do, insofar as spirituality is concerned. Still operating in the old philosophical paradigm of logical positivism, whereby the sum total of all that is must be constrained by empirical evidence, they are unwilling to speak new sentences that might accomplish new ends.

Dewey had just such mental blinders in mind when he labeled his 1929 Gifford lectures, *The Quest for Certainty*, by which he meant the faulty "spectator theory of knowledge," the old Greek idea that knowing is like "what was supposed to take place in the act of vision."[18] By contrast, he urged us on to operational knowledge, which he thought a better explanation of what true scientists do. Rarely content to watch and wait in the hope that random data will turn up patterns worth observing, scientists manipulate the world so as to get a controlled glimpse of it. "We perform various acts with a view to establishing a new relationship" with whatever it is we want to know. That is the very essence of a scientifically controlled laboratory experiment. Sometimes the data are not amenable to such control—as in "astronomy, for example, [when] we cannot introduce variation into remote heavenly bodies." But then, "we can deliberately alter the conditions under which we observe them."[19] Jews who deny spirituality on the grounds that they are not scientific have a very limited view of science. The issue is hardly how the world operates or the physical laws which are indeed a matter of scientific investigation. The issue is the relationship we establish in advance between ourselves and the data in question: the conditions, that is, under which we observe them. By conditions, I mean as well our conditions internally—what we are prepared to say and to find out about the very phenomena that are also describable empirically but not only empirically.

Spirituality is what's left when we throw away Wittgenstein's ladder; it is what cannot be spoken of in scientific sentences but what people talk about anyway. It is thinking differently in Rosenzweig's sense, thinking, that is, by speaking differently, by trying out new sentences that may find resonance within us as we contemplate the relationship between what we say and the deeper aspects of what it is that we experience.

Notes

1. *Merriam Webster's Encyclopedia of Literature* (Springfield, MA: Merriam Webster, 1995), s.v. "Romanticism," 964.
2. J. J. C. Smart, "Metaphysics, Logic and Theology," in *New Essays in Philosophical Theology*, ed. Anthony Flew and Alasdair MacIntyre (New York: Macmillan, 1955), 15, 17.
3. The relative numbers according to age group: Spiritual Inclination scale—14 (over age 65), 21 (ages 35–60), and 28 (under age 35); Spiritual Mentorship scale—19, 22, and 28; Involvement with God Scale—32, 36, and 42; Religion and Prayer Scale—19, 22, 27; Spiritual Experience Scale—20, 22, 25.
4. Ben Rogers, *A Life of A. J. Ayer* (London: Vintage Books, 2000), 9.
5. Ibid, 45.
6. Steven Beller, *Vienna and the Jews 1867–1938* (Cambridge and New York: Cambridge University Press, 1989), 16.
7. A. J. Ayer, *Language, Truth and Logic*, rev. ed. (New York: Dover, 1946), 108.
8. Ibid., 115.
9. Rabbi Joseph B. Soloveitchik, *Halakhic Man* (Philadelphia: JPS, 1983), 19–21.
10. John Dewey, *The Quest for Certainty* (New York: Paragon Books, 1929), 111 (italics his).
11. Rogers, *A.J. Ayer*, 247.
12. Ludwig Wittgenstein, *Tractatus Logico-Philosophicus* (London: Routledge and Kegan Paul, 1922), #6.42.
13. Ibid., 6.53.
14. Ibid., 6.54.
15. Ibid., 6.522.
16. Franz Rosenzweig, "The New Thinking," in *Philosophical and Theological Writings*, ed. Paul W. Franks and Michael Morgan (Indianapolis: Hackett, 2000), 109–39.
17. See discussion in Hilary Putnam, *Jewish Philosophy as a Guide to Life* (Bloomington: Indiana University Press, 2008), 31–33.
18. Dewey, *Quest for Certainty*, 22, 23.
19. Ibid, 84, 87.

The Middle Realm, the Creative Process, and the Creator in Religious Education

Jerome W. Berryman

Religious education involves learning a particular language system with its connotations and traditions. It teaches for fluency in speaking and living, so *how* religious language is learned is as important as *what* is learned. This article proposes that if children are invited into the middle realm to learn religious language, which involves being fully present and being in relationship rather than merely talking or thinking *about* it, they are likely to develop a kind of playful orthodoxy, which deeply roots them in their tradition and yet allows them to be open and flexible. This is because the language becomes associated with the creative process, which flows out of the middle realm.

Both theologians and those who study evolution agree that creativity is a primary characteristic of humankind. It is one of the main reasons why our relatively weak species has survived, but it also makes us one of the most dangerous creatures on earth. Given this situation and its dangers, how are we to proceed with religious education to help keep our species *constructively* creative in the "image and likeness" of the Creator?

The middle realm has much to do with answering this question, because it affects how religious language is learned. Seven analogies will be used to indirectly understand the middle realm and to understand how creativity originates. The creative process will then be discussed by describing its structure of five steps. Finally, we will discuss how the unity of the creative process divides into

REV. JEROME W. BERRYMAN has spent close to forty years creating a methodology, constructed of pedagogy and supported by a theology, known the world over as Godly Play. He has written numerous articles and books. Discover more of the educational theory of Godly Play in volume 1 of *The Complete Guide to Godly Play* and *Teaching Godly Play*.

psychological, social, biological, and spiritual dimensions as children develop. These dimensions acquire their own vocabularies and research traditions, but religious education and practice can help support and help reunify the middle realm in a conscious and non-naive way in adults. When the four dimensions of the creative process are reunified in people they become constructively creative, like the Creator, and the goal of religious education is accomplished.

The Unconscious Unity of the Middle Realm

The middle realm is like a room with seven windows. If we enter the room with children we can know it from the inside but this knowledge is difficult to articulate. It is neither subjective nor objective, so when it is consciously analyzed it disappears. Still, it is important to have a sense of what this realm is like to guide religious education. An example of an approach to religious education that values the middle realm is Godly Play,[1] which has provided the experience upon which this article is based.

Godly Play helps children cope with the existential pressure at their boundaries by inviting them to enter classical theological language with their senses, intelligence, and contemplative silence as they move the artifacts of Godly Play lessons to explore the art of making existential meaning. This indirect approach allows them to use their own creative process to cooperate with the Creator and the community of children to bring their ultimate limits within their awareness without being overwhelmed and to move towards becoming creative people in whom flow, play, love, and contemplation provide the central core in which their relationship with the Creator and other creatures can flourish.

The Psychiatry Window: Winnicott's "Transitional Space"

The first window we will look through is the work of Donald W. Winnicott (1896–1971), an English pediatrician and psychiatrist, who summarized his thoughts about "transitional space" in his last book *Playing and Reality* in 1971. Transitional space is where infants cannot yet distinguish between "me" and "not me." It is where spontaneity rules and children are not yet required to be compliant or assertive. Winnicott thought that transitional phenomena stay with us at some level into adulthood. He wrote:

This intermediate area of experience, unchallenged in respect of its belonging to inner or external (shared) reality, constitutes the greater part of the infant's experience, and throughout life is retained in the intense experiencing that belongs to the arts and to religion and to imaginative living, and to creative scientific work.[2]

Adults experience living in three realms, like children. There is the outside and the inside, but there is also an intermediate area of experiencing to which our inner and external lives contribute but which is different from either. It is a resting place in the vague awareness that all three realities are important and real but for the moment there is no urgency to choose which to dwell in.

Winnicott also noticed that objects sometimes take on the characteristics of this "intermediate area of experience." He called them "transitional objects," because young children are not asked to choose whether they are objective or subjective. Baby blankets, a thumb, and even unexpected realities, like a bit of wool, are charged with a sense of being part of the child and yet remaining other than the child. They live unchallenged in an intermediate world of inner and outer, self and other, and being alive yet not quite alive.

The energy of transitional objects sometimes lingers into adulthood, as Winnicott suggested. Linus, a character in the cartoon strip *Peanuts* by Charles Schulz, carried his baby blanket everywhere. When Lucy challenged him about what he was going to do with it when he grew up, he told her patiently that he planned to have it made into a sport coat. Most adults have a few special things and memories of childhood that remain strangely alive to them as adults.

Winnicott went further. He viewed therapy as serious play in the transitional space between the patient and the therapist. When the qualities of transitional space and play are absent in the relationship, the therapy is likely to be unsuccessful, because the energy, creativity, mutuality, and safety needed for clients to change are drained out of the relationship. Understanding Winnicott's transitional space can help us grasp the importance of the middle realm in religious education, because they are similar, but the middle realm cannot be reduced to transitional space.

The Semi-Sleep Window: The Hypnagogic State

The second window for viewing the middle realm is the analogy of the hypnagogic state between waking and sleeping. This has been interesting to people as different as Aristotle, Swedenborg, and Edgar Allan Poe. Alfred Maury gave this state of mind its English name in 1848, but its study has continued to the present. In 1987 Andreas Mavromatis published *Hypnagogia: The Unique State Between Wakefulness and Sleep*. About 70 percent of adults have experienced this fluid state of mind where connections blend in unusual ways.

Herbert Silberer, briefly a member of Freud's group in Vienna, called cognition in this state "autosymbolism." He wrote a paper in 1909, admired by Freud and based on self-analysis, in which he argued that during this state, one experiences *images* of thought. A famous example was the experience of August Kekule (1829–1896), a German organic chemist. He saw molecules forming into snakes while he dozed by the fire. The snakes put their tails in their mouths. When he was fully awake he worked out the chemical structure of the benzene ring, based on this image. The hypnagogic state is important for understanding how religious language is experienced as images absorbed by children, but it is not the same as the middle realm, which is both broader and deeper. Still there are suggestive parallels. In Godly Play, the calm, slow, deliberate movements of the presentations and the peacefulness of the storyteller help children relax in a kind of hypnagogic state.

The Window of Wholeness

The middle realm evokes the whole person, which might be depicted as three concentric circles, each with its own kind of knowing. We are born into the largest circle, which connects infants and young children to the expansiveness of the Creator and yet intensely draws them to parts of the whole, such as a tiny pebble or flower. Both remarkable abilities, which to adult reason look like an odd juxtaposition, involve the knowing of the spirit by contemplation.

Maria Montessori compared children's power of attention, so often missed by busy adults,[3] to the intensity of mystics contemplating the Creator. She based her educational approach on this deep spirituality and considered children's love of learning to be part of their spirituality rather than their spirituality being something to be learned about.[4]

The boundless circle of children's spiritual awareness includes a smaller, more defined circle, which involves the knowing of the body by the senses. This is where young children first sense pleasure and pain, but their sensory discrimination rapidly becomes more refined as they grow older. Montessori created a number of materials—such as finely graded color tablets, bottles containing different scents, and bells for matching sounds—to help children fine-tune their body-knowing.

A third and smaller circle, fitting within the first two, involves the knowing of the mind by reason. It develops last and in our culture tends to overwhelm the two larger circles of knowing by its authority and analytical power. This tends to repress them, but they don't simply disappear. Spirit-knowing and body-knowing remain powerful, so sometimes their unacknowledged reality erupts in distorted ways with tragic consequences.

In the middle realm the potential of these three modes of knowing are equally acknowledged and carry equal weight as is evidenced in Godly Play. This is important for learning how to make existential meaning with religious language, because the existential limits to one's being and knowing challenge the whole person's existence, so coping must involve the whole person as well.

The Window of Being

The middle realm is also analogous to the view of "being," as considered by philosophically informed theologians. This tradition considers "the play of being" to involve the One, the self, nature, and other people. The Platonic practice of philosophy influenced this view, which appeared as early as Philo of Alexandria in the first century and later among Christians, especially in Alexandria and North Africa. This interest expanded during the Middle Ages when the Neo-Platonic tradition influenced Jewish, Islamic, and Christian philosophers. It was revived in Italy during the Renaissance, and a contemporary example is the Christian theologian John Macquarrie (1919–2007). His description of being sounds like, but is not the same as, the middle realm:

> We ourselves are, and only through our participation in being can we think of it or name it, and only on the basis of its self-giving and self-disclosing to us can we know it. Thus if we say anything about being, we are also saying something about ourselves. Talk of being, however it may express itself grammatically, is neither subjective nor objective talking, but holds these two together. So

it must be repeated that it is not metaphysical talk, since this tries to take being (or, more likely, the sum or totality of beings) for the *object* of a rational investigation.[5]

The Creator's being, according to Macquarrie, does not refer to a single being, a property, a class of things, a substance, or the totality of all that is. He also distinguished being from becoming, appearance, or the ideal. Talk of being must be limited for the most part to saying what it is not, a kind of *via negativa*. This protects and at the same time points to the Creator's incomparable presence.

An analogy of being, such as one between creatures who create and the Creator who creates, points in the right direction but remains inadequate. This is why Macquarrie argued that the Creator's being must be considered as "letting-be," an action, rather than a status, substance, or matter of logic. This letting-be is the gift of the Creator's self and permeates the middle realm for children to experience as they learn the art of making existential meaning with religious language. Letting-be is what Godly Play attempts to support and participate in, when God is invited to come play the game of discovering how to make existential meaning with children. Unfortunately, this quality also adds to the difficulty of describing or defining the middle realm.

The Window of Art

Art invites us into a boundary state between ordinary and imagined reality to better understand both. If an actor on a stage turns toward the audience and fires a gun, the audience can ponder how this feels, because the experience is safely framed by the stage with its curtains. After leaving the theater, however, if someone points a gun at you in the street it is better to defend yourself.

Art is like the middle realm. An example is *The Velveteen Rabbit*, published in 1922 by Margery Williams. She invited the reader into an imaginary, Victorian nursery to listen while two toys, the Velveteen Rabbit and the Old Skin Horse, discussed the nature of reality:

Real isn't how you are made," said the Skin Horse. "It's a thing that happens to you. When a child loves you for a long, long time, not just to play with, but REALLY loves you, then you become Real."

"Does it hurt?" asked the Rabbit.

"Sometimes," said the Skin Horse, for he was always truthful. "When you are Real you don't mind being hurt."

"Does it happen all at once, like being wound up," he asked, "or bit by bit?"

"It doesn't happen all at once," said the Skin Horse. "You become. It takes a long time. That's why it doesn't happen often to people who break easily, or have sharp edges, or who have to be carefully kept. Generally, by the time you are Real, most of your hair has been loved off, and your eyes drop out and you get loose in the joints and very shabby. But these things don't matter at all, because once you are Real you can't be ugly, except to people who don't understand."[6]

As the story progressed, the Velveteen Rabbit kept a little boy company while he suffered with scarlet fever and then was thrown out with other infected things when the boy got well. The Velveteen Rabbit wiggled out of the bag and hopped away, even though his "coat had worn so thin and threadbare from hugging that it was no longer any protection to him."

It is as if the author turns to the reader at the end of the story with some questions implied by the narrative. Did you experience what it is like to become one of Winnicott's transitional objects? Do you have the courage to be loved into being a real adult by a real child, even if it hurts? Can you imagine yourself "hopping" into a whole new level of reality, like the Velveteen Rabbit did when he became a "real" rabbit? Finally, was the end of the story an indirect way of saying that the Velveteen Rabbit died? Narrative provides an open text for asking such questions. Stories and other kinds of art are integral to learning how to speak religious language and personally become the meaning it guides one towards. Children are better at this than adults, so Godly Play always leaves the invitation to art open.

In the Godly Play room, which is an analogue of the middle realm, the teaching objects, such as those designed for the teaching of narratives from the Hebrew Bible and New Testament, are beautiful and strong but still invite care. The materials and the presentations were worked out with children over many decades, but they still need *to be made* real, like the Old Skin Horse said, by really loving them.

The Window of the Unconscious

The unconscious involves processes that are not open to introspection, yet can have a major impact on behavior. Friedrich Schelling

(1775–1854) coined the term "unconscious" and Coleridge (1772–1834) introduced it to the English-speaking world. Freud, Jung, and others continued to map this largely hidden landscape in the twentieth century, but it has remained difficult to study directly by rigorous empirical methods. Since religious language operates at the unconscious as well as the conscious level, this analogy to the middle realm is also important to consider.

One way to gain access to the unconscious is by hypnosis and trance. These terms conjure up images of "mind control," but that is a mistake. They actually refer to rather ordinary acts such as hearing (chanting, storytelling, murmuring a mantra, drumming, etc.), kinesthetic experience (dance, storytelling with movement, rituals, etc.), sight (visual storytelling, a mandala image, art, beauty, etc.), scent (perfume, pheromones, incense, flowers, etc.), taste (fasting, herbs, tea, etc.), and spiritual practices (centering prayer, yoga, Sufism, walking a labyrinth, pilgrimages, etc.).

Milton Erikson was a gifted and controversial therapist, who was very sensitive to all of the above modes of communication. Andre Muller Weitzenhoffer was a friend of Erikson, but was also a critic. In *The Practice of Hypnotism,* Weitzenhoffer wrote, "Were I to strictly limit this book to a scientifically founded hypnotism, I would have to disregard much of Milton Erikson's post-1960 contributions and, more particularly, most of that which has been referred to as the Eriksonian approach." He went on to caution the reader about the ambiguity in the whole field of scientific hypnotism. The "signs of hypnosis . . . are equivocal and none are unique, single or in combinations."[7]

Still, there was something useful as well as controversial about Erikson's work. His special abilities as a therapist were related to biography. He grew up in a farming family, dyslexic and colorblind. He overcame his dyslexia by training himself to use an autohypnotic trance, but at seventeen he contracted polio and was severely paralyzed. Death seemed the only possible outcome, but he again used self-hypnosis. This time he recalled "body memories" and began to talk and move his arms. He was finally able to walk with a cane and went on to become a psychiatrist. In his fifties he developed post-polio syndrome, so once again he used self-hypnosis to control his pain, but this time he remained confined to a wheelchair. When he died in 1980 at the age of seventy-eight, he left his wife, eight children, and a lasting legacy of healing relationships.

Erikson used hypnosis and trance to remove irrelevant stimuli in communication and to sharpen his awareness of the unconscious in himself and other people. This enabled him to intuit the logic of what was going on unconsciously and respond in like terms, engaging people at the level of their fundamental being and knowing. The middle realm cannot be reduced to hypnotism, trances, or any aspect of Erikson's approach to therapy, but there are intriguing similarities, which can help us pass through the gates of consciousness, when mentoring children, to enter the unconscious, where the Creator is always at play and religious language has a special relevance. What I hoped to do in Godly Play was to slip through the gates of consciousness, straight into the ocean of the unconscious, because that is where the action is and where God truly comes to play.

The Dream Time Window of the Species

We began our indirect approach to understanding the middle realm by discussing Winnicott's transitional space in the development of individual human beings. We close by considering an analogy from the development of our species.

Steven Mithen's *The Prehistory of the Mind* combined archeology, prehistory, and modern cognitive studies to understand the origins of art, religion, and science (tool-making) among humans. Mithen believes that the cause of the creative explosion among the Cro-Magnons in southern Europe some thirty thousand years ago can be understood by investigating the Walpiri of the Central Australian Desert. What is interesting about this approach for our purposes is that Aboriginal art has a kind of indeterminacy, like the art of the Cro-Magnon people. Much is left open for interpretation, which actively involves the onlooker in a state of mind somewhat like the middle realm.

When the Walpiri make circles they refer to "campsites, fires, mountains, waterholes, women's breasts, eggs, fruit and other items. The intended meaning of the circle in any one composition can only be identified by the associated motifs."[8] One needs to take part in the images to get a feel for them and to know something about the context to understand them. Meaning is a function of associations, which operates much like the origin of meaning in the middle realm.

Aboriginal children are supported by their culture to develop their ability for multileveled interpretation. They begin by making naturalistic, univocal images, such as a fish. The literal fish becomes the *outside meaning* and the *inside meaning* develops when the child matures and becomes initiated into the ancestral world when the image of a fish is connected to the Ancestral Beings. The fish becomes "a potent symbol of spiritual transformation of both birth and death." Fish are interesting for children to paint because they swim, are fun to catch, and are good to eat, but they are also, as Mithen says, "good to think."[9] The additional layers of meaning do not replace the literal fish, because Dreamtime and everyday events are one.

Mithen and others have argued that Cro-Magnon people made meaning much like the Australian Aborigines do today. This is reflected in the way they buried their dead, including children, and other religious practices, by the tools they made, and by the art they created. The middle realm is like both Dreamtime and the explosion of creativity among the Cro-Magnons, but it can't be reduced to either. There is always more than can be expressed, because the Creator is involved, which is central to religious education.

The middle realm, then, shares similarities with transitional space, the hypnagogic state, and communication with and by the whole person. It is held together by being, invites one to enter in like art does, is largely unconscious, and is related to the explosion of creativity in our species, which is like Dreamtime. When religious language is learned in such a setting it becomes deeply rooted but also remains open and creative, because it is associated with the creative process to make existential meaning.

The Middle Realm and the Origin of the Creative Process

The indeterminacy and theological mystery of the middle realm stimulate scanning for a way to encompass both, which leads to the development of the creative process in the child. In 1926, Graham Wallas published *The Art of Thought*, which helped begin the modern study of creativity, but he focused on adults after the process was already developed. He argued that the process has four steps: preparation, incubation, illumination, and verification. By 2012, R. Keith Sawyer had published the second edition of *Explaining Creativity: The Science of Innovation*, a much broader study, which includes a comprehensive history of the concept's interpretation.[10] We will use five steps to describe how the creative process feels as it moves in a circle from opening to closing to opening again.

Opening

The creative process opens when one's assumed world is challenged. The indeterminacy that results stimulates the creative process to open in a hard or soft way. A hard opening is when one's world is shattered by a tragic loss such as the death of a loved one. A soft opening results from overflowing richness, such as a beautiful sunset. The wonder that arises from both hard and soft openings sets scanning in motion to find a more adequate worldview in which such events can be accounted for.

Scanning

Scanning transforms wonder into a new worldview. It can take a few minutes or many years. Once scanning begins it moves relentlessly though sometimes unconsciously toward new and more adequate meaning. The search is inevitable, but the insight is not. Frustrations such as internal rigidity, repression, or external factors can block discovery, so sometimes people get stuck in scanning and are unable to move away from the event that prompted the scanning or find the more adequate closure they long for. One of religious education's tasks is to help children open softly, scan, discover existential insights, develop a life based on such discoveries, and find a soft closure that is always ready to open again because of the safety derived from being deeply rooted in one's tradition.

Insight

Insight can be correlated with a burst of brain activity. There is "a spike of gamma-wave rhythm," which is the highest electrical frequency generated by the brain. Insight can be predicted by a steady rhythm of alpha waves, emanating from the right hemisphere about eight seconds before the insight takes place.[11] Neurological maps confirm that we are not "imagining" things when we sense that the creative process is at work or when an insight is about to happen, but they only chart what is felt during the process without commenting on causes.

One of the many interesting things about insights is that they seldom arrive completely formed. An insight might begin as a piece of a picture, a bit of the song, or an odd jumble of words for a poem. Working out what one has discovered involves the fourth step in the process, which is also critical for religious education.

Development

The development of an insight is optimally channeled through one's special interests and capacities, as Howard Gardner's theory of multiple intelligences shows. In 2011 he looked back to 1983 when *Frames of Mind* was first published to bring his theory up to date. "I am sticking to my 8½ intelligences, but I can readily foresee a time when the list could grow, or when the boundaries among the intelligences might be reconfigured."[12] The frames of knowing Gardner recognized in 2011 were: linguistic, musical, logical-mathematical, spatial, bodily-kinesthetic, interpersonal, intrapersonal, and naturalistic. The one-half frame was existential, which acknowledges that some children are drawn toward ultimate questions. People in religious education have long understood that some children have a special sensitivity to such concerns. In Latin there was even a term for such a child, the *puer senex* or old child. Despite some critical queries, the successful use of Gardner's theory in education for over thirty years has established it.

Gardner specifically related his theory of multiple intelligences to creativity in 1993 in his *Creating Minds: An Anatomy of Creativity*.[13] This book provided significant examples for the then seven frames of mind. An insight might be developed in intra-psychic terms like Freud, in mathematical terms like Einstein, in visual art like Picasso, in music like Stravinsky, in words like T. S. Eliot, in dance like Martha Graham, or in social terms like Gandhi. This clearly shows that religious education is not just about words. Mentors need to be attuned to the many ways children make meaning so their insights can be appropriately supported and equally respected.

Closure

The need for closure varies across individuals, situations, and cultures. It might take the form of an emotional conclusion to a difficult life event or involve the mastery of a cultural uncertainty. Simple closures answer questions in the same terms they are asked, but an ultimate question involves being at peace with mystery, which cannot be reduced to a simple solution, and which is a special interest of religious education.

Closure might be hard or soft, like the opening. A hard closure is firm and protective, but a soft closure is relaxed and curious about events that arise to challenge it. Closure is also related to the creator's decision-making style, the will-to-close, and the need to balance the lure of perfection against what is "good enough" to carry one's new idea forward to completion, communication, and usefulness. On the other hand, closure is sometimes *forced against one's will* by internal or social pressures or both. Closure, therefore, is very much part of the whole circle of the creative process and its continuation.

The creative process has a kind of fractal quality. In the same way that a head of cauliflower or a bunch of broccoli has florets and sub-florets the creative process is self-referencing. Each of the smaller parts resembles the whole. Human life from birth to death is the overarching opening, scanning, insight, development, and closure. The scanning at the macro level results in the insight of the creative process itself and the development of the process differentiates into the psychological, social, biological, and spiritual dimensions. Each dimension generates additional discoveries, but the macro closure is for them to be rejoined consciously in a non-naive way. This results in a creature who is pervasively integrated in the Creator's image, which is religious education's goal.

The Conscious Integration of the Middle Realm as Creator

The integration of the creative process in the four dimensions has to do with complexity, but complexity is not the opposite of simplicity. The opposite of simplicity is intricacy, which suggests something involved or perplexing. Integration suggests being closely connected and yet distinct like the creative process is, when it appears in its psychological, social, biological, and spiritual forms as flow, play, love, and contemplation.

The Psychological Dimension of the Creative Process: "Flow"

When the creative process is working smoothly life seems to flow. The study of flow took a leap forward in 1975 when Mihaly Csikszentmihalyi published *Beyond Boredom and Anxiety*. He argued that creativity appears in a middle range of activity between the extremes of tedious rigidity and anxiety-producing chaos.[14] In 1990, he described flow as the optimal experience.[15]

Flow involves concentration so deep that one's sense of self disappears. Time is altered and the experience is enjoyed for itself rather than for any product that might result. When feedback is relatively immediate and the goals are clear, then flow continues as long as one's skills are challenged without being overwhelmed.

People will always seek happiness, Csikszentmihalyi warned in *The Evolving Self*, but when they lack the discipline and knowledge to be creative they will settle for activities that only *simulate* the creative process. Fake flow is "wasteful or destructive, and in such cases, the result of seeking enjoyment is entropy, rather than harmony."[16] Religious education, therefore, needs to challenge children and provide them with skills to support the flow of their existential creativity. One of the most important parts of flow for Godly Play is to affirm what is *personally* new for children. The goal is not for children to create a completely new idea for society to accept, but to create what is new for them, which supports and stimulates their developing creativity. When children discover something for themselves, as the Montessori tradition has long advocated, it is not forgotten. This is why it is so important for children to discover the art of making meaning with classical theological language.

The Social Dimension of the Creative Process: Play

Play overlaps flow. Even Csikszentmihalyi conflated the two at first. The subtitle of his 1975 book about creativity was: *The Experience of Play in Work and Games*. As he gained clarity, however, he energized other students of creativity such as Howard Gardner, who noted in his *Creating Minds* that when Csikszentmihalyi asked him, "Where is creativity?" instead of the usual, "What is creativity?" the scope of his study changed and took on new life, giving the creative process its social dimension.[17] The social "where" of creativity continued to be developed by Csikszentmihalyi[18] and Gardner,[19] who were joined by others, such as Jonah Leher, who emphasized the importance of the composition, style, and environment for creative teams.[20]

Play is always social even when its creativity appears to be solitary. Perhaps, the most radical view of play's social dimension was that of Johan Huizinga, the Dutch historian. He claimed that play defines our species. We are primarily players (*homo ludens*) instead of makers and users of tools (*homo faber*) or reasoning creatures (*homo sapiens*). Huizinga's view of play has often been misunderstood. He argued that play is not an element *within* culture, but that play *is* culture, which is a more challenging idea and links culture inextricably with social creativity.

Garvey wrote that "play is pleasurable," "has no extrinsic goals," "is spontaneous and voluntary," and "involves some active engagement on the part of the player." The fifth quality is that "play has been linked with creativity, problem solving, language learning, the development of social roles, and a number of other cognitive and social phenomena.[21] The social dimension of the creative process has the characteristics of play, which help describe this aspect of religious education and echoes the form of creativity in the other three dimensions.

The Biological Dimension of the Creative Process: Love

The biological dimension of the creative process is found in healing and health, but what could be more biological than "making love," which can result in the *creation* of new life, as well as health! Love, as the key biological manifestation of the creative process, is seldom noticed because: "From the beginning of the twentieth century to its end, influential accounts of love included no biology."[22] In 2000, the authors of *A General Theory of Love* set out to rectify that situation. They observed that people are drawn together by a "limbic resonance," which makes the match while the neocortex makes up reasons why the match is right.[23] The limbic system is where our "emotional intelligence" resides, which developed before the neocortex, so it can override our rationality, which makes an exclusively philosophical view of love inadequate.[24]

Jaak Panksepp and Lucy Biven identified our seven old brain systems as: seeking, rage, fear, lust, care, panic/grief, and play.[25] Only love and lust in their system refer explicitly to love, but all seven affect systems seem to revolve around it. Love is seeking. It moves toward newness, satisfaction, and creativity, but is complicated by the rage associated with competing for scarce resources. Fundamental fear is not learned. It is a basic warning about danger during seeking. Lust is what pushes us toward creating offspring but nonsexual caring for offspring and each other is also part of love. Panic and grief come from the potential or actual loss of care and, finally, play is a way to cope with the conflicts between systems without rage and with care.

The kind of language most appropriate for connecting our thinking and emotions is poetry, because it bridges the neocortex and the limbic system. Robert Frost wrote that a poem "begins as a lump in the throat, a sense of wrong, a homesickness, a love sickness. It is never a thought to begin with."[26] This explains why the poetry of religious language is often important to connect our thinking and emotions about love.

One of the most widely used love poems in Christian celebrations of marriage is that of Paul (I Cor. 13). He wrote that love is freely given and received. It is patient, kind, not jealous, not boastful, not arrogant, and not rude. Love is also deeply engaging. It bears, believes, hopes, and endures all things, so it lasts forever and has no extrinsic goal. That is why jealousy, arrogance, and boasting are not part of its reality. People without love are as empty as their language is. They are like "a noisy gong or a clanging symbol." Love is very important for learning the art of how to use religious language to discover and support human flourishing.

The Spiritual Dimension of the Creative Process: Contemplation

Christian history often traces contemplation back to John Cassian (c. 360–435), but he learned about contemplation from the solitaries and groups of men and women already living in the deserts of Egypt in the fourth century. In 415 he settled near Marseilles in modern France and built the Abbey of St. Victor, whose spiritual practice shaped Christian monastic life to the present. A modern manifestation of this tradition is centering prayer, known from the writings and retreats of the Trappist monk Father Thomas Keating and others. Centering prayer is a blend of ancient traditions and has been practiced widely both inside and outside the cloistered life since the 1970s.

One of the classical Christian definitions of contemplation is that of Richard of St. Victor from the twelfth century. He wrote, "Contemplation is the free more penetrating gaze of a mind suspended with wonder concerning the manifestations of wisdom."[27] The opening with wonder to seek unity with the Creator shares the same basic characteristics as the other three dimensions of the creative process. We often think of the creative process as something people do, but the wordless practice of contemplation shows that the creative process is also something people are.

Csikszentmihalyi's flow, Garvey's play, Paul's love, and Richard's contemplation do not perfectly match, but the differences enrich rather than challenge each other. For example Csikszentmihalyi's description of flow fills in, rather than contradicts the characteristics of love, play, and contemplation. Csikszentmihalyi and Garvey have both added helpful nuances to Richard's "more penetrating gaze of a mind," his "suspension with wonder," and they have extended the meaning of his "manifestations of wisdom." These shared characteristics of the dimensions, therefore, help interpret and enrich each other as well as disclosing the overarching creative process and the mixed individual and specific uses in daily life.

The characteristics of flow, play, love, and contemplation are also related to the structure of the creative process, which was discussed in the second section. The *opening* is connected to the giftedness and voluntary aspect of the four dimensions. You cannot compel someone to enjoy flow, to play, to love, or to contemplate. *Scanning* is linked to the deep engagement and searching quality in all four dimensions. *Insight* is associated ironically with engaging this process for itself with little thought of any product that might result. One cannot force insights. *Development* connects flow, play, love, and contemplation to specific problems. *Closure* brings satisfaction and enables the discovery to be communicated in order to be effective.

The potential is always present for the four major dimensions of the creative process to be renewed and integrated in a non-naive way by the flow of creative energy. Many people have moments when flow, play, love, and contemplation come together, but this integration can also become a stable way of life. When this stability and integration is communicated to children as they learn religious language, mostly in nonverbal ways, and associate it with the creative process, then it is most likely to be of help to support the journey in community toward a mature spirituality, based on the Creator's self-disclosure.

Conclusion: The Foundation for Religious Education

The middle realm is a state of consciousness that is open and indeterminate. It is the source for the creative process, and contributes to integrating the whole person by the integration of its flowing, playing, loving, and contemplating. The indeterminacy allows the parties in the relationship to meet in the middle in a space that belongs to neither but is open to both. The wonder and openness of the middle realm provides the place for the creative process to spring from, and eventually to have the potential to re-integrate the unity we were born with.

As the creative process develops in the different dimensions of life, religious education contributes to re-integrating the whole person by religious language and creative community. The integration of flow, play, love, and contemplation not only discloses and supports the image of the Creator in the child but also enables the likeness of the Creator to flourish in adults and contributes to the constructive creativity needed by the whole human community and our planet.

Notes

1. Godly Play® is a well-developed approach to children's religious education. It was created by Jerome and Thea Berryman and has been in development since 1960. Many kinds of supporting publications are available, but the primary text to investigate its method is: Jerome W. Berryman, *Teaching Godly Play: How to Mentor the Spiritual Development of Children* (Denver: Morehouse Education Resources, 2009). An overview of the literature and spiral curriculum for Godly Play may be found in: Jerome W. Berryman, *The Complete Guide to Godly Play,* vol. 8 (Denver: Morehouse Education Resources, 2012), 156–69.
2. D. W. Winnicott, *Playing and Reality* (London: Tavistock Publications, 1985), 14.
3. Maria Montessori, *The Montessori Method* (New York: Schocken Books, 1964), 172–73.
4. Maria Montessori, *The Secret of Childhood* (Notre Dame, IN: Fides Publishers, Inc., Dome Edition, 1970), 140. The connection between Montessori and Godly Play is a major theme in Jerome W. Berryman, *The Spiritual Guidance of Children: The Montessori Tradition and Godly Play* (Harrisburg, PA: Morehouse Publishing, 2013).
5. John Macquarrie, *Principles of Christian Theology,* 2nd ed. (New York: Scribner & Sons, 1977), 106.
6. Margery Williams, *The Velveteen Rabbit, or, How Toys Become Real* (New York: Random House, 1986), 14–15.
7. Andre Muller Weitzenhoffer, *The Practice of Hypnotism,* 2nd ed. (New York: John Wiley & Sons, 2000), 97, 224 .

8. Steven Mithen, *The Prehistory of the Mind: The Cognitive Origins of Art, Religion, and Science* (London: Phoenix Paperback, 1998), 179.

9. Ibid.

10. R. Keith Sawyer, *Explaining Creativity: The Science of Innovation*, 2nd ed. (Oxford: Oxford University Press, 2012), 15–34.

11. Jonah Lehrer, *Imagine: How Creativity Works* (New York: Houghton Mifflin Harcourt, 2012), 17, 139.

12. Howard Gardner, *Frames of Mind: The Theory of Multiple Intelligences* (New York: Basic Books, 2011), xxi.

13. Howard Gardner, *Creating Minds: An Anatomy of Creativity Seen Through the Lives of Freud, Einstein, Picasso, Stravinsky, Eliot, Graham, and Gandhi* (New York: Basic Books, 1993), xiii–xiv, 37.

14. Mihaly Csikszentmihalyi, *Beyond Boredom and Anxiety: The Experience of Play in Work and Games* (San Francisco: Jossey-Bass Publishers, 1975), 35–54.

15. Mihaly Csikszentmihalyi, *Flow: The Psychology of Optimal Experience* (New York: Harper Perennial, 1990), 43–70.

16. Mihaly Csikszentmihalyi, *The Evolving Self: A Psychology for the Third Millennium* (New York: Harper Perennial, 1993), 197–99.

17. Gardner, *Creating Minds*, 37.

18. Mihaly Csikszentmihalyi, *Creativity: Flow and the Psychology of Discovery and Invention* (New York: HarperCollins, 1996).

19. For Csikszentmihalyi one center of the creative process is the "the domain." It is where "a set of symbolic rules and procedures" reside. In Gardner's terminology this is "the work" and includes the relevant symbol system of the domain in which the creative individual is working.

   A second center is "the field," which for Csikszentmihalyi includes "all the individuals who act as gatekeepers to the domain." For Gardner this part of the creative process is called "other persons" and includes family and peers in the early years but later expands to rivals, judges, and supporters. Gardner, *Creating Minds*, 9. An idea, which is personally novel, becomes socially significant through the interaction of individuals, domains, and fields. Ibid., 36.

   The third center of activity is "the person," who works in a particular domain (or sets up a new domain) and moves beyond personal creativity into being creative socially when the field accepts the new idea. Csikszentmihalyi, *Creativity*, 27–28. Gardner noted that a creative person "solves problems, fashions products, or defines new questions in a domain in a way that is initially considered novel but that ultimately becomes accepted in a particular cultural setting." Gardner, *Creating Minds*, 35.

20. Jonah Lehrer, *Imagine: How Creativity Works* (New York: Houghton Mifflin Harcourt, 2012), 139–74.

21. Catherine Garvey, *Play: The Developing Child*, 2nd ed. (Cambridge: Harvard University Press, 1990), 5.

22. Thomas Lewis, Fari Amini, and Richard Lannon, *A General Theory of Love* (New York: Random House, 2000), 6.

23. Ibid., 63.

24. Daniel Goleman, *Emotional Intelligence* (New York: Bantam, 2005), 80–83.

25. Jaak Panksepp and Lucy Biven, *The Archeology of the Mind: Neuro-evolutionary Origins of Human Emotions* (New York: W. W. Norton and Company, 2012), 32–38.

26. Quoted without a source in Lewis, Amini, and Lannon, *General Theory*, 34. The source is a letter from Robert Frost to Louis Untermeyer (January 1, 1916).

27. Richard of St. Victor, *The Twelve Patriarchs; The Mystical Ark; Book Three of the Trinity*, trans. Grover A. Zinn (New York: Paulist Press, 1979), 157.

A Transformational Model for Jewish Education

Rami Shapiro

What to Expect from This Essay

The intent of this essay is to kick-start a conversation on a radical redesign of Jewish education: what it is, what it does, and how it is delivered. To accomplish this I begin by defining my terms. In and of themselves, words like "God," "Torah," and "Israel," and phrases like "sacred teaching" and "spiritual learning" tell us nothing and function as mere buzzwords pretending to content they do not have. You need not agree with my definitions, of course, but they form the basis of my argument. This essay is a compass needle pointing us toward transformation and not a map leading us to it. What I offer here is an achievable vision of Jewish education that can be rolled out fairly quickly and that can provide us with quality learning for decades to come.

General Definitions

The following definitions are intentionally broad. My goal is to provide us with a framework in which to reimagine just what Judaism and Jewish life can be in the twenty-first century. If you feel the need to fill holes in the definitions that follow, shovel away.

Judaism is the Jewish people's ancient and on-going efforts on behalf of *t'shuvah* and *tikkun*, returning to our true nature as *tzelem Elohim* (Gen. 1:26; understood as vehicles for godliness) and transforming the world through justice and compassion in fulfillment of our mission to be a blessing to all the families of the earth, human and otherwise (Gen. 12:3).

God is indefinable, but the Names of God found in our tradition give us the following sense of the Divine: God is *Ein Sof,* the

RABBI RAMI SHAPIRO, Ph.D. (C81) is an award-winning author, poet, essayist, and educator whose poems and essays have been anthologized in over a dozen volumes, and whose prayers are used in prayer books around the world.

unmanifest infinite from which and in which the finite emerges; *YHVH/Ehyeh-asher-Ehyeh*, the manifest finite arising from and in *Ein Sof* as a wave arises from and in an ocean; *Elohim*, the creative birthing and dying of finite reality in the divine sea of infinite possibility; and *Anochi*, the singular, infinite, nondual, and indefinable consciousness that is God, nature, man, and woman.

T'shuvah is turning from *mochin d'katnut* (narrow mind) to *mochin d'gadlut* (spacious mind), and thereby achieving *behirut*, clear insight into the unity of woman, man, nature, and God that leads naturally to a life of *tikkun*.

Tikkun is engaging the world in a way that promotes universal justice, compassion, and dignity for all life forms rooted in the realization of the unity of all life, in and as the One who is all life.

Torah, both written and oral, is the collective teachings of the Jewish people regarding life, its origins, its meaning, its purpose, and how best to live it. Torah is a human document that contains both timeless wisdom and time-bound bias. As liberal Jews we affirm the former and set aside the latter. Following Hillel, we see Torah's essential message as promoting justice and compassion ("What is hateful to you, do not do to another" [*Shabbat* 31a]), and we reject as false all interpretations that lead to the contrary.

A *Jew* is a person who identifies as a Jew, who makes Jewish culture her primary vehicle for celebration and meaning, who practices *t'shuvah* and *tikkun*, and adopts or adapts mitzvot, the cultural artifacts of Jewish life, as her central means for doing so.

"Sacred Teaching" and "Spiritual Learning"

Nothing is sacred in and of itself, but only becomes sacred when a community deems it to be so. Take *sefer Torah* for example. Why do we stand when the Ark is opened? Why do we march the Torah scroll through the congregation and invite people to touch and kiss her? We don't do this with other religious books such as the New Testament, Koran, or Bhagavad Gita. Indeed, we don't demonstrate this kind of reverence when a copy of Gunther Plaut's *The Torah: A Modern Commentary* is carried into the shul.

We stand for *sefer Torah* not because of Torah herself but because we have labeled this particular expression of Torah—this handwritten scroll—as sacred, and we honor the sacred by standing. It is the meaning we attach to Torah and not the scroll itself that matters."Sacred" means nothing outside the sociological parameters of the group decision as to what is and what is not sacred.

The notion of "sacred teaching," therefore, means teaching that which the community holds sacred. Defining just what that is would be a rich and fruitful task on the part of different Jewish communities—clergy, educators, and laity alike—but well outside the scope of this essay. For the purpose of this essay, the Jewishly sacred is any Jewish ritual object, mitzvah/action, or Torah/teaching that merits the additional label "spiritual."

This, of course, begs the question: What is spiritual? Simply put, something is spiritual if it has the potential to shift people from *mochin d'katnut* to *mochin d'gadlut*.

Mochin d'katnut is that level of consciousness associated with self and at times selfishness. It is close to the "I" of Martin Buber's I-It, the "I" that sees the world and everything in it as a means to one's personal ends. The world of I-It is consumptive, obsessed with the commodification of all morals, values, and actions, and devoted to the zero-sum ideal where winners take all, justice is retributive, and success is defined by how much money you have and how much power you wield.

Mochin d'gadlut is that level of consciousness similar to the "I" of Martin Buber's I-Thou, the "I" that sees itself a part of rather than apart from God, the Greater Reality that embraces and transcends the natural world. The world of I-Thou is collaborative, with values rooted in human freedom rather than the "free market," and committed to building a non–zero sum society founded on cooperation, distributive justice, and compassion for all life, human and otherwise.

While both I-It and I-Thou are natural and necessary to the healthy functioning of both individuals and societies ("If I am not for myself, who will be for me? If I am only for myself, what am I? [*Pirkei Avot* 1:14]) we live in a time and place where *mochin d'gadlut* and a nonzero I-Thou world are viewed with suspicion if not distain. The military–industrial–financial–media complex, having captured and turned politics, patriotism, and mainstream religion to its own ends, promotes an I-It agenda that seeks to erase reason, science, spirituality, and I-Thou sensibility from both the public and private spheres.

Challenging this agenda by promoting and training people to make the shift from *mochin d'katnut* to *mochin d'gadlut* should be the task of Judaism. To the extent that we make this the heart of our Judaism and central to our efforts at Jewish education, we make

Judaism relevant, revolutionary, and intrinsically compelling to millions of people, Jew and Gentile alike, who are looking for a prophetic and deeply spiritual alternative to a commoditized market-driven religion in league with a no less commoditized market-driven civilization.

If "sacred teaching" is teaching the tools of making this shift from *mochin d'katnut* to *mochin d'gadlut*, then "spiritual learning" is the internalization of these tools in such a way as to actually achieve the shift. "Spiritual learning" is transformative, but contemporary Jewish education is rarely so.

Transmission or Transformation: The School as Museum

Judaism is an ancient civilization, and like all ancient civilizations it has produced lots of artifacts. Any serious attempt to educate Jews in Judaism requires a basic understanding of these artifacts. But learning about ancient Jewish artifacts doesn't translate into living spiritually rich Jewish lives any more than digging up human remains from the Pleistocene period makes one a Neanderthal.

Jewish educators do a fine job, and in many cases an excellent job, with regard to transmitting knowledge about the artifacts of Jewish life. Where we fail is teaching our students to use these artifacts in a spiritual way: that is in a way that will lead to *t'shuvah* and *tikkun*. There are two reasons for this. First, far too many of our leaders and educators fail to live spiritually transformative lives themselves. If our teachers are not engaged in using Jewish artifacts to shift from *mochin d'katnut* to *mochin d'gadlut*, we cannot expect them to pass this knowledge on to their students. Second, given the penchant for artifacts as artifacts rather than as catalysts for transformation, we spend most if not all of our classroom time on transmission and leave transformation to others. These others, sad to say, often turn out to be swamis, sheikhs, lamas, roshis, and other spiritual teachers from every religion but Judaism. Having transmitted a dead Judaism, many Jews seek elsewhere for a living transformative spirituality.

In effect we have turned our schools and even our synagogues into museums where the focus is on transmitting information about the artifacts of Jewish life rather than transforming the lives Jews actually live.

What does it mean to be a museum? Take, for example, the Israel Museum in Jerusalem. The museum houses a rich and inspiring collection of Jewish artifacts, religious and secular, representing different stages of Jewish civilization, and different aspects of Jewish life. As the visitor walks through the museum's many galleries she learns about the objects she sees—a variety of *chanukiyot* used by Jews from ancient to modern times or the various fashions of Middle Eastern Jewish couture, to name but two. She gets a feel for how Jews lived throughout our history. And yet none of what she sees or learns is alive. Even if there is an interactive exhibit where, for example, she is invited to dress up as a Yemeni Jewish bride, it is always just that—dress-up, make-believe, pretend. The world she encounters in the museum is not her own, and the artifacts she is shown are mere curiosities and largely irrelevant to her life and how best to live it.

Teachers operating in a transmission-oriented "museum" school are in effect docents. The docent's task is to transmit information about the museum's collection of artifacts in an entertaining and cogent manner, and the training of docents naturally focuses on those artifacts and how best to transmit information about them. A good docent knows a lot and transmits what she knows to her charges. A good visitor learns a lot and comes to appreciate what she knows. Much is transmitted; no one is transformed.

You Are How You Eat: An Example of Transformational Learning

Spirituality is by definition transformative, shifting the learner from *mochin d'katnut* to *mochin d'gadlut*, and in so doing awakening her to the Greater Reality of which she is a part. Jewish spirituality achieves this by adapting the artifacts of the Jewish past to the needs of the Jewish present. The spiritual educator isn't a docent but a rebbe, charged not with transmitting knowledge but with transforming learners. The educator-as-rebbe helps each student become a mensch, and uses the tools of Judaism to do so. Judaism is a means to a greater end, and not an end in itself. To illustrate what I have in mind, let's focus on the teaching of kashrut.

In the transmission model of Reform Jewish education, kashrut is an artifact, a set of laws and rules that one is expected to learn, but not necessary live. In fact, Reform Jews often say that we teach the past only to justify our rejection of the past. Of course, this isn't how we put it, but it is how most of us hear it and live it. Students are taught the origin, laws, ethics, techniques, and politics of kashrut without any expectation or obligation to keep kosher themselves. We say that we have to know what it is we are rejecting, but rejection is still the norm.

And how could it be otherwise? In the late 1990s the Reform rabbinate sought to promote kashrut among the laity. But the kashrut we offered was an artifact from an ancient past completely at odds with the norms by which most Reform Jews live. The people resisted, and the rabbis backed down. Dubbed the Cheeseburger Rebellion, this event is a perfect example of how the transmission model differs from the transformational one.

In the transmission model we bring kashrut-as-artifact out from the musty storeroom of the Jewish museum and ask people to embrace it as it was. In the transformation model, however, the study of kashrut isn't about kashrut itself, but about transforming one's relation with consumption and adapting rather than adopting the principles of kashrut to do so.

In the transformation model of learning, kashrut is defined not as a set of ancient and fixed practices, but as a set of timeless principles calling us to elevate all our consuming to the highest moral, ethical, and environmental values to which we can aspire. Learners are *expected* to keep kosher as a way of living the principle of *tikkun*, a way expanding their sense of compassion for and responsibility to all life. It may not be the kashrut of the Orthodox family down the street, but it is kosher nonetheless, and it is vital that we affirm it as such.

Notice I'm not speaking of eco-kashrut, or Reform kashrut, or liberal kashrut, but simply kashrut. No hedge, no doubt, no hemming and hawing, just a bold affirmation of an authentic Judaism rooted in timeless principles applied to our time without regard to how other Jews act or what other Jews think.

Every time we hesitate in our teaching, every time we wax nostalgic about a halachic lifestyle most of us would never adopt, we delegitimize Reform Judaism and pass on the message that Reform Judaism isn't authentic. We have no need to defame any other Judaism; we must simply take care not to use the standards of another Judaism to measure the authenticity of our own. If it is true that Orthodoxy is the only authentic Judaism, then we should stop promoting a faux Judaism and join an Orthodox shul. If we believe in what we are doing, if we believe that Reform is a vital spiritual path of transformation, then we have no need to look over our shoulders or to keep up with the Soloveitchiks.

In other words, there was nothing wrong with Reform rabbis deciding to renew the standing of kashrut in Reform Judaism in the 1990s. What was wrong was defining kashrut by halachic norms of the 1890s.

What we should have done, and what teachers of a transformational model of Judaism must do, is this: First, identify a real personal or social need, in this case the need to free ourselves from a consumptive lifestyle that defines all people as consumers and reduces all relationships to commodities. Second, show how this issue is something Jews have wrestled with for millennia. Third, explore how Jews have dealt with this in the past. Fourth, extrapolate from the past principles and values that are applicable to changing the situation in the present. Fifth, empower the individual to apply those values to her own life in her own way. And sixth, ground communal solidarity in shared principles rather than shared practices.

Remember, we aren't demanding a behavioral standard per se. We aren't defining what kashrut is, only how it functions spiritually. We are only requiring that our members engage with kashrut as we teach it—a practice calling us to elevate all our consumption to the highest ethical, moral, and environmental standard we can achieve. What anyone's personal kashrut will look like is up to the individual, but the community requires that each individual do the best she can with the principles we hold sacred.

Jew Is a Verb

For thousands of years we Jews have defined ourselves by bloodline: A Jew is a person born of a Jewish mother. In recent decades Reform and Reconstructionist Jews have broadened the role of blood to include people born of a Jewish father but not a Jewish mother. To the latter we added a behavioral component: people claiming Jewish lineage through the father must have been raised as Jews, something not asked of a person born of a Jewish mother. Converts to Judaism are also expected to live as Jews, leaving the definition of what "living as a Jew" means to the rabbis doing the converting, and the community with which the convert chooses to affiliate.

While not abandoning other definitions, the transformational approach to Judaism applies the behavioral element of patrilineal descent and Jew-by-choice to all Jews: A Jew is what a Jew does, and what a Jew does is *t'shuvah* and *tikkun*: strive to shift from *mochin d'katnut* to *mochin d'gadlut* by applying Jewish principles and adapting mitzvot to her life in such a way as to make her living a vehicle for compassion and justice, and a blessing to all the families of the earth.

The transmission model of Jewish learning has no need to define who is a Jew and no need to set standards for being a Jew. It is focused on transmitting facts about the artifacts of Jewish life and need not insist or expect students or teachers to engage with these artifacts outside the classroom.

Again, go back to our Israel Museum example. The Israel Museum is open to everyone, Jew and gentile. Docents need to be well-educated in the Jewish artifacts they are sharing, but being Jewish themselves is irrelevant. The same is true with the transmission model of Jewish education, the school-as-museum. Chances are there are many gentiles attending Jewish schools and many teachers in these schools who aren't Jewish. Even teachers of specifically Jewish subjects need not be Jewish when the material being transmitted is the artifacts of Jewish life rather than the transformative principles of Jewish living.

If spirituality is to mean anything it must mean transforming oneself by moving from narrow to spacious mind. If spirituality is to merit the adjective "Jewish," it must require that one make this transformation using the principles and practices of Jewish life. If this transformational Jewish spirituality is to work within the context of Reform Judaism, it must allow a wide range of creative expression of these principles and practices, a range far beyond what other forms of Judaism may accept. But it cannot abandon the notion of living Jewishly altogether, and the community must prescribe and enforce its own level of spiritual activism.

Am I saying that only Jews can engage in sacred teaching and spiritual learning? No. I'm saying that only those who live the principles of Judaism and use Jewish artifacts to effect spiritual transform from narrow to spacious mind can engage in Jewish sacred teaching and spiritual learning, and we must help all our educators to do so.

Spiritual Learning Requires Spiritual Teachers

If we are going to move from the transmission model to the transformation model of Jewish education, if we are going to focus on sacred teaching and spiritual learning, we will have to train our educators differently. The docent/transmission model will not work in a transformational setting. We will have to teach our teachers to use the artifacts of Judaism as catalysts for the transformation of Jews. And that means a new kind of educational training for our local synagogue teachers that will require them to make the transformation themselves.

The rebbe/transformation model requires our teachers to have a deep understanding of the artifacts of Jewish life, not only how they have been used in the past, but also how they could be adapted for use in the present. They would have to use these artifacts in their own lives, and they would have to continually experiment with and adapt Jewish texts, teachings, and mitzvot to their own lives as they move from *mochin d'katnut* to *mochin d'gadlut*. Without personal experience of transformation through Jewish living, one cannot be a rebbe as I am using the term.

While there are notable exceptions, by and large our clergy and educators are trained within the transmission model of Judaism-as-artifact, synagogue-as-museum, and rabbi, cantor, and educator as docent. Therefore they cannot be expected to make a 180-degree turn toward a transformational model of leadership and education on their own. If there is going to be a spiritual revolution in Reform Jewish life, it isn't going to be a grass-roots effort only and must be driven from the top, in this case by the Schools of Education at HUC-JIR. While HUC-JIR is aware of the problem, and has put the issue of spirituality on its agenda, the focus is still too much on transmission and not enough on transformation.

The reason for this is simple, if painful. Our laity is largely ignorant of the artifacts of Jewish life, let alone how they might be used as catalysts for spiritual transformation, and our clergy are hardly trained in the art of spiritual transformation. While we are taught about prayer, we aren't taught how to pray or how to teach others to pray. While we are taught about God, we aren't taught how to realize God. While we are taught how to lead services and life-cycle events, we aren't taught how to use these to transform the lives of the people we are leading. While we are taught how to sing, we aren't taught how to teach our congregants to use the voice as a vehicle for transformation.

If our educators must become rebbes, our rabbis and cantors must become *baal shem* (shamans), "medicine women" and "medicine men" who can use the medicine of Judaism to heal the shattered spirits of our people. And they cannot do this on their own. Reinventing rabbinic and cantorial education is not the topic of this essay, but we would do a great disservice to our educators if we imagine the problem of Jewish education lies with them alone. It doesn't. If they must change, rabbis and cantors must change as well. And if rabbis and cantors don't change, any change on the part of educators will be shallow and short lived.

Training for Transformation: Let Google Be Google

Sacred teaching and spiritual learning—what I am calling education as transformation rather than transmission—takes time, and, as almost any Jewish educator will tell us, there just isn't enough time left for transformation when all our efforts focus on transmission. The solution, however, isn't to transmit less, but to transmit differently.

As I prepared to write this essay I took a look at the academic catalogs for the Master of Arts in Education at HUC-JIR in New York and Los Angeles. The curriculum is rigorous, deep, and designed to produce the highest-quality docents for the transmission of the artifacts of Jewish life. But docents don't need M.A. degrees, let alone doctorates.

While there are those high-level Jewish educational programs that need people with graduate level degrees in Jewish Education, most of the Jewish educating that goes on around the world doesn't. And even if it did, synagogues couldn't afford to hire people who have earned these degrees, and, even if they could, HUC-JIR couldn't produce them fast enough.

We are doing a phenomenal job producing well-educated graduates who understand both the meta-dimension of learning per se and the artifacts that they are trained to transmit. The problem is that the world for which we are training them is dying, and because it is dying the educational model we are training them for is failing. We are essentially training docents for museums fewer and fewer Jews choose to attend.

Rather than train our high-level educators to be teachers in the classroom, we ought to train them to be educational artists and entrepreneurs in the cloud. Rather than send them out to transmit what they know to hundreds of students, we should send them up (into the cloud) to transmit what they know to millions of students and, just as importantly, to the local teachers who deal with these students on a daily or weekly basis.

Here is my rule of thumb for transformative education: *Let Google Be Google.* Anything our students can learn by running a Google search should be learned by running a Google search. Asking our teachers to be stand-ins for Google is asking the impossible: first, because no one person can possibly know what Google knows; and second, because what people really want to know they can't find on Google and can only discover in deep conversation with teachers and peers, something our teachers are often unprepared to hold, and our classrooms ill-suited to host.

In other words, Google is superior when it comes to transmitting knowledge, but it fails miserably when it comes to discovering meaning and transforming lives. Only teachers can do that, and they can only do that when they aren't forced to play Google instead.

The Role of HUC-JIR: Creating Educational Creatives

If the onus of sacred teaching and spiritual learning falls on local rabbis, cantors, educators, and synagogues, it will fail. If all we are doing is calling forth a new set of buzzwords to banter around synagogue boardrooms in hopes that this will somehow reinvent Jewish education, we are fooling ourselves and failing our communities.

If we want sacred teaching and spiritual learning we will have to create it, promote it, and sustain it from the top. No one else has the resources, financial or educational.

What we need, and what our Schools of Education should be producing, are educational creatives: people who can invent new ways to transmit the artifacts of Jewish life that are challenging, compelling, engaging, and open to anyone with Internet access. What HUC-JIR should be building is our own cloud-based Kahn Academy.

Salman Khan, an MIT and Harvard Business School grad, created the Kahn Academy in 2006 to provide "high quality education to anyone, anywhere." At present the Academy offers over 4,000 eight-to-nine-minute video workshops in dozens of subjects. His vision is that students learn the basics online and then use classroom time to go deeper.

If we are serious about sacred teaching and spiritual learning, we must do the same. Here is what I think must be done:

1. HUC-JIR should establish and fund a task force in transformational Jewish education charged with creating a curriculum for the transformational Jewish classroom complete with standards for both students and teachers.
2. In consultation with rabbis, cantors, and educators around the world, the task force would identify core artifacts of Jewish life (historical, textual, philosophical, etc.) along with core transformational values of Jewish living related to them. Emphasis here is on "core"; we are looking for the bedrock artifacts and values of Jewish living; the minimum every Jew should know and do. We can expand beyond these over time.
3. HUC-JIR would then create its own cloud-based Kahn Academy, call it HUCademy if you will. Linking the best and brightest of our graduate students and faculty with their peers in media (our schools are in New York and Los Angeles for goodness' sake!). HUCademy would produce eight-minute teacher training videos on various facets of each artifact and value, along with a parallel series of eight-minute videos for students of various age groups. These materials would be made available on a subscription basis, and the fees synagogues would pay to access this material would help cover the cost of producing it.
4. Teacher-training webinars with HUC's education professionals would help teachers around the world learn how to use the material in a transformational classroom setting. The HUCademy materials would be the docents, and we use the Internet to train teachers to be the rebbes.
5. As HUCademy proves its worth, HUC-JIR would establish a Department of Transformational Jewish Learning to continually deepen and expand online transmission-based resources as a foundation for transformational work in both synagogue classrooms and synagogue communities at large.
6. In addition to the basic curriculum required by all graduate students in Jewish Education, students majoring in Transformational Jewish Learning would be trained in creative writing, media production, social media, and related areas needed to be producers of cutting-edge Jewish educational materials designed for cloud-based distribution and access.

All of this could be done within three years, and a transformational revolution of Reform Jewish education could be fully underway within five years.

Turn On, Tune In, Transform

This section describes how HUCademy might work in a synagogue classroom setting.

Imagine a teacher wants to explore the history, meaning, and usage of mezuzot. Today, she might spend classroom time studying the relevant texts, looking at different designs of mezuzot over the centuries, and then have her students make their own mezuzot that they would then take home. This is solid activity-based learning. But it isn't transformative.

With the HUCademy all this transmission can be taught in a few eight-minute videos produced by HUC students and faculty, which our learners can watch via the Internet at home with their parents. One video gives the textual roots and historical background of mezuzah. A second shows different mezuzot from different times and places, and ends with contemporary mezuzot created by Jewish artists from around the world. A third video guides students and their parents in making their own mezuzot, offers them a link where they can download the scroll that the mezuzah houses,[1] shows them how to attach mezuzot to real doorposts in their home, and teaches them how to recite the *b'rachah* while doing so. A very brief online quiz whose results are sent via e-mail to the student's local teacher, lets that teacher know the student is doing the assignment and grasping the material.

The assignment given by the teacher is for all students to watch the videos, make and attach their own mezuzot, film themselves making and attaching mezuzot via a smart phone, and share their video with their teacher and classmates (and perhaps their peers around the world) on a classroom blog or Facebook page. This fulfills the transmission element of mezuzah-as-artifact without using a minute of class time.

When students do come to class having already made, affixed, and shared their videos, class time can be used to explore how mezuzot can be used to help make you a mensch in every room of your home.

For example, a mezuzah on the living room doorpost reminds us to make the conversations that happen in that room holy. Asking what that might mean leads naturally to exploring the Jewish principle of *sh'mirat halashon* (avoiding gossip and hurtful speech) and learning to speak compassionately and yet honestly with one another. HUCademy video on right speech could be shared, and the conversation deepened.

We might do the same with the issue of kashrut mentioned earlier. How might we use the principle of kashrut to effect transformation by defining kashrut as lifting our individual and community consuming to our highest moral, ethical, and environmental standards? As always we begin with transmission: What is kashrut? Where did it come from? How has it been understood in the past? Why does it matter in the present? All of these questions can be addressed through HUCademy videos: four questions, four videos of nine minutes duration. In less time than it takes to watch an episode of *Glee*, our students can learn the basics of kashrut. This is transmission; now on to transformation.

Transformation requires action, so imagine our teacher asks her students to make a list of areas of their lives where kashrut might matter. Among others, these four will surely be mentioned: what we eat, what we wear, what our parents' drive, and what gear we own (smartphones, televisions, and other electronic devices). The class is now divided into four teams, with each team focusing on a one area of concern. This will be a multi-week project.

During the first week students are asked to explore the nature of their engagement with their topic. Let me use just one team as our example. Each member of the "food team" is asked to take a close look at one or two foods she or he eats: how it's made, how the workers who make it are treated, how it gets to the supermarket, how healthy it is to consume, how advertising is used to get us to consume it.

If I were on that team, I would look at French fries, and more specifically McDonald's French fries. Within seconds I would find out that raw potatoes are almost fat-free, yet almost half the calories of McDonald's fries comes from fat; fat that must be added to the potato; fat that seems to account for a rise in obesity and all the health problems obesity brings. That doesn't sound all that kosher when I know that kosher means "fit" as in fit for human consumption.

A McDonald's video easily found via Google shows me how McDonald's makes French fries, and I can't help but notice that the potatoes seem quite healthy until the they are bathed in sugar (dextrose), salt, and fat as part of the manufacturing process. Googling on, I discover that adding sugar, salt, and fat to our foods is how the food industry hooks us into eating more and more of what they make. Sugar, salt, and fat are to the food industry what nicotine is to the tobacco industry. Again it just doesn't seem kosher. But I love them! I share what I have learned and the link to the video with my classmates via my smartphone in fulfillment of the first week's assignment. We can't help but comment on each other's discoveries.

During weeks two and three, students are asked to apply the principles of kashrut to their eating. What do I do with my beloved French fries? I decide to abstain from French fries, but not from eating at McDonald's. So I go to McDonald's and, with the help of my parents and smartphone, I explore my options. I film myself tasting the salad and fruit sides, and create a personal diary of how they stack up to the fries. I share my research with my teammates, and solicit their advice on how to go fry-free.

My parents call a friend who is a nutritionist, and she is willing to meet with me to talk about French fries and French fry alternatives. She doesn't know anything about kashrut, but that's fine. I'm making that connection by myself. I film my interview with the nutritionist and share it with my teammates along with clips from videos she suggests I watch online. Again I invite feedback.

In preparation for their fourth Sunday class, the teacher asks her students to compile a short documentary, one from each team, showing what each team did. On the fourth Sunday, the videos are shown and discussed as a lead-in to the bigger discussion: How will I live a kosher life? Not *will* I live a kosher life, but *how*. The expectation is on Judaism as the art of living one's principles not just holding them. So how will I live my understanding of kashrut?

Drawing from the experiences of each team, students are asked to prepare and share their own kosher plan, and are then asked to live by that plan for the next few weeks, keeping the class up to date on their progress and setbacks on a blog they created for the class called "My So-Called Kosher Life."

At the end of this process, parents are invited to join with students to watch some of the documentaries, share what is on the blog, and engage in a larger discussion of how, as a family, they can live a meaningful kosher life.

In this transformational context teachers aren't so much imparting knowledge to their students as they are drawing out wisdom from them. Knowledge our students can get from the Internet, and HUC-JIR should be the premier center for Jewish knowledge creation. But wisdom they will discover by engaging with teachers and peers in a conversational classroom setting.

Conclusion

HUC-JIR could become a global production company for Jewish education, providing synagogues and Jewish day schools with the highest quality online material at minimal cost, allowing even the smallest Reform community access to the best teachers and most creative educational materials available, while at the same time allowing the Reform Movement to establish a level of quality control surpassing anything we have seen thus far.

Students would be tested and held to certain grade-level standards established by HUC-JIR, but most of this knowledge transmission would take place online at home and/or in family-centered or peer-centered learning groups inside or outside the synagogue. Local educators would monitor their students' progress and would be available to tutor students who are having difficulty, but classroom time would be spent largely on activities that go beyond filling heads to those that transform hearts and minds instead.

The transformational model respects the artifacts of Jewish civilization but doesn't restrict Jewish civilization to them. On the contrary, the transformational model of Jewish education recognizes that there is no one epoch or set of artifacts that defines Jewish life; that Judaism is what Jews make of it; and that a living, spiritually transformative Judaism for the twenty-first century, no matter what shape it may take, is as valid as any expression of Judaism from the past.

Where the transmission model makes learning about Jewish artifacts the centerpiece of Jewish education, the transformation model uses these artifacts to shift the consciousness of student and teacher alike, moving them, and through them the world, from narrow to spacious mind, and from zero-sum to nonzero living. The transformation model is at the heart of what I would call sacred teaching and spiritual learning.

Note

1. I understand that a printed scroll isn't kosher, but as vehicles for transformation, a mezuzah with a printed scroll works just as well as one with a kosher scroll.

Section Two: Children's Jewish Spiritual Education

Avirah Ruchanit—Creating a "Spiritual Atmosphere" for Jewish Teens

Moshe Ben-Lev

If you have the opportunity to spend some time with teens, you will know, especially from their confirmation year, that when asked what they are most looking for from a synagogue their answer is invariably, "spirituality." This is not surprising when according to the 2008 National Survey on Spirituality by Synagogue 3000,[1] 50 percent or more of Jews want to know how spiritual exploration, meditation, and sacred text can relate to their lives. The irony that teens want the same as their parents is not missed on teen educators, who know that deep down, teens, although rebellious on so many levels, often follow the same values as their parents. According to *Engaging Jewish Teens: The Study of New York Teens, Parents and Practitioners*, a 2011 study conducted by Brandeis University's Maurice and Marilyn Cohen Center for Modern Jewish Studies, "Ritual observance is at the bottom of the list for both parents and their children. Still it is remarkable that many parents do not place high importance on involvement in a Jewish community, and some place relatively low weight on their child's Jewish identity."[2] In a culture that values academic achievement, personal growth, physical well-being, and the ability to be placed in a good affordable college above all else, it is not surprising that spiritual

MOSHE BEN-LEV, MA is director of Education at Northern Virginia Hebrew Congregation in Reston, Virginia. He was born and educated in London, UK, at Jewish Free School and has worked in various Reform, Conservative, and Reconstructionist congregations for over twenty years in formal and informal Jewish education. He made *aliyah* in the 1980s and studied Biblical Archeology at the University of Haifa. He is a graduate of Jewish Studies from Baltimore Hebrew University.

Sa

health, religious practice, and a community of values and belief is often overlooked or seen as worthless. However, although poor at marketing and public relations outreach, the synagogue could and should be able to rigorously reach out to families and teens by selling the unique and rare qualities of its programming and services as a community center with its expertise in guiding the individual in spiritual and personal growth, and the ability to take the isolated individual and offer them a community with so many possibilities. Our synagogue institution aims at fulfilling that human need to belong to a community.

For younger children, the sense of a spiritual need is not perhaps articulated in the same manner as teens but is at the forefront of their desires when they enter a synagogue. *T'filah* when led by a dynamic song leader, rabbi, and cantor with plenty of interactive music and movement can be uplifting and truly *z'man kodesh* (sacred time). However, the process and tools that are utilized in attaining a sense of spiritual connection is palpably different. Although teens reject organized prayer services post *b'nei mitzvah,* younger children embrace a sense of *ruach* (spirit) through a meaningful prayer experience. According to psychological development, teen rejection of organized religion is both normal and appropriate. However, let us not be fooled into believing that this automatically means that they are not in need of something deep and spiritually fulfilling in their lives. The challenge is to find that bridge that triggers both desire to search for a meaningful relationship with all that is offered through a synagogue experience and a series of carefully constructed avenues to test and experiment with those possibilities offered. The following article explores various programs, tools, opportunities, and possibilities that congregational schools can consider in creating an atmosphere that promotes spiritual connection for teens.

Creating a General *Avirah Ruchanit*

Understanding the premise that prayer alone does not necessarily create a spiritual connection for many Jews, my direction is the creation of what I call an *avirah ruchanit* (a spiritual atmosphere) in order to encourage students to make those connections with *k'hilah* (community) and each other. While we automatically think that our synagogue building is a *makom kodesh* (holy place) we should not assume that our children feel the same way. It is what occurs in the building that creates an *avirah ruchanit*. An education program where behavioral issues and bullying are an issue and where teachers are unable to control their students is clearly not the kind of environment that promotes any sense of *ruach* or *k'hilah*. This is also an environment where learning tends to be minimal, friendships are dormant, and morale is low. Using simple social and emotional learning techniques, teachers can take back their classrooms. An authoritarian approach may instill a sense of order, but does nothing for student connection, relationship building, or in creating both a physical and spiritual sacred space. With social emotional learning (SEL), teachers are taught to make an effort to connect with students by taking time to get to know them. Lessons begin with a check-in time, a personal moment of reflection. Students are encouraged to talk about themselves and share in a safe environment. This is further enhanced by utilizing teaching techniques that promote collaborative learning. Cooperative learning groups, a modified differentiated learning format, and project-based learning, all encourage students to work together to teach each other, learn as a group, and get to know one another. One hears synagogue educators report that students who have been in class since kindergarten barely know each other when they reach confirmation! This further supports the belief that traditional teaching methods are failing to create community. Fortunately, many professional educators and Jewish institutions have realized the weakness in this format and are now pursuing new approaches to strengthen and improve engagement and educational programming.

An Immersive Environment for *Avirah Ruchanit*

Another related concern is the perception that congregants often see the religious school and synagogue as two separate entities with two different cultures. In order to change our paradigm, we need to look at ways to bring them closer together.

Regardless of how we envision Jewish education in our congregations, we cannot succeed in creating spiritually fulfilled and committed Jews if we do not fully engage parents and families as a unit and teach that Judaism is an "everyday" religion. If families are not encouraged to take our Jewish blueprint into their daily lives and are unfamiliar with our Jewish ritual and practice, it is our duty to preach a Judaism that is centered in the home with the synagogue as a community-based center that encourages and educates our members to make their home a place of *avirah ruchanit.*

While we talk with them about the personal need to nurture their soul or tell them that communal prayer is a spiritually uplifting experience, many families fail to see the value of a formal prayer experience. Unfortunately this comes hand-in-hand with a narrow view on God, spirituality, and belief. Our traditional message as educators and clergy has been, "unless you commit to attending a service, you are spiritually devoid of any connection with God." This simplistic view seeps into the classroom environment unless consciously challenged and corrected. It is no coincidence that many liberal synagogues have adopted meditation, *nigunim* (wordless songs), yoga, drum circles, and so on as a means of creating a spiritual connection with prayer. Our goal is to encourage alternative ways to connect as each adult must find his or her own path to spiritual growth and prayer. The same can be said of our youth. For example, Orthodox Rabbi Aryeh Kaplan explains that "Jewish meditation enables the one in prayer through mantra meditation, contemplation, and visualization within a Jewish context to use meditative techniques to enhance prayer using the traditional liturgy such as the *Amidah* and the *Shema.*"[3] For teens that become discouraged or disconnected with our formal liturgy, this approach of prayer choices and possibilities has the distinct opportunity of enabling them to find a deeper and more culturally meaningful connection with Judaism.

With the *avirah ruchanit* concept in mind we should look more closely at how we teach students *t'filah.* It is common practice today regardless of denomination to place an equal emphasis on Hebrew learning that balances *keva* and *kavanah.* The words themselves, although substantially taken from Torah text and often set in a poetic setting that evokes God through the beauty of language, are not clear enough in a modern Diaspora world. *Kavanah* is that spiritual inner emotion that, evoked or triggered by the words, brings us closer to a spiritual understanding and relationship with God and *Am Yisrael.* For children we invest a great deal of our energy on *kavanah,* often having no choice but to compromise the language portion of a meager teaching time. Educators struggle and battle with this balance every time they teach *t'filah.* While they do go hand in hand, a sound bite of Hebrew teaching is problematic without reinforcement. We must acknowledge that similarly to adults, not every child will see the personal value in prayer. Once this truth is accepted, it is understood that beyond those students who simply cannot become proficient in attaining Hebrew and prayer literacy, there are those who have no desire or motivation to learn Hebrew simply for the sake of fulfilling some requirement imposed upon them to reach a goal that they are ambivalent about to begin with! Perhaps a different approach is needed. Key to that approach is offering parent-oriented classes that teach basic Hebrew and prayer in order to assist students in learning at home. The impact of a successful adult Hebrew class can significantly impact both the attitude and level of student's Hebrew knowledge.

Social and Emotional Learning

When developing an *avirah ruchanit* in our schools, we should explore the tools developed through a social emotional learning method. It seems obvious that when applying SEL to our education plan, we must utilize Jewish values (*midot*) as a common way to instill a sense of Jewish ethics, spirituality, justice, and fairness. Many schools teach and use such terms as *rachmanut* (compassion), *derech eretz* (doing the right thing), *kavod* (respect), and *tikkun olam* (fixing the world)—all *Pirkei Avot* (Ethics of the Ancestors) concepts and phrases we use commonly in our religious schools. Although we teach *midot* and talk about the virtues of enabling students to use them as a framework for their Jewish identity, the goal should be to model them within our approach to Jewish education and offer opportunities for our students to do so within our institutions. We need to create an environment that not simply teaches Jewish tradition, history, practice, and Israel but also nurtures and consciously allows students to find their own path to Jewish living and spiritual growth. This is the meaning of *avirah ruchanit* that exemplifies what it means to be a relevant, vibrant Jewish community that connects its values to real life.

Midot and the application of these concepts to real-life situations is often overlooked in our religious schools when we miss opportunities to discuss and debate with our students when something occurs in our world and community. When the Columbine school massacre took place on April 20, 1999, many of our public schools avoided talking about this tragedy for fear of angry rebuke from parents and students. The synagogue schools in my region developed a series of programs that centered on a *midot*-based approach to a secular event. If we chose to set these events aside because they did not align themselves with our curriculum or lesson plan, we did a great disservice to our students and families. We cannot advocate for a Judaism that is relevant, far-reaching, and home-based steeped in a marriage between tradition and modernity if we fail to meet our families' spiritual needs during times of national and community crisis. Fortunately, many educational resources that address such events as they take place are being developed by such organizations as the Jewish Community Relation Council, Jewish Federations of America, and the various denominational movements. Thanks to the Internet, we are also fortunate that regional events that are monitored nationally are accessible as they are created by those Jewish communities.

Creating *Avirah Ruchanit* as a Teen Partnership

Within the last five years, a great deal of resources and brainpower has been invested in teen engagement—from URJ's Campaign for Youth Engagement[4] to Jewish think tanks such as the Rose Community Foundation[5] and the Jim Joseph Foundation.[6] The Cohen Center for Modern Jewish Studies has commissioned a number of surveys and reports on teen engagement over the last twenty years. In their December 2000 report, *Being a Jewish Teenager in America: Trying to Make It,* they concluded that, "As expected at this developmental stage, three-quarters of the teenage respondents were preoccupied with a search for meaning in life. Among these, only 40% thought it important to find that meaning through their Jewishness. For these teenagers, being Jewish was about remembering the Holocaust, countering anti-Semitism, being ethical, and making the world a better place, caring about Israel, or feeling a connection to other Jews."[7] In my work with teens over the last two decades, I have concluded that an *avirah ruchanit* is created when certain components exist within a synagogue-based teen program:

1. *Variety of offerings.* We know that a cookie-cutter approach to programming for teens does not work, because each teen follows a unique and personal connection to Judaism. The more

cerebral student, for example, will be enticed with an in-depth discussion on Mishnah or Talmud, while the very sociable student may be looking for an environment that solely nurtures relationships, finding fulfillment in, for example, a Jewish cooking class or a socially based option. The choices must be diverse and relevant to the population. Finding a balance between teen needs and interests and educational goals are a challenge that must be met. Each new group of teens has its own unique culture. In order to serve the corresponding group, the educator must be familiar with both the individuals and the group being served.

2. *Hiring young and dynamic teachers*. It is crucial that the right personality with a skill set that embraces and encourages teens as well as inspires them be hired to engage them. Relationship-building is a key to success, and the synagogue and Jewish community as a whole must carefully consider how to attract, train, support, and retain young Jewish professionals.

3. *Pathways of engagement*. For various reasons teens disengage and in many cases attempt or desire to reengage in our synagogues. A rigid teen program that offers few options beyond a stringent one-night-per-week program will detract teens and their parents from remaining or returning to our fold. Flexibility, creativity in design, and reaching out to teens and their parents will yield a more inclusive and inviting program. Over the years I have offered various days of the week with different curriculum emphasized. These can be short-term project-based programs, social action events, or a small *chevruta* study option as well as an individual study component where the student receives a teacher as a guide whom they meet with on occasion while studying or researching at home. The essence of creating such a program of engagement is to be as flexible as possible. If teens sense that you are genuinely willing to meet their needs, their response will be positive and will often result in a higher rate of retention as teens feel a stronger connection to the synagogue as a welcoming environment.

4. *Connecting with teen culture*. In recently teaching an eighth/ninth grade class, I learned from them that the Internet and relationships developed through the Web are as meaningful to them as a school friend who they spend time with at the

mall. These strangers become virtual friends who they share their deepest thoughts and hopes with. Geographical obstacles have been overcome. While their parents may find this disturbing or potentially dangerous, it has become our teens' reality. While not all of us embrace this cultural shift, we must address it if we want to remain connected and relevant to our teens. While we can and should talk about the pitfalls of this kind of relationship, we can also talk about what it means to show *kavod* and *derech eretz* in all of our relationships with those we interact with. There are many lessons to be taught when we acknowledge that this is our teen's lives. Teen culture changes and we must adapt to that change while using our Jewish toolbox to make relevant, poignant connections that will help our teens grow, feel connected to our synagogue as a place that meets their needs in life, and as a safe and nurturing environment with a teen *avirah ruchanit*.

5. *Mentoring*. The use of a social emotional learning methodology has taught us that relationships that are meaningful between students and teachers create positive and long-lasting change and enable students to accomplish more in the classroom. I have also found that SEL creates an *avirah ruchanit* by creating a stronger and deeper sense of *k'hilah*. Five years ago, along with my clergy, we created a mentoring program. We divided the high school population among cantor, rabbi, and education director. We began the school year with a ten-minute individual meeting where we discussed the student's life, our program, the educational choices and path we had to offer, and Judaism and their secular lives. Towards the end of the year, we met again with our students to evaluate the year, look ahead, and discuss life in general. The impact of this approach has been enormous. We personally connect to each teen, creating opportunities to engage more often and naturally. With some additional training on mentoring techniques, we have learned how to make good use of our meeting times and how to sustain a long-lasting connection.

   An additional outcome that we had not planned for was the desire for our teens to mentor younger teens and children.

6. *Hadracha (a leadership program)*. Using a combination of teaching resources from both the secular and Jewish world, I

created a leadership curriculum that is geared towards two components: teaching leadership skills from a Jewish prospective and taking those skills and knowledge and adapting them to the synagogue community. Students have created their own social action opportunities, assisted in our K–6 programs beyond being a *madrich/a*, and have joined synagogue committees, boards, and lifelong learning classes. In addition, they are now planning their retreats and writing programs. This concept is an example of teaching relevant, hands-on materials that are then utilized and expanded upon. Teens embrace opportunities that enable them to shine, take control of their learning, and make an impact on the lives of others.

7. *Social action programming.* Creating a regular, exciting, and multi-topical program that offers regular opportunities to help others and makes a real difference in the world resonates strongly with teens. It is partly due to the mandated student service learning hours that middle and high school students in America are asked to complete and the sense that doing good for others is developmentally appropriate. Much work has been achieved in the Jewish sector as it connects with Jewish culture, values, and teaching. Such organizations as the Jewish Teen Funders Network[8] and the Jewish Youth Philanthropy Initiative[9] have created some wonderful opportunities for Jewish teens, both affiliated with synagogues and nonaffiliated, to engage in philanthropic work. It should be noted that these programs were not created to replace congregational schools' social action programs but rather to enhance them. Our religious schools should invest heavily in creating social action projects within their own curriculum. Local, national, and international organizations welcome teen involvement and commitment. Interfaith opportunities, Israel connections, and internal synagogue needs should be included. In working with Jewish Foundation for Group Homes,[10] for adults who are mentally challenged, I have seen such a sense of *avirah ruchanit* and *rachmanut* on the faces of our teens that I am assured that we achieved one of our goals of creating *menschlichkeit* in our teens.

Kavod (respect) goes both ways especially with teens who view the world through a prism of justice and injustice. If teens feel irrelevant, discounted, or ignored in being active partners in their own Jewish education, we will lose them. Finding opportunities to connect in ways that are not offered in their everyday lives but are relevant, meaningful, and worthwhile will mean the difference between a successful Jewish teen program and experience and one where teens leave in droves following their b'nei mitzvah.

Teachers as Spiritual Guides

Another key to successfully creating a congregational school that inspires and entices families while advancing an avirah ruchanit is to hire and train motivated teachers that can nurture and encourage students to search for spiritual connections. This cannot be achieved without a clear and direct vision shared by clergy and education director. Michael Zeldin sees this synergy as one that must be organic in nature:

> [Clergy and directors of education] must encourage teachers to realize their human and Jewish potential, and to guide them as they share themselves with others. Their primary responsibility is more interpersonal than administrative. As mentors to their staff, they must be given the organizational and material support necessary to nurture those who have direct contact with students. They must provide teachers with a vision of what is possible when Jews engage each other in learning and growing as Jews. Investing in the "human capital'" of the congregation—its teachers—will go a long way in fostering commitment to a vibrant Jewish future.[11]

I would add further that in many cases, as the only consistent Jewish role model outside the family, congregational teachers have the additional responsibility of carrying the burden of all that is Jewish upon their shoulders. It is our jobs as congregational educators to make those shoulders broad and strong.

Some years ago, I took part in an experimental project that brought education directors and fourth-grade teachers together to talk about their own relationships with God. The program was based around the concept that if we were comfortable talking about our own views of spirituality, faith, and God, we would do a better job teaching our students and thus would be able to be more effective. Ultimately as the sessions progressed we became entrenched in definitions, religious dogma, and creating barriers. It was clear that a clinical approach to a subject that is based around emotion, trust, belief, and personal relationships cannot be sufficient to use as a teaching tool.

Creating opportunities and encouraging a nurturing environment and a positive experience make it possible for young children and teens to connect spiritually. Key to creating a successful *avirah ruchanit* is the hiring and training of teachers that are comfortable with their sense of spirituality and can transmit that sense to their students. A teacher that is not able to delve deeply with their own relationship with God will be unable to imbue that onto their students. In an era in which synagogue schools struggle with finding and hiring teachers who are competent, passionate, able, and inspiring, it is often the case that a teacher who is ambivalent with their own relationship with Judaism is hired without asking these fundamental questions. I would argue that without an introspective spiritual journey, it is difficult to ignite any passionate interaction with students over such a fundamental cornerstone of our education program, Jewish identity building. It is imperative and should be a major part of teacher training for teachers to search within themselves, through text study and guidance, a path to their own feelings about God, faith, and belief. Avoiding teaching or tackling these topics makes it difficult for teachers to have a frank and open discussion when answering any questions related to God or belief that students might have. I recall some years ago when confronted by a sixth-grader who openly stated in class that God did not exist and that religion was nonsense, that I needed guidance from my principal on how I should deal with this opinion. He handed me an article to read that he felt addressed this issue from a synagogue movement perspective. Whether I agreed with the article or not, I was instructed to verbatim regurgitate the article's contents. Only later I understood that I should not dictate a particular ethos or halachically based answer but rather guide my students through a lifelong search that I hope will be rewarding, fulfilling, and spiritually uplifting. For teens, the possibilities are boundless as long as they think broadly and creatively.

In his book *The Road to Whatever: Middle Class Culture and the Crisis of Adolescence*,[12] Elliott Currie talks about how middle-class American teens are neglected, abandoned, and worse. He attributes much of this to the failure of various institutions to support teens and nurture their growth towards a healthy adulthood. One such criticism is aimed at the lack of a safe environment for teens to share their feelings or views when topics arise that deal with real-life issues and making difficult choices. The congregational school has a unique opportunity in enabling teens to talk about such issues as teen depression, suicide, substance abuse, relationships, and more. Opening up your classroom to mental health experts and trained Jewish educators and clergy who can work together can make those crucial connections to looking at issues through a Jewish lens. We have a unique opportunity to give teens a safe place to express their inner selves and reveal their unique *n'shamah* (soul). Finally, this may help clergy and educators to identify those teens who are in need of both spiritual and mental health guidance. Teens often feel isolated and misunderstood. The synagogue can be a refuge for teens as they are accepted without judgment in an environment that helps nurture their spirit through professionals who know and care for them. Unfortunately, I agree with Currie when he states that many of these issues are not acknowledged as problems within our society. Many organizations that have attempted to address issues of mental health in a congregational setting have found doors closed and leadership deaf to the reality that faces teens and adults in our community. Until we can face these issues honestly and with an open mind, we will continue to miss an opportunity to make a lifelong difference to our congregants.

The Spiritual Retreat

Another missed opportunity to create and nurture *avirah ruchanit* is through retreats, *Shabbatonim* (Shabbat retreat), and special weekend programming, which are all events that require enormous planning and resources and yet, when successfully executed, can provide a forum to process the knowledge taught during the years. It will provide the unique opportunity for families to experience, question, and grow together. The design of our school year does not often enable us to be either reflective or continuous in our approach to sustaining and expanding those seeds that we plant. For example, while we may have successfully conditioned our group of children and adolescents to begin a process of creating a more meaningful grade or group *k'hilah* whilst in an intense formal/informal synagogue setting, we don't often think of these opportunities as a new foundation on which to build a *k'hilah* that will foster and grow into a strong, vibrant, and long-lasting community. We have essentially created our *avirah ruchanit* and then let it fester or dissipate never to be realized as a potential for maintaining a healthy and continuous *chavurah*. Producing a *Shabbaton* that consciously uses the format as a springboard for creating opportunities for nurturing a *k'vutzah ruchanit* (spiritual group) and testing the teaching already imparted should be at the heart of what we are trying to achieve when we offer such opportunities. In order to successfully achieve this, one would need to take into account the group dynamic, culture, and the *avirah* before planning the program. This takes skill and flexibility, and it will require a group of teachers along with education directors to work together with a long-term plan that deliberately takes into consideration the future educational goals in the coming years of religious education. In other words, these meaningful opportunities should be seen as a beginning in a continuum of learning and *k'hilah* and not as either an end goal, or as is often the case, a one-off, isolated event that would translate into a meaningless or, even more, a missed opportunity. Much of the buzz following a summer break centers on a Jewish camp experience. Our students, and especially our teens, view our schools as the antitheses of that model of engagement. What makes this kind of experience unique and resonates with our youth? According to the Foundation for Jewish Camps, which commissioned a study in 2011 entitled *The Long-Term Impact of Jewish Overnight Camp: Evidence from 26 U.S. Jewish Population Studies on Adult Jewish Engagement*, "The analysis indicates that they [campers] bring, first of all, an increased inclination to practice Jewish behaviors in their lives. Secondly, they bring an increased inclination to values and seek out the experience of Jewish community. The bonding experience of camp not only builds a long-lasting taste and yearning for community; it also creates habits of Jewish practice. It makes Judaism part and parcel of life's most joyous moments. Moreover, those moments are experienced as integral parts of life in a beloved community."[13]

In other words, this environment has consciously and with real purpose fostered and nurtured successfully an *avirah ruchanit*. *Shabbatonim*, while significantly shorter in length, still enable us to create an environment that can guide preadolescents and teens towards an honest and genuine experience that connects them with community, prayer, and Judaism. Taking the camp philosophy into account and adapting its essence into such an event is both powerful and meaningful. However, we should also be aware that it is further an important opportunity to promote, build, and connect our youth groups and our school programs. Deliberately blurring the lines between formal and informal education for teens in particular enables a more in-depth look at a holistic approach to Judaism. For example, whenever I run a teen retreat, I always include the youth group leaders as well as the teachers in the programming. I always end the retreat with an *asefah*, a kibbutz style gathering or meeting where teens come together to share views, ideas, comments on the teen program, and their Jewish education as a whole. Recommendations are made by the teens and considerations are taken into account. In this way, teens know that they have a voice in their Jewish education, teachers have some great ideas when planning courses, and everyone feels invested. This in itself is a spiritual moment of *k'hilah*.

When contemplating retreats and *Shabbatonim* it is important that the program and content be planned with a vision in mind. If you are introducing a new concept or path for your teen program, a retreat is a great opportunity to begin that process. Over the years I have chosen *hadracha*, social action, and a blending of youth group and school program into themes that have been springboards for a yearlong program. Using the arts or providing a specialist or guest allows a unique experience to occur. A balance between what your program will look like weekly and an exciting and inspiring kick-off campaign works well when planned with care and thought. The opportunity to have a mini-camp experience should be an inspiring, exciting, and energizing one. It should be used as a beginning of something new and creative.

Conclusion

In the words of Rabbi Saul J. Berman, director of Continuing Rabbinic Education at Yeshivat Chovevei Torah and Law professor at Stern College and Columbia University School of Law:

> We may not be able to directly cultivate the experience of God's presence in our classrooms, but we could shape them as safe places in which people could talk about the experience of God, could engage in God talk, without embarrassment and without

the fear of ridicule. We could certainly explore all texts, and all Jewish experiences which we provide in educational settings, from the perspective of what they reveal about human virtues which we aspire to achieve. And we could benefit from a more profound awareness that God desired not only personal improvement, but the formation of an ideal society in which social justice is the religious foundation of the social order.[14]

More importantly, we need to change our vocabulary when we talk about how we approach teens.

The Jim Joseph Foundation report *Effective Strategies for Educating and Engaging Jewish Teens* highlights the important distinction between education and engagement:

> We acknowledge that education and engagement are not, by strict definition, the same thing. Engagement is about getting people to participate in something, while education is about having them learn something. In many cases they can be combined, but engagement does not necessarily include deep learning. We believe it is also important to consider engagement approaches because they may be what is needed to get teens to the "learning table."[15]

Each child who enters our synagogue and takes part in our programming deserves to be given the opportunity to develop a strong sense of spirituality. It is the responsibility of teachers, clergy, and education directors to address and nurture the internal and external emotional connection we hope we can develop with each child in his or her relationship with God and *Am Yisrael*. How we achieve that is by creating an *avirah ruchanit* in our synagogues. This means making a conscious effort to develop a program that enables this *avirah* to exist. Using social emotional learning techniques from the first moment that a child enters our religious schools and building a strong relationship with teachers and students will be the building blocks in creating a mutual trust and respect that will grow throughout a child's religious education. This will help immensely in building *avirah ruchanit*. We must also take into account that no single effort or program can reasonably be expected to address the challenge of Jewish teen education and engagement. Training teachers in areas that include talking about God, spirituality, and asking and answering difficult questions will help develop a level of personal and professional comfort in addressing issues of faith and guidance in developing a stronger and more meaningful relationship with God and Judaism. Working with our curriculum to ensure that opportunities are frequent, having open and honest dialogues with our teens, and guiding students of all ages to find their own paths to spiritual growth, will also substantially alter how youth view the synagogue community and their own world at large. In encouraging a stronger connection with *Am Yisrael*, we must balance the Jewish world with the secular one and allow room for discussion and reflection of current events. Our biggest challenge now and in the future is to provide families with the tools to create their own *avirah ruchanit* in their homes. We have spent resources, energy, and time developing our synagogue program while neglecting the very essence of what Judaism teaches us; we live and practice it every day and not simply on the occasional Shabbat or religious school session. *Ruach* is not an easily manufactured feeling but one that occurs through positive experiences, deep personal immersion into one's self-conscience, and a strong sense of belonging and sharing with a people who have the same belief systems as us. In 2014 we know that not every child is given these opportunities at home or the synagogue. When Experiments in Congregational Education was formed, it was done so with the express desire to unite ALL constituents of education and culture in the synagogue. It was understood that significant transformative change in how we connect our youth and adults to both our congregation and to an enriched Jewish life could only happen by working with all parties invested in the synagogue community both inside the institution and at home. The same must be emphasized with guiding our youth on a Jewish spiritual journey. It must be a conscious and concerted effort to develop an *avirah ruchanit*, for without it we will miss another opportunity to engage children, young adults, and families who are searching for a deep and meaningful religious experience that is relevant to their present lives.

Notes

1. Synagogue 3000, *2008 National Survey on Spirituality*, http://www. synagogue3000.org/system/files/pirituality questionnaireformatted WITHSTATS V3.pdf.
2. Amy L. Sales, Nicole Samuel, and Alexander Zablotsky, *Engaging Jewish Teens: The Study of New York Teens, Parents and Practitioners* (Brandeis University, Cohen Center for Modern Jewish Studies,

November 2011), www.brandeis.edu/cmjs/pdfs/EngagingJew-ishTeens/EngagingJewishTeens111011.pdf.

3. Aryeh Kaplan, *Jewish Meditation: A Practical Guide* (New York: Shocken Books, 1985), 5–6.

4. URJ's Campaign for Youth Engagement, urj.org/cye/.

5. See the Rose Community Foundation at www.rcfdenver.org.

6. See Jim Joseph Foundation at jimjosephfoundation.org.

7. Charles Kadushin et al., *Being a Jewish Teenager in America: Trying to Make It* (Brandeis University, Cohen Center for Modern Jewish Studies, December 2000), http://bir.brandeis.edu/bitstream/handle/10192/22989/JAS.pdf?sequence=1.

8. See The Jewish Teen Funders Network at www.JTNF.org.

9. See Jewish Youth Philanthropy Initiative at www.PJLL.org.

10. See Jewish Foundation for Group Homes at www.jfgh.org.

11. Michael Zeldin, "Rethinking Jewish Education," *Reform Judaism* (Spring 1995): 50.

12. Elliott Currie, *The Road to Whatever: Middle Class Culture and the Crisis of Adolescence* (New York: Holt Paperbacks, Henry Holt and Company, LLC, 2004).

13. Steven M. Cohen et al., *The Long Term Impact of Jewish Overnight Camp: Evidence from 26 U.S. Jewish Population Studies on Adult Jewish Engagement* (The Foundation for Jewish Camp, 2011), www.jewishcamp.org/static/website/uploads/Camp_Works_for_Web.pdf.

14. Saul J. Berman, "Perspectives on Jewish Education: Searching for Spirituality in Education," *Jewish Educational Leadership* (Winter 2007), www.lookstein.org/online_journal.php?id=136.

15. Jim Joseph Foundation, *Effective Strategies for Educating and Engaging Jewish Teens* (March 2013), www.jimjosephfoundation.org/evaluations/effective-strategies-for-educating-and-engaging-jewish-teens/.

Good Grief: Helping Jewish Children Live with Death

Jennifer Gubitz

"She's not alone, sweetheart," my grieving mom promised. "She's buried very close to Aunt Patty's grandmother and Aunt Mildred's family is a few feet away, too." No one had thought to buy a plot for her yet. My Aunt Judy's death by suicide was premature and wholly unexpected. Liberal Judaism treats suicide as illness and allows for full burial rites within a Jewish cemetery, but even though Aunt Judy's burial site (near someone we called aunt, but who was unrelated to us) had far more to do with logistics than the cause of her death, my eleven-year-old mind decided that being buried far from my Bubbe and the family plot was what it meant for her to be shunned, punished, and ostracized for killing herself.

Unsurprisingly, when the school year began, like the location of her burial, I experienced that sense of being on the outskirts—the secret of my aunt's tragic death buried deep within me. It was a confounding loss, leaving a breach that even decades later remains open and painful. I had so many questions about the nature of her death and even more about death itself. Did she know she was dead? What happened to her soul after she died? Why does anyone have to die at all? Can't we just all live forever? Does this mean I will die, too? And how will I die? Will my parents die? The questions, the curiosity, the grief, and the fear were endless. And the answers to my questions were not something anyone around me—in my public school or religious school classroom—was talking about openly.

RABBI JENNIFER GUBITZ (NY12) serves Temple Shir Tikva in Wayland, Massachusetts. An HUC-JIR Tisch Rabbinical Fellow, she is a graduate of Indiana University's Borns Jewish Studies Program, and she grew up as a song leader at URJ Goldman Union Camp Institute in Zionsville, Indiana. This article is an extension of her HUC senior thesis under the direction of Rabbi Dr. Carole B. Balin.

The *Shulchan Aruch Yoreh Dei-ah*[1] starkly intones, *ein aveilut hakatan* (there is no mourning for a child). In our modern day, we would understand this statement to be false. We know that children experience the grief of mourning. The *Shulchan Aruch* as a body of Jewish law is pointing specifically to the requisite ritual obligation of mourning—that a child under a certain age is not halachically bound to observe those rituals. However, in the same conversation, the scholars of *Yoreh Dei-ah* focus on the various times when a child *may* participate in mourning rituals for the sake of education.

Jewish life-cycle education centers on the breadth of ritual milestones that punctuate the arc of Jewish living. From birth to earth, our youth learn about *b'rit milah, simchat bat, b'nei mitzvah*, wedding, and mourning rituals. There are a number of life-cycle curricula that help guide children through the rituals connected to Jewish funerals and mourning. With regard to this final stop in the Jewish life cycle, children might visit a cemetery and a funeral home with their religious school class, map out the details and symbolism of shivah, make condolence cards, explore memory on a scavenger hunt throughout the synagogue, or discuss the meaning of the *Kaddish* liturgy.[2]

While current curricula focus on how Jewish rituals brilliantly and intuitively guide us through the process of mourning a loss, what can clergy and educators do to address the spiritual and emotional ramifications of loss? What of a child's inner questions: How does it feel to be in the cemetery? How will it feel to visit someone I love who is buried there? What will it feel like to attend a funeral or to mourn the death of someone I love? What can I do when someone I care about is sad and in mourning? When children's feelings are voiced, they have the power to transform. Unspoken and unaddressed, they have the capacity to fester and to darken a child's spiritual and emotional development.

And fester they have. These days, our teens are literally crying out. Over the last five years, the core of Reform Jews suffered multiple tragic and untimely deaths that left communities of teens, parents, congregants, and clergy reeling. In each case, these tragedies led to outpourings of grief on social media like Facebook. Though NFTY responded immediately by organizing an online response with resources for grieving teens, many continue to post their grief on the Facebook walls of those who passed away for years after these tragedies. These walls are covered with short sentiments ranging from "We miss you!" and "Hope things are going well up there!" to lengthy and detailed descriptions of a youth group event or Israel trip. In many ways Facebook and other social media function as a modern-day memorial book, like the *memorbücher* (memory books) that originated as far back as the First Crusade and were created to commemorate the long lists of the dead. Indeed, the millennial generation's response to death is a very public act. Might it even function as a mechanism for expressing some sort of theology of the afterlife?

Though impossible to measure, it would seem that these particularly public sentiments of grief and mourning fulfill a fundamental human need. They comfort. They console. They allow people, especially young people, to mourn outwardly, unabashedly, and publicly. But what about the content of their Facebook posts? Do teens really believe that the dead are reading their Facebook wall from some far away, heavenly place? Though some "magical thinking" might underlie the posts, most teens who experience the death of loved ones respond publicly because they have few other places to turn. They are unequipped to face the reality of what they are experiencing and feeling. As young people, this may be the first time they have faced the death of a loved one or especially a peer. Perhaps they have not been exposed to or educated about Jewish rituals for mourning. It may be that they have not been helped to formulate beliefs about death and the afterlife. They may not have had a safe space to articulate their questions and fears about death. Rather, in the face of tragedy, they grasp for meaning. Is this the ideal way for our kids to grieve? In what ways can we better equip them to cope with the death of a loved one from a much earlier age? How can we create opportunities to address life's deepest questions and fears about mortality?

As Rabbi Alvin Fine wrote, "Birth is a beginning and death a destination. And life is a journey." We cannot avoid death, and we cannot avoid the grief we will experience when faced with death. While the best of curricula cannot prepare one for the pain of loss, we owe it to our children to create open channels of conversations about death, dying, and the afterlife, if possible, before they are faced with these difficult circumstances. If we can offer our youth an opportunity to experience the journey of life in its fullest by creating safe spaces for exploration of their deepest questions and fears about death, perhaps when faced with inevitable loss, they can draw from a wellspring of emotional resiliency to experience, as Charlie Brown said best, "good grief."

From *Kiddush* to *Kaddish*:
Fighting Our Fears to Teach Our Children

We are a people whose daily actions sanctify the holiness of life. Like many synagogues, at the conclusion of Shabbat services at Shir Tikva in Wayland, Massachusetts, we invite up young children to join for *Kiddush* and *Motzi*. It's a sweet moment that directly follows the somber *Kaddish* liturgy. Though those two prayers share the three-letter Hebrew root *kuf-dalet-shin* (k-d-sh), we teach children the blessing for wine (*KiDduSH*) long before we teach them the blessing to commemorate death (*KaDdiSH*). Perhaps children intuit the necessity of remaining silent during the *Kaddish*, noticing the change of energy in the room. Some may even ask "Mommy, why is that person crying?" or "Who are those people on the list the Rabbi is reading?" or "Why are those people standing?" More likely, children may not even be present for the *Kaddish*, having left when the rabbi began the sermon, returning only when it's time for *Kiddush*.

Explaining the *Kaddish* is not a conversation we wish to have. But when death arrives, as it inevitably does, and grief strikes, the conversation we hoped we'd never have to have with our children must occur. What, then, is the barrier that prevents us from talking with our children about death?

> Rav Nachman showed himself [in a dream after his death]. Rava asked him "Was death painful?" Rav Nachman replied. "It was a painless separation . . . But were the Blessed Holy One to say to me, 'You may return to that world where you were before,' I would not wish to do it, for the fear of death is too great." (BT *Mo-eid Katan* 28a)

As Maurice Lamm, in *The Jewish Way in Death and Mourning*, writes: "We are deathly afraid of death."[3] Known clinically as thanatophobia, the fear of death is pervasive. We may fear death for a variety of reasons: We may fear the physical pain endured in the dying process; we may fear death for the emotional pain it causes us and our loved ones. Thanatophobia may be the result of religious dogma that teaches adherents that reward or punishment will occur in death; or more starkly because we "fear of the possibility that nothingness follows life."[4] Perhaps, we simply have less experience with death and dying in our modern milieu and we fear the unknown.

This was true in the 1960s when Dr. Herman Feifel pioneered the scientific and academic study of death, known clinically as thanatology:[5]

> Today we live increasingly in a "death free" milieu, but in an earlier, predominantly rural America, death was commonly present in homes. It was personally experienced by young and old alike...[and] was necessarily experienced by all as a natural, inevitable, and ever possible aspect of the human condition. Children were not "protected" . . . a recognition and acceptance of death became an integral part of their informal education.[6]

Feifel observed the clinicalization of death that resulted in a shift from a historically "death-accepting to a death-avoiding society."[7] Death generally took place removed from home life; many people died in hospitals or nursing homes—environments that were generally not child-friendly and that further institutionalized the process of death and dying. Cultural influences also pushed the process of death and dying to the margins:

> Much in our American culture conspires to remove death from our minds and even our feelings. In television, the movies, and other expressions of our mores, emphasis is on the preservation of youth and the denial of aging. Death, though threatening and difficult to handle, is made remote . . . Estranged by our civilization from the basic realities of life (of which death is a part), we have lost contact with the daily struggle for life of animals in field and forest. We have less and less contact with nature, with the death of livestock, and with the slaughtering of animals for food. Death has become for us foreboding, frightening, repugnant, and mysterious.[8]

Death was all but taboo, Feifel noted.[9] Death, Rabbi Earl Grollman perceived, was "a dark symbol not to be stirred—not even touched—an obscenity to be avoided."[10] Especially when it came to children, while "most modern parents are convinced that they should be honest in discussing the biological processes of birth… when it comes to life's end, they may fall strangely silent."[11]

After two World Wars, the Holocaust, atomic warfare, and scientific advances leading to longer life expectancy, Feifel decided that the taboo needed to be lifted. Though his 1959 publication of *The Meaning of Death* was criticized by people who did not want to discuss the meaning of death, Feifel's groundbreaking work led to a flourish of activity on the thanatology scene in the 1960s and 1970s. Colleges and universities began to teach about death, dying, and bereavement; there were many significant publications by scholars spanning multidisciplinary fields (among them Richard Kalish, Robert Kastenbaum, our own Rabbi Earl Grollman, Daniel Leviton, and Edwin Shneidman). Elizabeth Kübler-Ross's *On Death and Dying*, which emphasized DABDA,[12] the five stages of grief, universalized the bereavement process. Academic journals such as *Omega, Death Studies*, and the *Journal of Thanatology* appeared. Cicely Saunders began the hospice movement; and numerous professional organizations with a focus on thanatology convened.[13]

Ironically, even today in our emotionally open and scientifically informed age, conversations about death—emotional, scientific, or other—are relegated to whispers. Why? For adults, it may come as a surprise to learn that we share similar emotions about death as our children.[14] Rabbi Grollman, in *Explaining Death to Children*, reflects on Ralph Waldo Emerson's observation that "Sorrow makes us all children again."[15] We don't want to talk about death, especially with our kids, because we, too, struggle with the topic. It causes immense discomfort. It scares us. It activates feelings of sadness and pain. And as Grollman citing Simone de Beauvoir notes, in some ways, by talking about death or mourning a loss, "we are taking part in the dress rehearsal of our own burial."[16] How frighteningly true. And yet, if we continue to remain tight-lipped about these topics, when death does occur, not only will children have few emotional resources to confront the loss, their parents may be unable to support their child because they too are in mourning. How, then, can clergy and educators move our communities from *Kiddush* to *Kaddish*? How can we guide parents to explore their fears in order to address the spiritual and emotional needs of their children? How can we utilize Jewish death education as a framework to nurture spiritual and emotional resilience for our children?

Jewish Death Education: Nurturing Emotional Resiliency

Most commonly, families face death, dying, and bereavement in a reactive mode. However, Dr. Daniel Leviton speaks of the proactive strategy of "primary prevention" as the first aspect of a three-pronged approach to teaching about death before (though difficult to control) one experiences it.[17] Our sacred texts understood this "primary prevention," as well. In the *Shulchan Aruch*, the *D'risha*[18] teaches that if children are to learn about and participate in the rituals connected to death and dying, it should be *m'shum agmat nefesh* (in the absence of grief).

When, then, is the right time to begin conversations about death? The grades during which different synagogues introduce death as part of the Jewish life cycle vary throughout the country from as early as third grade to eighth grade. In particular, for those that use the URJ's CHAI Curriculum, end-of-life content is introduced in Levels 5 and 6. While there is no *wrong* time to focus on the end of life, a proactive approach to Jewish death education will help remove the taboo around death and enable Jewish youth to engage in the topic before they are consumed by *agmat nefesh*, adrift with grief and confused by unanswerable questions.

Death is ever-present in children's lives whether adults are aware of it or not,. Children talk of death frequently in daily routines, using death-related terms when they play computer games or video games (e.g., "He is out of power.") as well as indoor/outdoor games (e.g., "If you cross the line or step on the line, you are dead."). Children also experience death in fairy tales and storybooks: Characters die from eating poisonous apples or are devoured by hungry wolves.[19] While children may not comprehend death as fully as adults do, lacking the ability to understand nuances and abstraction, they do grasp more than we might expect. Though parents may worry that their children are not emotionally mature enough to learn about death and dying, studies on the subject suggest otherwise.

The widely accepted study by Hungarian psychologist Maria Nagy shows that children develop their ideas about death in a stage-like progression.[20] Her conclusion that "children pass through several stages before arriving at an adult concept of death"[21] is congruent with the research and theories of developmental psychologist Jean Piaget, who studied cognitive development for youth.

While every child is different, Nagy observed three distinct developmental stages during which children grasped various aspects of death and dying. Generally, she observed that they "moved from the idea that death is not final to death is final but avoidable, to death is final and inevitable."[22] These developmental stages, however, are only landmarks for how a child might engage with learning and understanding death concepts. Age, personality, maturity, family circumstance, general life experience, and many other factors play a role. Children who have experienced death, even of an animal or insect, may grasp the concept better, as do those whose parents are open about the subject. Research shows that when parents squelch conversation about death and dying, withhold information, or give evasive answers to difficult questions, "they foster confusion and increased anxiety in children."[23]

Most parents want to raise resilient and emotionally thriving children. Jewish death education with a spiraled and developmentally appropriate approach can build resiliency in kids *and* in their parents. Helping parents through their own anxieties about death and building on their hopes and dreams for their children's emotional strength can create openness to conversations about death and dying that can transform not only children, but entire families.

As our partners in the work of Jewish death education, the first vital step to Jewish death education involves clarity of communication with parents about how topics surrounding death and dying will be taught to their children. In building this trust, parents can come to understand that Jewish death education does not have to be radical, scary, or avoided, rather, prepping parents for how we will teach their kids will also educate them. Being clear with parents that while developmentally their second-grade child, for example, may not understand the concept of death permanence and universality, a teacher will focus on what a child *can* understand: personal emotions and feelings of sadness, anger, and fear; compassionate ways to comfort and care for sad friends; or gratitude for special memories of deceased loved ones. There is value in inviting parents into this conversation: What are the qualities of heart and mind that a child who faces death might feel? What do children need in order to cope? How can my child develop inner reserves of empathy that shape compassionate outward interactions with the world around her?[24]

A first step to teaching children about death is offering them a vocabulary—a language for how to talk about death within a Jewish context that creates spaces for noticing and then articulating related emotions and questions. Some kids will be able to express feelings associated with loss, while others will have a sense of these feelings but struggle to name them. Brainstorming lists of possible emotions people feel in general and then zeroing in on emotions (sad, depressed, angry) or behaviors (crying, yelling, hiding) that are closely linked to loss and grief can assist in further conversations about death and dying. Offering music, art, or theatre as modes of emotional expression are helpful for all children, and especially for those who are less verbally articulate.

Creating a safe space where students know their questions and feelings are honored and important is the palette for using shared vocabulary. This safe space may later become the context and community where in times of loss kids can share their grief. In those times, shared language and experience of learning and processing together will enable peers to offer genuine empathy and support. While group conversation can be useful to understanding the how-tos of end-of-life rituals, the personal nature of a child's enduring questions and deepest fears about death may feel quite private and kids may not feel comfortable initially (or ever) sharing them aloud. Making available a question box open for anonymous inquiry or utilizing private writing exercises or art activities can offer openings for private expression and voicing curiosity. Some children may initially express discomfort with conversations about death, behaving inappropriately and disruptively in attempt to avoid the conversation. Some kids may laugh. Some may be silent. Regardless, it is critical to create a safe space where all of these diverse behaviors are ultimately welcome.

Nurturing a disposition of compassion, caring, and empathy in children at an early age is a primary goal of Jewish death education. In the field of moral education,[25] this ethic of caring explored in depth by Nel Noddings in *Caring: A Feminine Approach to Ethics and Moral Education* develops a concept of caring *for* another and being cared for *by* another as the ethical ideal.[26] Most children grow to understand implicitly from being raised in loving homes what it feels like to be cared for, emotionally nourished and supported, clothed and fed, and helped when they ask or even when they don't. They eventually learn to care for others, to share, to express concern, and to offer help. Jewish rituals related to death and dying extend the circle of care that kids understand early on in their own families. To develop an awareness and comfort with how to express care and concern in times of mourning, utilizing role-playing or bibliodrama, is an engaging, active, and useful method.

For example, consider the experience of Moses and Aaron after their sister, Miriam, dies in Exodus 20. Moments later, the Israelites assemble against the brothers, angered by the sudden absence of water, which midrash connects with Miriam's death. Utilizing bibliodrama, a theatrical method of bringing Torah to life as popularized by Peter Pitzele or Amichai Lau-Levi's Storahtelling, a teacher might set up a scene like this: "You're an Israelite and you are angry that you have no water. It's hot in the desert and you've been wandering for days. But your leaders, Moses and Aaron, just lost their sister, Miriam. Even though you're angry and thirsty, what might you say to them?" Bibliodrama shrinks the distance between text and self. Narration is often dropped and the child-turned-actor is guided to dialogue directly with Moses. The narrated "I would tell them I'm sorry" becomes an embodied "Moses, Aaron, I'm so sorry for your loss." The internal experience of sympathy becomes more real when articulated in first-person. Simultaneously, exploring sympathy and compassion through Torah stories creates *enough* distance that no child must act out their own possible loss.

This is where the how-tos of death and dying—how to show empathy and compassion, what to say to someone who is sad and grieving—converge with the development of emotional resiliency. Through role-playing, helping a child to see another child's perspective or to feel another child's experience and emotions, even just for a moment, will build inner strength for when actual experiences of loss become reality.

The medium of art is another modality through which emotional strength can be fostered. As an element of developing compassionate responses to grieving friends and family, children might design condolence cards or artwork that express sympathy, care, and concern. We understand through artistic and architectural responses to national tragedy just how meaningful and cathartic artful tributes to death can be. Offering children examples of appropriate phrases to write on a condolence card—"My deepest sympathies," "*Hamakom Yinachem Etchem,*" or "May the One who heals broken hearts heal your heart"—not only provides vocabulary, but models compassionate language for face-to-face connections, as well. Consider creating a class set of stationery with these consolatory phrases that can be used throughout the school year for times when students experience a loss.

Addressing concepts of the after-life, which are often mysterious and underdeveloped for Jews of all ages, can also be explored through art. Inviting kids to express through art their understanding of Jewish beliefs of the afterlife—*Gan Eden, Sheol, olam haba*, or *t'chiyat hameitim*—can utilize creativity to develop a sense of wonder and curiosity. And because we simply don't know what happens to us after we die, exploring these indeterminate possibilities through art broadens a child's capacity to grasp uncertainty. Rabbi Dr. Michael Shire once explained to me that "a child who begins to grasp the uncertainty and indeterminacy of living can eventually learn to grasp loss too."

As children begin to experience death over the course of their young lives—from seeing crushed insects or wilted flowers, or grieving the loss of a beloved pet or the mournful death of a family member or friend—they develop a deep capacity for coping and compassionate care. My colleagues Rabbi Neal Gold and Cantor Hollis Schachner and I found this to be true as our Boston-area congregation faced tragedy locally and nationally. But even before the Newtown tragedy or Boston marathon bombings of 2013, the following scene transpired:

"When we leave *t'filah* today, we need to be very, very quiet and calm as we walk through the halls. Someone in our congregation lost someone very special in her life and is sitting shivah with her friends upstairs in the library." As Cantor Schachner led an open and interactive conversation with our third to sixth graders about how we might change our behavior in the hallways that afternoon, our students' attention was peaked. Silence swept over the room.

"Wait, there was a funeral here in *this* room today?" one rambunctious child yelled from his seat.

"Yes," I answered, "the sanctuary that we're in right now serves a lot of different purposes during the week. What are some of the ways you can think of?" The kids yelled out different answers, "*T'filah*! Presentations! *Shirei Yeladim* Choir Practice!"

"Wait," that same child interrupted, "there was a *dead* body in here today? That is sooo cool." While "cool" would not have been the descriptor of choice for most of our students, as we requested, they all left the sanctuary in calm and quiet silence. When one child started to run, another reminded her of the proper behavior—for our synagogue had momentarily been turned into a house of mourning. As kids began to depart, a fourth grade teacher came up quickly and said, "The kids want to know how old the person was who died."

Before anyone else could leave, we told them the following: "The person who died was very, very, very old and lived a very, very, very, very, very long and full life." A few kids breathed a sigh of relief and walked quietly off to class.

We were so proud of our students that day. They varied in age—and we didn't go into many details—but they *got* it. They could calibrate their behavior to show honor to the dead and offer comfort to the bereaved. Equally as important, they knew they could express their fears and ask hard questions of their teachers and their rabbis and cantor.

Sacred Urgency: Creating Space for New Growth

Rabbi David Wolpe writes:

> Death is the fire that consumes our life. Without it, there would be no space for new growth. The world would be choked; life would be rendered without poignancy and yearning . . . A world with no end would be life with no urgency. That is as much as we are given in life to understand.[27]

Even in our adult lives, we struggle to understand the deaths of our own loved ones, remembering the times when we were consumed by grief, choked by fear of impending loss, and confused why God would create a world of which death is a part. Perhaps we negotiated with God to spare us from these losses, hoping that God might protect us from feeling such pain, all the while knowing intellectually that death is inevitable, final, and universally the fire that will one day consume our life. But as Rabbi Wolpe writes, "Without [death], there would be no space for new growth."

Clergy and educators are in the business of naming—discussing the undiscussable, raising hard questions, pointing out the elephant in the room, offering context, vocabulary, safety, and support to face life's biggest challenges. We have an opportunity to create a sacred and safe space for new growth in the Jewish community by giving our youth the tools and education to face the inevitable experience of death and loss. From the groundbreaking thanatology movement to child developmental research to the tremendous wisdom of our Sages, it is clear that society benefits from open conversations about death, dying, bereavement, and the afterlife, and that at varying levels children are capable of learning about these topics that humans have confronted for centuries. And it is even clearer that Jewish death education enables children to assimilate what they know with how they feel, cultivating numerous qualities of emotional resilience—teaching kids empathy, compassion and care, reflectiveness, emotional awareness, awe, and reverence.

One can never prepare for the shock of a tragic death, and even the deaths we are expecting cause tremendous grief, but Maurice Lamm reminds us: "The crises will come. If thinking on the subject is to be deferred, if there is to be no education *before* the crisis, what chance is there that we shall know how to handle the crisis when it arrives?"[28] By addressing these topics in our adult lives and helping our children integrate such learning into *their* lives, we can ensure that we will all live Jewish lives of meaning and purpose. And when death does come, and it always will, "good grief" will no longer just be the stuff of comics.

Notes

1. See *Shulchan Aruch, Yoreh Dei-ah* 384:5
2. These examples are sourced from: Julia Weisz, "Mourning and Loss: Family Education Curriculum" (Congregation Or Ami, Calabasas, CA); Shoshana Zonderman and Sigma Coran, "The Jewish Approach to Death: A Family Education Program for Fourth and Fifth Grade Families" (Rockdale Temple, Cincinnati, OH); CHAI Curriculum Lessons (URJ Press).
3. Maurice Lamm, *The Jewish Way in Death and Mourning* (Middle Village, NY: Jonathan David, 2000), xii.
4. John T. Deines, "Thanatophobia: A Historical Perspective," in *Bereavement Counseling: A Multidisciplinary Handbook,* ed. Mark B. Schoenberg (Westport, CT: Greenwood, 1980), 37.
5. Russian microbiologist and Nobel Laureate Ilya Mechnikov coined the term in 1901 from the Greek roots *thanatos* and *ology,* meaning the study of death-related behavior. Thanatos was the Greek god of death.

6. Herman Feifel, "The Meaning of Death in American Society: Implications for Education," in *Death Education: Preparation for Living*, ed. B. Green and D. Irish (Cambridge, MA: Schenkman, 1971), 114–28.

7. "Growing Old in a New Age," Center on Aging, University of Hawai'i, http://www.growingold.hawaii.edu/prog11.htm.

8. George R. Krupp and Bernard Kligfeld, "The Bereavement Reaction: A Cross-Cultural Evaluation," *Journal of Religion and Health* 1, no. 3 (1962): 226.

9. Herman Feifel, "The Thanatological Movement: Respice, Adspice, Prospice," in *The Thanatology Community and the Needs of the Movement*, ed. Elizabeth J. Clark and Austin H. Kutscher (New York: Haworth, 1992), 6.

10. Feifel, "The Thanatological Movement," 9.

11. Earl A. Grollman and Gisela Héau, *Talking about Death: A Dialogue Between Parent and Child* (Boston: Beacon, 1976), ix.

12. Denial, Anger, Bargaining, Depression, Acceptance.

13. Feifel, "The Thanatological Movement," 10.

14. Earl A. Grollman, *Explaining Death to Children* (Boston: Beacon, 1967), ix.

15. Grollman, *Talking about Death*, x.

16. Simone de Beauvoir, *A Very Easy Death* (New York: Putnam, 1966).

17. Daniel Leviton, "The Scope of Death Education," *Death Education* 1, no. 1 (1977): 41–56.

18. *D'risha* was part of the *Beit Yisrael* commentary by late sixteenth-century Polish halachist and Talmudist Joshua ben Alexander HaCohen Falk.

19. Joo Ok Lee, "Death, Don't Want to Talk about It!," paper presented at the annual meeting of the Association for Childhood Education International (April 12–15, 2006), 3, http://www.eric.ed.gov/PDFS/ED495287.pdf.

20. Robert Kastenbaum and Lynn Fox, "Do Imaginary Companions Die? An Exploratory Study," *Omega* 56, no. 2 (2007–2008): 124.

21. Ibid., 125.

22. Charles A. Corr and David E. Balk, *Children's Encounters with Death, Bereavement, and Coping* (New York: Springer, 2010), 27.

23. Sally B. Hunter and Delores E. Smith, "Predictors of Children's Understandings of Death: Age, Cognitive Ability, Death Experience and Maternal Communicative Competence," *Omega* 57, no. 2 (2008): 149.

24. In the introduction to *Growing Jewish Minds, Growing Jewish Souls: Promoting Spiritual, Social, and Emotional Growth in Jewish Education* (New York: URJ Press, 2013), xii–xiv, editor Jeffrey S. Kress

outlines what he calls centripetal and centrifugal elements of spirituality and emotion. Centripetal elements anchor one's inner being and encompass "issues of reflectiveness, sense of wonder, emotional awareness, dealing with frustration and challenges, goal orientation, creativity, empathy and appreciation of one's strengths . . . [C]entrifugal elements have to do with pro-social activities such as social justice and social action as well as positive everyday social interactions."

25. Field of education developed, adapted, and debated by Jean Piaget, Lawrence Kohlberg, Emile Durkheim, Elliot Turiel, Carol Gilligan, Nel Nodding, and numerous other scholars.

26. Nel Noddings, *Caring: A Feminine Approach to Ethics and Moral Education* (Berkeley, Los Angeles, and London: University of California Press, 1984 and 2003).

27. David Wolpe, "Death and Meaning," *Sh'ma: A Journal of Jewish Ideas* 34 (September 2003), http://www.bjpa.org/Publications/downloadPublication.cfm?PublicationID=10911, 1–2.

28. Lamm, *Death and Mourning*, xii.

Choose Life: Identifying and Addressing the Spiritual Needs of *B'nei Mitzvah* Students and Families

Goldie Milgram

What does it take to move from self-centered to mitzvah-centered living, which is the essence of becoming *b'nei mitzvah* and living as a Jew? Centering on mitzvah rather than self is a strategic shift. Before modernity, becoming *b'nei mitzvah* involved a parental mentoring process in order to set one's children upon a healthy path towards adulthood by offering a Jewish lens for living a life of goodness. The restoration of this perspective points us toward the spiritual needs of *b'nei mitzvah* youth and families.

Mitzvah-centered living does not mean selfless living. It requires cultivation of the self, attention to the development of character, and the capacity for resilience in the face of life's challenges. Rather than defining spirituality, this article will illustrate by example. I first developed the methods for *b'nei mitzvah* spiritual education while serving Project Kesher in Russia and the Ukraine, where Jews had little to no sense of how to live as Jews and little to no interest in God and Shabbat or daily services. What turned them on was a relational reframing of a great many mitzvot—especially those that can have an impact on the quality of daily living. What I taught was the Torah of Real Relationships.

Given the norms of Jewish education here in the West, it takes courage for educators to shift back towards traditional *b'nei mitzvah* goals and away from the narrow range of *b'nei mitzvah* preparation skills

RABBI GOLDIE MILGRAM (RRC93), director of Reclaiming Judaism, is an innovator of resources and programs in the field of Jewish spiritual education and development. Her newest book is *Mitzvah Stories: Seeds for Inspiration and Learning*, honored by the National Jewish Book Awards. www.ReclaimingJudaism.org, www.Bmitzvah.org.

that has become our norm. The world is a scary place and religious educators are dearly needed who can successfully convey the many profound and effective Jewish tools of survival for the human spirit for the sake of our children and for us. This is where Judaism excels.

Today's *b'nei mitzvah* and families respond best to active learning. They require more than an intellectual knowledge of Judaism acquired through text study; they seek real relationships with Jewish educators. They need us to be part of their lives in order to help them integrate the spiritual principles and practices they require to appreciate and navigate the amazing journey called life.

Conveying and Activating Life-Giving Principles

However much *b'nei mitzvah* families feel connected to or alienated from Judaism, their highest hope is for their children to "choose life," beginning with surviving the perils of the teen years. Reframing Judaism as a spiritual practice supports this core need. Let's begin with Alyssa's cohort. (All names have been changed for reasons of confidentiality.) We have given the participants a deck of Mitzvah Cards[1] with which they can playfully discover a spiritual slant on the meaning and relevance of Judaism. Here are a few examples:

> *sh'mirat haguf* (**guard your health**). Take good physical care of your body, the precious instrument upon which your soul plays life for God. (Gen. 1:27)

> *lo tikom v'lo titur* (**hold no grudges and take no revenge**). Address loss and anger carefully, without taking revenge or multiplying wrongs. (Lev. 19:18)

> *shalom bayit* (**co-create peace**). Undertake conscious acts of self-restraint, love, and generosity that may yield greater peace at home. (Gen. 18:13, Ps. 34:15)

> *t'kiyat shofar* (**heed the shofar**). Release resistance to needed change, as shofar blasts sound the call to engage in the healing of relationships. (Num. 29:1)

Everyone is asked to sort their deck of fifty-two Mitzvah Cards into the mitzvot they know and love, those they don't feel ready for, or are not of interest, and those about which they want to know more. They are never to be judged for their choices.

"Now, find someone you don't know well in the room to share a mitzvah that is important to you—even if you never realized it was a mitzvah in the first place. Be aware that anything someone shares with you is confidential, which means you can't talk about it outside of this room to anyone. Any questions? . . . Good . . . . As many youth-adult partnerships as possible will be appreciated. I'll give you a signal after five minutes to switch and listen to your partner . . . Time is up. If you don't already, please make sure you know your partner's name and thank him or her for doing this with you. Who has something to ask or share? Alyssa, go ahead."

"Rabbi Goldie, Bran and I disagree. I selected and interpreted the 'Set No Obstacles' card as more than meaning Braille signs in elevators and ramps for wheelchairs. I think it also means not putting obstacles in front of ourselves."

"Can you give us an example of what you mean?"

"I haven't applied to violin camp because I think I'm not good enough to get in. My teacher says I'm being too hard on myself and that I will definitely get in. That's me 'setting an obstacle' for myself, right? My parents say to apply, too."

I allow a silence to begin. When a student starts to call out, "You are the best violinist Alys . . .," I hold up my hand, even though the praise is sweet. Her violin teachers have tried this; the willingness and awareness has to come from inside of her.

Aaron plays flute with serenity beyond his years. I ask him to take his flute in hand and give us a gentle melody during which the rest of the participants will reflect on the "Set No Obstacles" mitzvah in order to see how it relates to them in their own lives.

Signaling for a pause in Aaron's music and after softly thanking him, I see that Alyssa's hand is already up. "Rabbi, does this mean it is a mitzvah for me to apply to violin camp? I really do want to go and the obstacle is judging myself ineligible right now." Across the room behind her, Alyssa's mom had wept softly during the reflection interval. Her father's back was to me, but he is now sitting forward on his seat listening to her closely—as is the whole group. A classmate calls out, "You are an amazing violist, Alyssa. I'd choose you!" I hold up my hand for stillness, saying, "Let's give her even more space to decide. The awareness of what a mitzvah means for you in your life today, and everyday, just like what happened to Alyssa, that is how holiness happens. It's called *k'dushah*. Can you all say that, please: *k'dushah*." They do.

Another hand, Ashley: "Like in *Kaddish*?"

"That's right, and like in the *Kiddush* over wine, too. In the Passover *Kiddush* is a line that reads, "Times we are free, holiness happens—*z'man cheruteinu mikra kodesh.*"
Others share their own obstacles, some set by themselves, some set by others. And then, "Rabbi Goldie!"
"Yes, Alyssa?"
"My parents, teachers, and you left me free to decide. And if it's a mitzvah not to set an obstacle, then surely it is a mitzvah to remove an obstacle! So I am definitely going to apply." The class bursts into applause and hoots of joy for her.
"How do you feel now, Alyssa, having made that decision?"
"Rabbi Goldie, it's like a miracle, I feel so light and free."

The capacity to move beyond the literal into metaphor typically arrives during adolescence. The difference between the interpretation of Bran, age 11.25, and Alyssa, age 12.5, clearly reveals the presence of this developmental divide.[2]

Reducing Social Isolation by Cultivating the Minyan of Your Life

Friendship is a central Jewish spiritual practice. This can be taught by inviting everyone present to sit and create a list of those for whom you would try your best to show up in times of suffering, as well as times of celebration, whom you believe would also do the same for you. Ask them to not include parents, grandparents, siblings, or pets.

"I saw some of you erasing. What led you to take someone off your list? Sam, yes?"
"I realized that a student at my public school who I always help out when he has trouble with his math homework doesn't really care about me at all. He always wants to come to my parties because they are at our beach house in a great spot, but when my mom almost died he never called me to do anything with him. He ignores me unless he wants something. He's a false friend. So I took him off my list."
A mom raises her hand: "I gave a long hard look at my business associates and thought of only one that is a real friend who shows up for me as much as I do for her. The others just want to get ahead. Why should we include them in the bar mitzvah? Our actual family lives so far apart from one another we need our gathering to reconnect and rebuild our relationships. And

why should my son have to invite all seventy-five classmates? I'd rather he have just his three close friends with whom he hangs most days. Isn't that more meaningful and honorable a mitzvah? I mean no offense to this group, I'm just thinking that authenticity matters and family connections are impossible when a whole class has to be invited."

A father: "I agree. We are all good people here, but these events get huge, loud, and meaningless. The kids know who are really true and honorable friends. Too many *b'nei mitzvah* celebrations and they begin to burn out and become cynical."

A mom: "My older son had his bar mitzvah preparation in a much smaller congregation, where there are only a few *b'nei mitzvah* each year. He was so hurt when he wasn't invited to one of his classmate's service and party."

"A small class is an important case to consider. The formal definition of minyan, the minimum number for a supportive community of prayer and care, is ten who have attained *b'nei mitzvah* age. Certain parts of the service cannot be offered without a minyan present, such as the *Bar'chu*, Torah reading, and the *Kaddish*. There are many mitzvot where we show up to help complete strangers—including ensuring there is a minyan for prayer. Why might our Sages have set a quorum for a service that includes Kaddish?" The floor is open for thoughts and feelings.

After the discussion, we continue with noting that our Sages emphasize empathy as a spiritual practice (i.e., acting with awareness of the impact of our choices upon the feelings of others). They set this principle under the mitzvah *lo tirtzach* (Do Not Murder") by declaring that causing someone humiliation or shame is like shedding his or her blood.

I hope older policies will be replaced by empowerment strategies, beginning with mitzvah-centered preparation of families to support them in making independent, honorable decisions. I also know that organizations are like cruise ships—those involved at every level have to be onboard with policy changes for healthy change to be able to take hold. A minyan used to be made of one's daily community—those who really do know your name and whose businesses and life stories were closely interwoven with yours. Everyone needs a minyan of good, true friends and the ability to discern who they are and how to be a good friend. Where, when, and how to set healthy boundaries is foundational to spiritual development for this stage of life. We spend a lot of time on this.

Cultivating Deep Listening

We focus early and often on nuancing the mitzvah of *Sh'ma*—by which we mean Listening O' Israel! Part of the spirituality of growing up is family members becoming better at listening to and understanding one another. The human spirit requires listening and validation in order to thrive. Here's an activity that has proven to be very effective. Parents and youth are asked to make a list of all of the feelings they are having about this time in their lives. They are not to consult with one another, though they are to sit in families while doing this. Then the youth reads his or her list aloud, to be repeated back, as much as possible, by the parent. A likely combination appeared on Arthur's inventory:

"Scared, excited, worried, curious, anxious, too busy . . ."
His mother responds: "Arthur, you don't have to be anxious. I promised not to come into your room without knocking ever again, and I won't."
Holding up my hand to pause the encounter, I explain that the important job right now is just to reflect back feelings. Clarification of what is meant by the feeling is the second step. "Arthur, what did you mean by anxious?"
"I'm anxious about standing up and speaking or singing in front of people."
"Yeah, me, too," comes from another family group, a high-pitched, female voice.
"Arthur," I ask, "what might support you to feel comfortable to do this vital life skill? Everyone, let's brainstorm some options in support of the challenge Arthur's anxious feeling reveals."
"Practice in front of a mirror."
"Make an art project or put on a play, and we'll be in it so you don't have to be on stage yourself."
"Go on the road with Uncle Stan, he's a salesman and can show you how he gets up his courage and creates his pitches."
"You just did it! You spoke in front of us. Do that some more."

The rule is that the youth gets to pick which option to implement. Arthur chose the Uncle Stan option. Now, continue with the youth listening to, and reflecting back, a family member's list.

Deliberation is one of eighteen awareness qualities (*midot*) for human development, an approach known as *musar*. These *midot* were expressed by Menachem Mendel of Satanov in 1812 in his book

Heshbon HaNefesh (Accounting of the Soul).[3] In the exercise above we paired the attribute of *deliberation* with the mitzvah of *shalom bayit* (co-creating peace at home in ways that make space for healthy love). Learning about the possibilities of shifting from reactivity into conscious living is very helpful, though difficult for adolescents. Youth and parents lean in closely for such shared life-learning opportunities.

The more supportive relationships our youth have going into their teen years, the better. We ask each group to make a list of those people they particularly admire for how they "do Jewish" and another list for people they know who share their talents and interests. Then we encourage them to make dates to interview some of these individuals and involve them in their *b'nei mitzvah* process.

A student with autism, to the point he couldn't possibly do public speaking, e-mails a Jewish fabric artist for such a meeting. They hit it off and she helps him to vision and create twelve tribes blessing panels. He used his own *yad* (a present from his grandparents) to point to each tribe's banner as its name appeared during the Torah reading. A student who loves writing contacts a local Jewish Israel columnist to meet. He develops a piece for *b'nei mitzvah* guests that he names the "Torah Times," in which he reports on information he'd found about a verse in his Torah portion that had captured his interest, the mixed multitude of slaves that left Egypt and covenanted along with the Israelites at Sinai. He conducts a discussion of reactions to the verse and his findings in lieu of a traditional *d'var Torah*. Guidance toward active community roles utilizing youth and family skills and talents is vital to post–*b'nei mitzvah* engagement and personal health.[4]

Seeking Answers to Core Questions

Part of what the human spirit requires is purposeful living. Students often ask whether there is a compelling reason to be Jewish, especially if one is already a good person. It is a reasonable question given that we are a non-dogmatic tradition. Is there a reason for us to exist beyond our sheer determination to continue?

"What are *your* ideas about whether the Jewish people have a mission? We don't actively seek converts to our faith. So why are we here?"

Ben: "To raise money for Israel?" Me: "That's part of the answer. What else?"

Casey: "To feed the poor?" Me: "Yes, also a great mitzvah and . . ."

Eventually, after many actions that are all essentially mitzvot are called out, I explain that: "Our mission encompasses every mitzvah you have mentioned and more. In the Torah, God tells us to *k'doshim tihiyu*. Who recognizes a Hebrew word in there?"

A father raises his hand. "*Kodesh*—holy."

"That's right, our mission is to become holy by knowing how to support each other through truly living the mitzvot in a free, life-giving way."

Another question at this developmental stage is whether the Torah is a literal document. Discovering that there are multiple legitimate levels of interpretation is foundational to spirituality and an adult appreciation of Judaism:

"In the Torah we read that Rebecca, who would later wed Isaac, fell off her camel the first time she met him. Now, how could that have happened? What could it mean? Was she just a total klutz? . . . Binah, yes?"

"She got so scared that a strange man was coming toward her that she wasn't paying attention to her riding and she fell off her camel. Plonk, splat. And how embarrassing!"

"Could be" (there's that developmental divide again). "What else could it mean? Could it be that 'fell off her camel' is an expression, a way people of that time used to talk, as in asking if someone is 'losing their marbles'? Bobby Schwartz, yes?"

"Could it mean falling in love at first sight?"

"Yes, that is another good option. All peoples' scriptures use folk sayings, just like we do today. Since falling in love isn't all that there is to loving relationships, we are going to consider the nature of love today. Would parents please come into the center of the circle and all of the youth sit on the outside. This exercise is where parents discuss the difference between falling in love and growing in love, and youth listen. We call this type of fish bowl exercise a *maagal chochma*—a 'wisdom circle'; we'll be doing them on lots of topics.[5] If anyone wishes to sit out, you are welcome to do so" (and so one parent did, given her marriage had ended two weeks before).

Next, the youth were invited to gather in the center to discuss what they observed in the parents' discussion.

"Several parents said they love each other more in some years or moments than others. Isn't love supposed to be forever? Why can't it last?"

"Great question. Lara, I also see your hand."

"They all agreed that wanting someone physically gets in the way of seeing who the person is, of knowing if they are a good person, or if you even share real interests. I had a boyfriend at camp this past summer and after a month back home I wondered what I had seen in him. It was like chemistry made us want each other. Almost all of the adults described something like that has happened to them."

"You heard that it is important to have shared interests, that physical attraction isn't enough, and you learned about that because of a camp boyfriend. Thank you so much for adding that helpful comment! Ken?"

"Mr. Magnus said growing in love is the most important kind of love, that it is hard work and takes a lifetime. How do we know how to do that?"

"What a great question. Perhaps one of the parents can offer an example?"

Why Add Spirituality to Jewish Education?

The capacity to nurture *nahat ruach*—the well-being of our students—requires us first to appreciate the origins of their spiritual needs and distress, e.g., *kotzer ruach*.[6] Here are just a few:

- Over 50 percent of these families are fractured by divorce, some twice during the childhood of our students.
- The *b'nei mitzvah* of today are typically wanted children. They often have older parents than the historical norm, and many of their conceptions required assisted reproductive technologies.[7]
- A good number of the students have subtle and even severe developmental challenges, as well as the early signs of eating disorders[8] and depression.
- Suicide is the third leading cause of death of young persons and accounts for 13 percent of all deaths among youth and young adults aged ten to twenty-four. "1 in 6 high school students has seriously considered suicide, and 1 in 12 has attempted it, according to the semi-annual survey on youth risk behavior published [in June 2012] by the Centers for Disease Control and Prevention."[9] Many struggle with gender identity without supportive recognition and mentoring.
- Menarche, the average onset of menstruation is now down to 12.5 years; it was 16 in the 1800s.[10] Sexual experimentation is well underway among our youth. Our girls start showing breasts between age 8 and 10, two years earlier than their educators' generations. Works by Steingraber[11] detail many studies

that show that girls who enter this new normal of early puberty report more anxiety, negative self-images, and suicide attempts. They are also more likely to abuse drugs, take up cigarette smoking, and drink alcohol than their counterparts. They are also often on the receiving end of physical and sexual violence. Being Jewish brings no statistical immunity.[12] Let me bring this closer to home for some readers—depending on the study, at least one third of clergy were sexually abused while growing up.

- There is a society-wide soul-deadening excess of consumerism. Our children taunt each other over fashion labels.
- Mortgage crises have led to widespread fear of one's family losing their home. Our communities are full of overextended families.
- Fewer Jews are in self-regulated family businesses and senior healthcare professions. Most have chaotic, stressed families where many parents are employed in megacorporations disrespectful of the personal aspects of life. High rates of unemployment and rapid shifts in which skills employers value render parents and older siblings anxious of remaining employed and despairing of being rendered redundant.
- Unhealed anxieties and fears of future persecution and loss driven by the Holocaust and other traumas abound.[13] We have been treating our youth less like feeling human beings and more like hard drives upon which to lodge all possible Jewish knowledge. It is as though any given child might one day, G-d forbid, be the "last Torah standing."

The attendant unruliness, broken spirits, and despair of our young people and families in an age of resurgent nuclear threats, global warming, and widely reported slaughter of innocents in our own schools, colleges, and inner cities is legitimately terrifying. Countries like Syria, which were at peace when our *b'nei mitzvah* parents or their children were born, now have governments that are slaughtering their own populace. Learning to live as a liberal Jewish minority in the age of roiling Christian, Islamic, and even Jewish fundamentalism is also of concern.

The flight to video games is rampant. A bat mitzvah student recently has told me, "These games teach survival skills that I could need—just look at the world. I've become really good at this. I won a house on an island and an enchanted garden. It's so peaceful there." Unlike in her home where warring parents wonder what they first saw in each other—while they also try to get her disabled brother to physical therapy appointments—this youth seeks fantasylands for security and happiness.

Jewish clergy and educators are largely unprepared to be of service in the face of all that I have described. The skills we teach, and the single mitzvah project our *b'nei mitzvah* are required to do, are but holy blanket scraps too tiny to begin to heal these wounds. New *b'nei mitzvah* perspectives are seriously needed. There are many authentic Jewish practices for releasing the tensions our families face, helping them discover a life-giving, mitzvah-centered Judaism.[14] For example:

Families arrive with their assignment, which is a picture of the students' parents (or guardians) before they had children. The families explain the stories behind the photos; some adults have also brought pictures of their own parents. We are fulfilling the mitzvah of *zachor* (remembering those who gave us life). Suddenly a young man interrupts: "I thought you hated grandpa!"

"It's more complicated than that," the father responds. "I'm sorry you got that impression. I need to tell you more stories about him—he was both difficult and fascinating. He taught me many important life lessons."

I interject: "Did you notice that there is no mitzvah in the deck titled 'Love Your Parents'? Let's explore why the mitzvah is to honor our parents. Why didn't the Sages say *love*?"

Separating them again into a youth and parent circle, a rabbinical student works with the youth, and I with their parents. The parents have lots of baggage about their families of origin. They quickly grasp the wisdom of not forcing such love. We shift to a discussion of how to receive adolescent bouts of hatred and rejection, while still holding their children in "love." Leaving a skillful parent to continue the group, I move over to the rabbinical student's section. I happen to have walked in while Talya—age twelve and three-quarters—is speaking; she's twelve and three quarters: "My mother doesn't understand me, or listen to me; she just wants things her way. I know I have to listen to her, watching her smoke her life away, my soul hurts so much. Is it because I love her or just hate her for being so awful and messed up? I can't tell the difference."

The rabbinic student reflects back in the manner we have found most useful—no fixing, just active listening: "Your mom smokes, is demanding, and doesn't listen to you. She doesn't understand you. Your soul hurts from watching her smoke and you aren't sure if you love her or hate her." Talya: "Like, yeah. That's so true. Is there a prayer for wanting your mom not to be so f__d up?"

Time is up and I step in. "For sure there is. We'll go there next week. Weather permitting our session will be at Telemark Park. Let's close today with your favorite Julie Silver song, 'Shiru L'Adonai.'"

Finding and Expressing the Prayer of One's Heart

Upon arriving at the park, everyone flops in a circle near me on the grass. Talya indicates she still wants to pray for her mom, and lots of us have our souls gummed up with things that are going on in our lives.

"I invite each of you to find a private place and pour out everything that's blocking up your happiness. Whisper or shout it out as though there is a listening God. Some of us think there is, some say not. We have agreed that we do create a Godfield, a powerful sense of God when we live in relationship to the mitzvot, and that prayer, when meaningful, is just such a mitzvah.

"So pour out everything, and if you run out of what to say, take a humming break and if there is more, you can start expressing yourself again. Go until you feel totally empty.

"Next, just look around you and wait to see if awareness arises, or, perhaps you will find something around you that is an answer or symbol for your hopes or prayers. You can break a stick or throw a rock at the ground."

I once thought nothing came of this practice for me, and then I tried again, leaned back against a tree and an eagle's nest was over my head. My husband and I had been on the road working for three years of my rabbinic teaching, traveling, and all of our stuff was in storage. The message was that it was time to create a nest together. We found a beautiful apartment, got furniture, and our laughter and love came right back. This practice is called *hitbodedut* (making yourself alone with God). I like to start with something like: "Holy One of Blessing, I am so frustrated by ____ or upset by ____ and also, I'm really angry about ____ and then there's ____ . . ."

At this age, young families aren't inclined toward long, quiet, sitting meditations. Something as active as *hitbodedut* works for most, and they can do it without us. There are also simpler approaches—like opening the ark and leaving the room to give each student private time to express the prayer of his or her heart each week. "Dear God, this week may be my first kiss. Did I pick the right person to have it with?" "Dear God, my mom's cancer is spreading, I'm so scared. Will my teacher be a good person with whom to talk about it?" The emerging field of Jewish spiritual guidance is termed *hashpa'ah*, a rich resource for expanding our service as Jewish educators.

Gratitude and Blessing

National studies on self-esteem show rising rates of young adult depression as linked to parental and societal tendencies to praise personal qualities.[15] Learning to appreciate others, the mitzvah of *hakarat hatov* (acknowledging the good), is more than expressing gratitude—research shows it is sharing the details of good behavior.

> Our *b'nei mitzvah* are off in the garden, writing vignettes of appreciated times with one or another parent/guardian. The parents with me are doing the same in regard to their son or daughter. It's the last week of this cycle of the program. When they return, the youths will invite their parents to walk with them and hear their appreciations. There will be tears and exclamations of surprise. I encourage the parents to save their reflections for integration into the words they will speak at the *b'nei mitzvah oneg* or reception. We primed them at the beginning of this practice with examples from sharings overheard over the years. For example:
> "Mom, I was remembering how you came to my room the night our dog Tiff died. How I fell asleep while you were still holding me."
> "Dad, it's so loving how you make pizza dough bread on the grill for us, when you can't even eat any wheat at all!"
> "Ben, I was remembering when you offered to skip your school event to stay with grandpa, because you didn't want dad and I to have to cancel our anniversary trip when his aide had called in sick. I cried with awe and joy."
> Next, we will have them ask each other with what they would like to be blessed in the year to come. They will write this down faithfully and each night pray for the blessing to be fulfilled for their parent or child. They love doing this. At times during the year they will also pray for what another student or family needs. They will also learn to ask God for what they need and discover that something inside of them shifts towards the possibility of things.

For this age group, God is best appreciated as a metaphor, e.g., the Bedrock of Life (*Tzur Hei HaOlamim*), *Maayan Raz* (The Wellspring of Mystery), or an awesome experience of Presence

(*Shechinah*). The young people discover God names that speak to them, that facilitate a meaningful connection. One girl, who hid from a predator cousin in a closet for an entire night, speaks of God as *Aron HaKodesh Sheli* (My Holy Closet). When I show her where this very idea appears in Psalms as "My Shelter," she glows and says in an incredulous voice: "So I have known God and am blessed just like King David!" I tell my students that I will always take their calls as priority, no matter what job I have. Some will dearly need this as a lifeline in challenging times, even if all I do is active listening and make a quality referral to local assistance.

Sometimes groups surprise the program facilitators by sharing the many things they have appreciated in the program and about each of us. They ask what we would like them to pray for *us*. We reflect and share honestly. We, too, are renewed in the process of the sessions and feel ever so blessed.

In Conclusion

Ours are the minds and hearts to which our youth and families come to find support for their spiritual needs, too. It is only human that we have our own spiritual needs, as well. Jewish spiritual education incorporates the mitzvah of *pikuach nefesh.* We need to nurture *our* spiritual lives, as well.

We want our children to live and thrive—to choose life. The time for Jewish spiritual education and development has arrived. May you be blessed to deepen and delight in this dimension of sacred service.

Notes

1. *Mitzvah Cards: One Mitzvah Leads to Another* (New Rochelle: Reclaiming Judaism Press, 2011) are available through Amazon.com. Discounted orders of a dozen or more are available through www.ReclaimingJudaism.org. Each phrase appears in Hebrew characters, transliteration, an inclusive interpretation intended to inspire discussion and practice, and the textual citation(s) with which our ancestors primarily associate each mitzvah.

2. A good discussion on adolescence and metaphor can be found in chapter 4, "Cognitive Development: Processes and Transitions," in Nancy J. Cobb, *Adolescence: Continuity, Change and Diversity,* 7th ed. (San Mateo, CA: Sinaeur Associates, 2010).

3. Menachem Mendel of Satanov, *Heshbon HaNefesh*, trans. Dovid Landesman (Nanuet, NY: Feldheim, 1996).

4. Thirty meaningful roles for youth and parents: http://bmitzvah. org/teachings/holy-rolers-who-are-you-becoming-community.

5. Goldie Milgram, *Make Your Own Bar/Bat Mitzvah: A Personal Approach to Creating a Meaningful Rite of Passage* (San Francisco: 2nd edition, Reclaiming Judaism Press, 2013).

6. Exodus 6:9, also see *Chumash Meirat Einayim*, Ikkar Siftei Chachamim (on Rashi 6:12), citation kuf (Jerusalem: Hotzaat HaTanach HaMefuar, 1995)

7. *2010 Assisted Reproductive Technology Surveillance*, http://www.cdc. gov/mmwr/preview/mmwrhtml/ss5209a1.htm; L.A. Schieve et al., "Estimation of the Contribution of Non–Assisted Reproductive Technology Ovulation Stimulation Fertility Treatments to US Singleton and Multiple Births," *American Journal of Epidemiology* 170 (2009): 1396–1407.

.8 Caroline Peyser, *A Guide for Addressing Eating Disorders in a Jewish Education Setting* (Jerusalem: Academy for Torah Initiatives and Directions, 2005), 14.

9. Meghan Neal, "1 in 12 Teens Have Attempted Suicide: Report," http://www.nydailynews.com/life-style/health/1-12-teens-attempted-suicide-report-article-1.1092622#ixzz2QrC4BwTJ.

10. Peter A. Lee and Christopher P. Houck, "Puberty and Its Disorders," in *Pediatric Endocrinology*, 5th ed., vol. 2, ed. Fima Lifshitz (Boca Raton: CRC Press, 2007), 275.

11. Sandra Steingraber, *The Falling Age of Puberty in U.S. Girls*, http://www.breastcancerfund.org/assets/pdfs/publications/falling-age-of-puberty.pdf.

12. Sharon Lowenstein, "Confronting Sexual Abuse in Jewish Families," *Moment* 15, no. 2 (April 1990): 48–53; Marcia Cohn Spiegel, "Spirituality for Survival: Jewish Women Recovering from Abuse," *Journal of Feminist Studies in Religion* 12, no. 2 (Fall 1996): 121–37.

13. Cheri Brown, "Unhealed Terrors." *Tikkun Magazine* (Winter 2011), http://www.tikkun.org/nextgen/unhealed-terror; Carola de Vries Robles, "Can We Invite God in Again?" *"Hashpa'ah* after the *Shoah* (Holocaust)," in *Seeking and Soaring: Jewish Approaches to Spiritual Direction*, ed. Goldie Milgram (New Rochelle, NY: Reclaiming Judaism Press, 2009).

14. Reclaiming Judaism, in collaboration with NewCaje offers a two-year distance-learning educator training in the principles, texts, and methods of Jewish spiritual guidance and education, http://www.ReclaimingJudaism.org.

15. "Praising Children for Their Personal Qualities May Backfire, New Research Finds," http://www.apa.org/news/press/releases/2013/02/children-self-esteem.aspx.

An Experiment in Spiritual Education: Teacher as Researcher, Student as Theologian

Joel Mosbacher and Wendy Grinberg

Is spirituality educable, or do teachers need a different approach altogether to cultivate spiritual development? Would it be worthwhile for high school students to explore their own ideas about God and existential questions in a supportive, student-directed series of conversations? We believe that more than being taught about God, people come to their own conclusions through a series of thought experiments, conversations, and experiences, testing out theories until they find one (or more) that speaks to them. Since people's ideas of God often change over time, it may be more important to give students the skills to revisit and revise their ideas rather than to instruct them in a particular theology.

The topic of this issue of the *CCAR Journal* was the impetus for the two of us to work together to explore an approach to talking about God with teenagers. We had worked together as a rabbi and an educator on the same synagogue staff from 1998 to 2001. Today we live in close proximity in a different state. Joel works in a congregation, and Wendy consults to congregations in the area of education.

RABBI JOEL MOSBACHER, D. Min. (C98) is the spiritual leader for the past twelve years of Beth Haverim Shir Shalom Synagogue in Oakland, New Jersey. He earned his Doctorate of Ministry from HUC-JIR, where his substantive paper focused on a spirituality curriculum for middle school students.

WENDY GRINBERG, RJE is a graduate of the Hornstein Program and Near Eastern and Judaics Studies programs at Brandeis University with fifteen years of experience in congregational and national Jewish educational settings. She is currently the founder and director of the Jewish Education Lab and clinical faculty at HUC-JIR's New York School of Education. She is also a student in the executive Ed.D. program at the William Davidson School of Education at Jewish Theological Seminary.

Method

We turned to early childhood education for a methodology. In the Reggio Emilia approach, teachers use documentation to measure student learning; share progress with students, teachers, parents, and administrators; and make decisions about the next steps in their curriculum. Thinking about spiritual education has evolved: David Hay and Rebecca Nye have described an approach to children's spiritual development that honors the individuality of each child.[1] Because it is likely neither possible nor desirable to outline a series of spiritual steps through which the teacher expects each child to progress, we thought applying the documentation/reflection model to this subject matter and this age group would be appropriate and instructive.

Rabbi Dr. Michael Shire describes "three elements of curriculum design [that contribute] to religious development in Jewish education: encounter, reflection and instruction."[2] Rather than try to provide all three of these experiences in this limited framework, we focused on reflection. Reflection is a chance for students to discuss "religious questions of meaning." In this phase, teachers act more as counselors and active listeners. Our suspicion was that while high school students may have had both opportunities for encounter and instruction, they may have had less of a chance to reflect and refine their own spiritual ideas.

Our questions were: Can we extrapolate the principles of early childhood documentation and apply them to older children in a curriculum about God and spirituality? What will happen if the teacher takes the role of observer/researcher and the students take the role of theologian? How will the students document their growth and questions, and can we use this documentation to determine what material and discussions to introduce to the class?

We should explain that while we did some research to understand the Reggio approach to documentation, we were not concerned with being purists regarding the theory or method. First, we were extrapolating the idea and applying it to high school students. Second, we think it is important to note that we are not researchers primarily but teachers, and we want to encourage others in our situation to experiment with different approaches to spiritual education that resonate and that might be fruitful for both student and teacher.

Therefore, we designed an experimental elective class for high school students wherein students would discuss their ideas about God and how God acts in the world, while Joel as the teacher would primarily record their thoughts. Later, he would reflect their ideas back to the students. Six students enrolled in the class, and attendance was inconsistent. The class met for five sessions (one that was planned had to be canceled due to weather). In planning the class, we anticipated the students playing a larger role in their own documentation. We felt this was an important adaptation of the documentation methodology for older students. At the beginning and end of each class, Joel asked the students to reflect on a text and/or question. He asked them to think if the discussions had changed their ideas in any way.

We thought that students might use technology like video diaries or online communal conversation tools to share their reflections, but in practice, while students sometimes submitted their reflections via their phones, mostly they used pencil and paper to record their thoughts. We think this was mostly due to the fact that students did not put much time into this class outside of the classroom, so they used what was most efficient and at their disposal during class time. We should also note that this use of technology would have been new and unusual for both the teacher and the students. We could have been clearer and more insistent about the need to incorporate these reflections and how to do that.

In between each class, we (the instructors) met by phone to review the students' comments and plan the next class. This collaboration time is an essential step to the documentation process as envisioned in Reggio. While the teacher spends a lot of time observing during class time, he/she should review the observations with a colleague after class to analyze progress and plan the subsequent class. This was a crucial part of the process for both of us. Insights about the material and the class became clear as a result of this collaborative reflection time. Wendy had a unique perspective, not having been to the class but reviewing the notes most of the time. On the other hand, when she did substitute teach, the roles were reversed. Having notes and reflection time allows the teacher to take a step back and analyze the learning taking place during class. The colleague provides insights that come from reviewing notes and listening to the teacher reflect. (We speak more about how this worked in the "Lessons Learned: Collaborative Planning and Reflection" section of this article.)

We spoke at length to plan the approach to the class, as it was a departure from conventional teaching. We outlined the best way to explain the methodology to the students. Joel explained the class was a place for the students to talk about their ideas about God. He told them that the class was private, but that it was also a research experiment for this article. He explained that students would share their ideas and he would reflect back to them in the hopes they would see how their own thinking was developing as a result of the class sessions. His role, he told the students, was to guide, help them reflect, ask quiet students to share, and make sure nobody monopolized the entire discussion.

After this explanation of the approach, Joel asked the students to write a reflection on the questions: What do you believe about God, and why? What's your big question about God you hope we'll talk about? Then he shared a simple translation of Maimonides' Thirteen Principles of Faith. The students discussed the text in a sort of free-flowing, self-directed discussion, during which Joel for the most part quietly recorded their comments on his tablet. For the final five minutes of class, Joel asked the students to write a reflection on how they were feeling about the discussion at that moment. Our goal for the first class was to introduce students to the method and get some feedback from students about our first experimental session. Student journals showed that four of the students felt the class discussion meandered, but that two thought it was still interesting.

We planned for some communication between the students and Joel in between sessions. There was one student in particular who sent his thoughts, but other than that, this did not happen. Students did hand in all of their reflections from each class, and Joel wrote comments on them, which he then returned to them in the subsequent class.

In the students' reflections and in reviewing their classroom comments, we thought there might be a discrepancy behind the idea of God that had been taught to the students in school (particularly God as a character in biblical stories or as a subject of prayer) and the way that the students experience or don't experience God in their everyday lives. Therefore we formulated the following question for the second session: How is the God of the Torah the same, and how different, than the God you experience? This was the focus of the second session's discussion. At the end of the class, Joel asked the students if their opinions had changed. Four of the students said they had not changed their views, but one said, "I'm more open." The other two students used the reflection to explore the idea of miracles and how God may act in the world. One student wrote additional reflections to the rabbi after the first and second classes. After this class he wrote: "Tonight I feel that a lot of opinions changed in the group . . . In theology there can be many answers that are correct . . . I believe that all questions can have multiple correct answers. Scientists want everything to be all black and white, but in truth there are all different shades."

For the third class, Joel asked the students to write a response to this question: It is said that God revealed the Torah in every language in the world. What does that mean to you? For the self-led discussion, the students considered different ways of understanding God: the Creator who no longer intervenes, a puppet master, a conscience, nature, or the One who metes out reward and punishment. The discussion included a debate about God's gender and the language we use to describe God, as well as if or how God intervenes in the world. There was also a discussion about the truth of different faiths and whether religion was a force for good or a source of conflict. At the conclusion of class, students revisited the initial question and reflected on the discussion.

In the fourth class, we wanted to steer the students away from generalizations about God as real or not real or religion as good or bad, to focus on their own experiences. We started with the questions: What is the evidence of God in your life? What proof is there that there is no God, if you don't believe? We were careful in our formulation to include a nonjudgmental option for someone who did not believe or was not sure of his or her beliefs. For the text, we read this selection from Harold Kushner's *When Children Ask About God*:

To ask "when is God" suggests that God is not an object, but a quality of relationship, a way of feeling and acting that can be found anywhere, but only if certain things (study, gratitude, self-control, helpfulness, prayer, etc.) are in evidence at that particular moment. . . .

Where, then, is God? He is not everywhere. He is potentially any-where; when people act and treat each other in certain ways, so that the Spirit of God flows between them, we can say that God is then present.[3]

Again they were asked to reflect for the last few minutes of class in writing. Wendy substituted for Joel during this week of the class. Her experience was slightly different because she had no relationship with the students. Also, the students didn't have a text in front of them but instead had it read to them. When the con-versation stalled, Wendy asked probing questions. One student, we'll call him Tom, who had been rather outspoken about his lack of belief in God as well as his belief that religion was a source of wars, voiced the following sophisticated theological idea towards the end of class. It seemed that he was struggling with the idea of free-will and a distant, abstract God. When another student said, "God could be like hope," Tom replied, "If there's a parent who doesn't take care for you or give you anything, then it's not really a parent. So if you don't have faith in God, and God never did anything for you, I don't really believe in God." Another student shared how her thinking was developing as a result of our discus-sions in her journal reflection: "This conversation made me think about how God isn't a Creator, but maybe a creation." At the end of class, Wendy asked the students to prepare a presentation for the last session that showed how their thinking had developed over the course of the class.

In the final session, students watched a slide show prepared with Prezi that synthesized some of the ideas they had expressed throughout the course. You can watch the Prezi here: http://bit.ly/godclassprezi. In synthesizing the comments from the previous classes, we saw that student thinking was around the nature of God, how people relate to/believe in God, the balance of power and control in our lives, and the nature of evil. Students also had a chance to present their own reflections on how their thinking had developed over the sessions. Some of the students had written re-flections that they read; others spoke from notes or extemporane-ously. Here are a few of the students' final reflections on the class:

I think the experience has been different. I like not just being taught to . . . God is such a complex and open topic that it's good to not just be taught about it. I came to see more of the arguments for and against believing God is real.

Before this, I didn't really believe in the whole God thing, and even though the class was a good experience, my views didn't change. We did have deep conversations though.

Before I took the class, I believed, but I didn't have an official—a formulated—vision of Him. Now I understand Him more, a strong force between people when we pray, the still small voice, and I think that God can work miracles. There are many. We just don't notice them. I think that there can be an infinite amount of interpretations of the Torah and an infinite amount of manifestations of God.

The class itself was helpful. If you want to ensure your beliefs, it was a helpful way to develop those ideas.

Taking this course has definitely changed the way I think about God. This class made me realize that everybody has very different views and opinions on God . . . When I was younger, I thought of God as a man with a long white beard and a large white robe who sat on a cloud and looked down upon his people. But then my thinking shifted—God was a tree, a lamp, a chair, the sky, God was everything all around us. God helped us to make the right decisions. My thinking shifted again once I started taking this class. I now realize that no matter what, you should rely on God. You can put your faith in God, or turn to God when things are hard or you need somebody to listen. But you should never assume that every bad decision, every wrong-doing thing is God's fault . . . Now I believe that's what God is: something to listen, something to pray to, something for people to believe in.

Lessons Learned

Documentation

Joel felt that being put in the position of researcher, documenter, and listener above all else was an incredible experience as a teacher. He was required and prepared to truly sit and listen to what the students were saying. This practice allowed him to listen more carefully for patterns, deeper questions, and significant insights. He also learned to trust the students, realizing that they could be responsible stewards of the conversation and that they were perfectly capable of carrying on a wonderful, often intense conversation without needing a teacher to manage it in any significant way. It allowed the students to practice respectful discourse and listening to one another—crucial skills for teens and young adults. This practice redefined what a teacher is for both students and teacher: not only someone who purports to have all the answers, but also a partner with a different perspective, someone who can offer reflections, invite deep and extended thinking, and learn from that interaction what might best serve the students going forward.

Taking notes during class allowed Joel to notice things that happened in the class that he had forgotten or missed completely. Wendy noticed that in reading over the notes, her perception of the class session changed dramatically. Often our impressions of the success of a class are not based on data; documenting student ideas gave us as teachers something concrete to help us evaluate students' growth. We think students also responded well to this process; writing down their ideas, and especially reflecting them back in the final session, legitimized those ideas and the exploration of different opinions in a Jewish setting. We believe it helped the students to feel heard when they saw their thoughts presented on screen. Because we want the students to continue to engage in dialogue with us during this critical time in their spiritual development, it was probably more important to us to communicate an openness and acceptance than to instruct them in theology.

Student Journaling

Requiring students to write reflections at the beginning and end of the class allowed the students to be reflective, notice things about their own views and how they changed. It allowed them to express things in writing that was hard for them to figure out how to say out loud; and it allowed them to say things privately in writing to Joel that they might not otherwise ever have shared out loud. On their own, more than a few of them were able to name their own growth patterns throughout the class. Others felt their beliefs were reinforced by class discussions. In addition, they seemed to remember and relate to material from previous classes in a much stronger way then they likely would have had they not been given the opportunity to write from class to class.

For example, one of the students (we'll call her Rachel), took the class at the same time she was preparing her speech for her bat mitzvah. Initially, she brought a draft of the speech that seemed insincere. In the course of a meeting with Joel, he realized that she was expressing doubt in her belief in God and a hesitation in expressing that, both to Joel and perhaps to her parent. In the meeting, Joel told her that sometimes the most devoted Jews ask the toughest questions. It seemed to him that the conversations in class and the conversations in bat mitzvah preparation were complementary, even one in the same. As Rachel volunteered with victims of domestic violence for her mitzvah project, she questioned why she should believe in a God who commands us to honor our parents while there are abusive parents in the world. In one-on-one meetings, Joel was able to introduce texts in which the Rabbis struggle with the definition of honor. Because of the two sets of conversations, Rachel seemed more open to acceptance of different interpretations of God and eased her fury against a God who would ignore this suffering. In the final session, she said, "I didn't believe in God before, and I still don't, but now I understand how people might believe, especially when you're struggling."

As the teacher, Joel felt having their writing was immensely helpful as he tried to gauge what they were and were not internalizing, what they were and were not learning from each other, and what they were and were not getting from the texts. It also allowed Joel to write to the students privately after class. This served many purposes: responding to individual questions and thoughts, extending the learning beyond the short number of in-class hours, legitimizing the students' ideas and pushing them to think even more deeply, and building the relationship between the students and the rabbi. We would like to explain these last two points with a few examples.

By writing notes in the student journals, Joel was able to affect the class dynamics. In the first few sessions, the boys tended to dominate the conversation, while the girls would sit more quietly. After discussing this in our reflection/planning meeting, Joel decided to address this in his written notes to students. He was able to privately invite the boys to make room for other voices to be heard and at the same time strongly encourage the girls to make their voices heard.

The chance to build a relationship with a clergy person and role model at this stage in one's spiritual development seems very important to us. When Wendy substituted, she noticed that the student who had been most engaged in discussions and had written to Joel in between classes approached the director of education before class. He asked if he could switch to a different class! After class, Wendy stopped the student, explained what she had observed, and asked why he wanted to withdraw. He said that he took the class to study with the rabbi, but that many of his friends were in a different class. We believe that this illustrates how the significance of building strong relationships with clergy in Jewish educational settings cannot be overstated.

Collaborative Planning and Reflection

For both of us, there was a critical value to debriefing and reflecting with a colleague during the process. These discussions gave Joel an opportunity to be self-reflective about his role in the classroom and, as we mentioned, gave us real data to consider in planning future sessions. Since Wendy only had the benefit of notes, she was able to see the big picture of what happened in each class and tie together themes that had arisen over a series of classes. Together we decided what the next session should look like. We were also able to discuss class dynamics and ways to respond to individual students and issues. The class was able to evolve over time, and had we had more students and more sessions, we believe we would have seen an even more fruitful, deep, and varied discussion among the students, with different students challenging different ideas. Having experienced this kind of collegial reflection, Joel now intends to incorporate this practice more often in all of his teaching. No doubt this will benefit Joel as well as the teachers with whom he collaborates.

Future Experiments

We would be excited to see this experiment replicated in different settings. There are a few changes we would suggest to the methodology.

Certainly, this was a small experiment, both in terms of the number of students in the class and the number of weeks that the class ran. We would expect to see more development if there was a more critical mass (making it harder for a few students to dominate the discussion) and if the class met more often and over a longer period of time. It was also somewhat challenging to have seventh graders and tenth graders in the same room. They are, obviously, at very different stages of their own personal and spiritual development, and there were times when those different stages clashed— sometimes the older students had questions that the younger students could not even comprehend, and sometimes the youngest kids asked questions that the oldest kids were challenged to allow for. For example, one student introduced a thought experiment about sacrificing one life to save three others, and if God participates in making such judgments and sacrifices. A younger student chimed in after a while with: "Why is everyone saying 'He'? How do you know that God is a boy?"

The topic of God and God's role in the world is also rather broad. We think the class could be improved with a clearer focus on the topic, although we hope that the teacher would allow for discussions to evolve organically. With more time to plan, the teacher could choose texts that honed in on the specific theme of the class, bringing different perspectives on that theme to each setting.

We would also like to see the students play a greater role in their own documentation. This is somewhat dependent on the culture of the institution, how often the group is meeting, and how much time students can be expected to focus on this content outside of classroom hours. In this vein, we suggest that the teacher devote time to writing responses to each student after each class. Joel started doing this about halfway through the course, but he feels it was one of the most successful parts of the experiment because it allowed students to deepen their own thinking and for him to individualize his responses to each student. It would also be interesting to introduce other creative opportunities during the class sessions for student reflection, different modalities that would include art, writing, and oral reflection. Video diaries would allow the students to see themselves expressing their ideas at the beginning, middle, and end of the process. As this is just a snapshot of the students' development, and we want the process of reflection and testing out of spiritual ideas to be ongoing, we would like to figure out ways to follow up with students after the classes have ended. Perhaps a segment of the synagogue or school blog could include reflections and stories of experiences, and students could be invited to contribute from time to time. We would like some way to check in with them after a period of time elapsed, to see what they have retained and how they have grown.

Other Applications

This experiment has caused us to ask some questions in general about religious education. The most valuable parts of the class were collaboration and listening. In our supplementary schools, when so many feel the pressure of limited time and the need to "cover" material, how would the experience be different for teachers and students if teachers felt their role was that of a guide and observer, with an emphasis on "uncovering" student beliefs? What would the effect be if teachers were assigned colleagues with whom to reflect and co-plan their lessons?

We are reminded of this tale:

A man lost his way in a great forest. After a while another lost his way and chanced on the first. Without knowing what had happened to him, he [the second] asked [the first] the way out of the woods. "I don't know," said the first. "But, I can point out the ways that lead further into the thicket, and after that let us try to find the way together."[4]

In the area of the mysteries of God, can we be partners with our students on a journey, like the two Jews in the tale? Perhaps our spiritual learning communities can be strengthened with a greater emphasis on listening, asking, and learning about and from one another.

Notes

1. David Hay with Rebecca Nye, *The Child as Spiritual Being*, rev ed. (London: Jessica Kingsley Publishers, 2006).
2. Michael Shire, "Nurturing the Spiritual in Jewish Education," *Ha Yidion* (Winter 2010): 13.
3. Harold Kushner, *When Children Ask about God* (New York: Schocken, 1995), 54, 55.
4. Rabbi Hayyim of Zans, in Martin Buber, *Tales of the Hasidim: Later Masters* (New York: Schocken Books, 1948), 213.

Practices that Nurture Young Jewish Children's Spiritual Development

Deborah Schein

Introduction

When I began my doctoral studies in 2005, there was no clear definition of "spiritual development" for young children living in the United States, yet researchers highlighted the need for a deeper understanding of this aspect of children's lives. I decided to ask early childhood educators for their definition and what activities and experiences they used to foster this part of their students' maturation.

This study found that spiritual development requires deep connections, basic and complex dispositions working together. The educators defined "deep connections" as children feeling linked to others, to self, and to nature. They also described how spiritual development supports other areas of development (cognitive, social, emotional, and physical), as well as leading children to ask big questions enabling them to think beyond themselves. One of the educators said:

> I think [in spirituality] . . . there is a connection with academic skills . . . and then there is scaffolding that builds on those skills . . . . I believe that it is the teacher's challenge to connect spiritually with every child in the classroom, academically and in a Buberian I-Thou way. The depth of that connection will determine the extent of the learning that will occur. This is not the transfer of knowledge of language arts, math, etc., but something less measurable.

DEBORAH SCHEIN, PhD is an early childhood educator and consultant. She specializes in professional development of teachers and nurturing the spiritual life of children.

A disposition is a child's nature, character, and temperament.[1] Basic dispositions refer to those things that make children wonder at the world. Complex dispositions refer to a children's ability to show empathy. Adults need to model these dispositions of wonderment and compassion. Spending time within spiritually rich environments, creating spiritual moments, is essential for their growth.

This article will analyze this theory of spiritual development using a Jewish lens and provide guidelines of practice for rabbis, early childhood educators, and parents to help nurture the spirituality of young Jewish children.[2]

Love and Attachment

Study Participants' View on Love

According to the study, love and attachment trigger something inside children that has the potential to awaken all domains of learning—cognitive, social, emotional, physical, and spiritual. Maria Montessori, a prominent educator described this process as the awakening of the child's spiritual embryo, defined as part of the "human . . . psyche, present at birth, housing the horme, . . . a vital force" that guides and propels each child toward growth, independence, and a desire to learn.[3] Simply stated, loving relationships stimulate the spiritual embryo.

Study participants agreed. "When we are born to this world . . . [we] are so dependent. Is someone going to take care of us? Love us? Of course, we aren't thinking these things, but we learn to trust based on whether their needs are taken care of, whether we are cuddled and loved."

Jewish Perceptions on Love

Judaism speaks about love and attachment too. Two prayers in Jewish tradition reinforce these notions. One commentary to the *Ahavah Rabbah* prayer suggests, "We [Jews] learn of our own significance through the love that is freely offered to us first by parents and later by others. This prayer teaches us that our ultimate worth, found in this love is 'rooted in divine love.'"[4]

Findings from Other Research

Montessori believed that the kind of love found between parents and infants is the kind of love that "should reign ideally [throughout] . . . the world."[5] Current researchers have validated these ideas, determining that attachment closely relates to touch and is needed to support and sustain healthy brain development.[6] John Bowlby, a British psychologist who pioneered work in attachment theory, wrote that close attachments to others provide a core around which other people's lives revolve, from infancy to old age.[7] Infancy is indeed the time when "the seeds of trust, hope, and love are developed through the actions of the infant's caregivers."[8] This is how neurologists describe what occurs in the brain when a child feels love and attachment: Rich connected experiences lead to brain function patterns that are constantly developing and changing throughout the first years of life. These experiences lead to an increase in the "sensorimotor cortex, thalami, brain stem, and cerebellar vermis, [which are part of the] central systems that subserve brain stem reflexes and visuomotor integrative performance" in infants.[9] Deep connections stimulate exploration and an infant's beginning awareness of self and others.

Practice #1: Feel loved, and then bestow love on others, especially children.

Pathways to Practice

Before an adult can support the spiritual development of a young child, he or she must feel loved and then model love. If you do not feel loved, then the steps that help nurture a young child's spiritual development might also help nurture yours. Begin by finding moments of wonder and demonstrating hospitality (*hachnasat orchim*).[10]

Many years ago, I visited a synagogue preschool, where I felt unwelcomed. Nobody spoke to me, no one said hello, and the director of the school never introduced me to the teachers or children. As children absorb everything they see and hear, they internalize this inhospitality. We need to find ways to model *chesed* (kindness) and *derech eretz* (proper manners)[11] not simply by greeting children by name and a smile, but by how we interact with everyone in the hallways, even the stranger.

A Young Child's Absorbent Mind

Montessori talks of the absorbent mind and says, "everything else waits on it."[12] She is referring to children's exceptional ability to learn unconsciously from the environment. At the beginning of life, infants who grow up in Jewish environments begin to learn about themselves as Jewish individuals and as part of the Jewish community. *B'rit milah* and *b'rit b'not* are most likely the first communal experiences absorbed by infants. Here the newborns are actually welcomed into the covenant of the Jewish people. Despite what we might think, the infants miss none of the religious or cultural nuances. Similarly, being present for Shabbat dinners or other holiday celebrations, hearing the *Sh'ma* recited, being blessed on Friday nights, listening to Jewish music, prayers, blessings, and Hebrew; smelling special foods cooking, seeing a mezuzah or other Jewish symbols are all experienced through an infant's amazing absorbent mind. Nothing goes unrecorded.

Practice #2: Place infants in beautiful Jewish environments so they have something Jewish and beautiful for their absorbent minds to absorb.

Pathways to Practice

First, introduce infants to a Jewish lifestyle and holiday cycle so that their absorbent minds drink in what a Jewish life looks like and feels like. In other words, do not leave infants and young children home; rather immerse them into Jewish life. Bring them to services and religious celebrations so that they can feel the fullness and authenticity of Judaism and learn the required behavior and mannerisms that go with being in those spaces. Create worship and celebrations in which children feel safe and comfortable either by purposely incorporating them in the community experience or by creating parallel opportunities for participation. As children grow, invite them to touch and experience beautiful Judaica up close. Guide them in touching sacred objects with care, appreciation, and respect. Encourage their sensual connection with the Jewish symbols and artifacts.

I have often heard loving adults telling children not to touch the gourds in a sukkah or the breakable *Kiddush* cup. I once visited a synagogue preschool that had a large glass cupboard filled with beautiful Judaica. I was told that parents had purchased the cupboard and all the items in it as holiday gifts for the school. As holidays approached, each classroom of children decided what items it would use for its celebration. Best of all, the cupboard was located in a prominent place for all to see and touch, providing adults daily opportunity to observe children's faces for signs of wonderment.

Adult Observation of Children

While children are using their absorbent minds, adults should be using their power of observation. What in the environment helps each child to feel wonder or to act kindly? For instance, a child who shows interest in gourds can be introduced to the wonderment of other plants and encouraged to cook something to share with others. Another child, who is more interested in the structure of the sukkah can be encouraged to explore other types of shelters possibly leading to an interest in helping the homeless or building a small home for a pet. The Book of Proverbs tells us to "teach a child according to his way." To do this, each child must be closely observed, truly known, and seen with a positive lens. This is a good way to nurture children's developing sense of self and their spiritual development.

Practice #3: Closely observe children to discover what triggers their attention and passions, then add dimension (breadth and depth) to the experience to stimulate both mind and spirit.

Pathways to Practice

John Dewey, an American philosopher; Reggio Emilia educators from Italy; and Lev Vygotsky, a Soviet psychologist, believed that young children learn best socially constructing knowledge from social and collaborative experiences rather than from straight teaching.[13] In other words, children learn by playing with other children, while having dialogues with friends and supportive adults.[14] Provocation (intellectual challenge) is a Reggio Emilia technique used for this type of learning. In other words, not every experience needs to be entertaining. Young children flourish when confronted with challenges.

I recommend that adults learn to view young children as having "rights instead of needs," strengths instead of weaknesses.[15] Seeing children in this light—recognizing who they are at the moment and the potential they hold—guides adults' behavior as they interact with children and helps youngsters construct the individuals they will become. To achieve this, children should not be viewed as simply cute or helpless. They must engage in meaningful activities within carefully prepared environments.

Spiritual Moments

The educators spoke often about the important role the environment plays in nurturing children's spiritual development, but describing this connection proved complex. First, they had a difficult time defining spiritual development, and then they found they had few words to describe its connection to the environment. After analyzing the grounded study interviews, the concept of *spiritual moments* emerged in place of environment, activities, or experiences.[16]

One participant said, "I have never been asked this question. I don't really have the words to answer." Another participant said, "When you see it [a spiritual moment], you know it. But, if we are not paying attention, we can even miss it, not even recognize it. [They are like] emotions . . . reflection, . . . inner contentment; all seem to be a part of a spiritual moment."

Yet another participant said, "I have these moments every day. I have taught for over twenty years. Those moments happen very fast, the eye contact and the engagement."

Spiritual moments are best described using Schwab's concept of milieu[17] and the Reggio Emilia understanding of "the environment as a third teacher."[18] Milieu speaks of situations and surroundings as well the tonal qualities of a moment.[19] The environment can act as an educator by being flexible and transformable so that children and teachers might use it to collectively explore big projects of learning.[20] A big project occurs when children work together with their teachers using art to share their knowledge and questions. Some educators refer to this as making learning visible.[21]

As children work together they strengthen deep connections, gain a sense of wonder, and perform acts of kindness. An environment that is organized, beautiful, and stimulating is most conducive to this kind of learning.

Participants eventually described several spiritual moments in time, in space, in nature. They spoke of the big questions that connect young children to something beyond themselves.

A Jewish Perspective

Heschel also spoke of spiritual moments using a Jewish perspective. He described sacred moments that go beyond abstract thinking of science to "ultimate insight . . . when we are stirred beyond words [to] wonder . . . and radical amazement . . . [as we] discover the unknown" and beyond.[22] A good way to acknowledge such moments is simply to be present, and it is in the present moment where young children usually reside.[23]

Practice #4: Support children in their ability to be present in the moment. *Heneini* (I am here).

Pathways to Practice

To support children in being present, adults need to step back and look at the schedule of a child's day. I can remember teaching at a Jewish preschool and every Tuesday, the children and I were in our classroom together for only forty-five minutes during a six-hour day. The rest of our time was spent in music, gym, and Hebrew. For the very young child, it is better to integrate these activities into the flow of the children's time in the classroom, rather than taking children away from the carefully designed classroom. For instance, music can take place outdoors, during morning group time, or as children are waiting to line up, etc. All the activities are important and necessary for healthy development, but we are often unaware of the consequences of disrupting the child's play. Children need enough time to be fully present in any one of these moments.

Spiritual Moment in Time

Spiritual moments require routine, order, quiet, calm, and time. When children are not rushed, they are better able to predict and anticipate the order of events.

One participant described the reality that exists in many early childhood programs in the United States today. She said:

> We are so caught up with standards . . . that sometimes we don't have the time to actualize the goodness within ourselves. There is no checklist for this. It gets lost in the craziness of what we do.

Although there is great truth to this, parents and educators can teach children how to take deep breaths and to enjoy quiet moments. Adults should consciously try not to fit too much into an activity or a day.

Practice #5a: Provide children with patterned and predictable time to play, where they are encouraged and supported in choosing their own activities and cleaning up after themselves.

Pathways to Practice

When I worked at a cooperative preschool, a school where parents rotated in to work with me in the classroom, I discovered that the children had no responsibilities. The children were often loud and disorderly. As they played, the parent for the day cleaned up after them. I went to the school board and explained the situation. The parents agreed to stand back and encourage the children to clean up themselves. We simplified the classroom environment and added time in the day for the children to clean up. The outcome was a classroom of young children learning to be responsible. This eventually produced a more orderly, quiet, and calm school.

Similarly, when participating in Tot Shabbats or holiday celebrations, wholeness is achievable by asking young children to help with some type of preparation and cleanup. I have found that even one-year-olds are capable of placing a cup on a table and clearing it away after using it, especially when offered guidance and opportunity to practice. Children come to learn that activities require time for preparation and clean up in order to be experienced fully.

Jewish Perspective of Time

Heschel wrote that Judaism sanctifies time over space.[24] In his book *The Sabbath,* Heschel wrote that "time is the heart of existence" and meant to be shared rather than controlled.[25] In Jewish homes and classrooms, spiritual moments in time are easily achievable through rituals. "Rituals and routines work together to create secure environments that nurture relationships between infants and caregivers [and strengthen] the bond between parents and child . . . and between teachers and parents."[26]

Practice #5b: Provide rituals that incorporate Jewish prayers and blessings. Encourage children's participation in the preparations and experiences of holy days to sanctify time.

Pathways to Practice

There are so many ways to create spiritual moments for Jewish children. Families and preschools already do many of these rituals.

Here are a few examples: Begin each day with prayer. At home, recite the *Sh'ma* with a young child or sing a song as the child is awakened with light kisses and hugs. Congregations and schools should consider offering parenting and spirituality programs to help families bring such rituals into their home.

At school, the day begins with *Modeh Ani* or a morning song sung with gusto and appreciation of a new day. To extend this ritual, educators can place a vase of freshly cut flowers in the middle of a morning circle or pass around a mirror reflecting the faces of the children who are present. Furthermore, Shabbat rituals highlight the passage of a week, just as holidays mark the changes of seasons and the passage of a year. The *Shehecheyanu* marks time as well. I recite this prayer when children lose a tooth, learn to tie their own shoes, or do a new mitzvah. Such acts are markers in the timeline of the child's life.

As a classroom preschool educator, the children and I would begin each Thursday mixing dough for Shabbat challah. On Friday, we would bake it. By midyear, the children could measure, pour, stir, and kneed. During these moments, children were absorbing the passage of a week that culminated with the wonderful smell of challah baking. When my own children were young, we would also welcome Shabbat with the simple rituals of singing and dancing.

I found other ways to make time sacred in my preschool classes. For Sukkot we always planted bulbs that would miraculously blossom in time for Pesach or Shavuot. I planted potatoes to store for Chanukah, and I have always wanted to plant barley for the counting of the Omer. Nature and the Jewish holidays create a spiritual tapestry for young children.

I once taught a Jewish education course for teachers entitled Holidays through Horticulture.[27] The students did plant barley, and we explored the connection of nature to the Jewish festival. Celebrating the seasons is a great way to sanctify the passage of time.

Spiritual Moments in Space

Participants described the need for play spaces that are beautiful, stimulating, organized, and pleasing. They used words such as aesthetics, beauty, intentionality, and perspective to describe such environments. Rather than the typical book corner, reading center, or rug area, they recognized the need for thoughtfully selected materials. They also discussed the concept of "less is best."[28] Children need fewer toys and more items that are capable of stimulating wonderment and exploration in a social setting. Unfortunately, this notion of spiritual spaces surpasses what is typically available to most children in the United States. One participant commented:

> We American early childhood educators have tried to fill the environment with scientific explanations when, quite frankly, I think we should be creating environments that could be producing questions, wonderment, and curiosity about the world rather than answers to things . . . To teach children their colors appeals to the lowest part of brain development, not to mention a real lack of spiritual or cognitive development. You reduce it to a name of a particular kind of color that robs all of the other possibilities.

A walk can provide a child with multiple shades of green, as can mixing varied amounts of yellow and blue paint together. Therefore, there is no need to teach children colors. More can come from guiding children in using a paintbrush in a serene setting. Teaching robs children of wonderment and does not support their questions or interests. The names of colors are learned through the child's absorbent mind. For instance, when a child is asked, "Which color sweater would you like to wear today, the blue or the red?" the child begins the process of learning colorness. By the age of two most of our children know their colors.

In environments where less is best, plastic objects, clutter, toys that are not cared for (puzzles with missing pieces, broken toys, or toys stacked upon each other), and commercial products (Disney dresses and Ninja action figures) would all be eliminated. In their place would be wooden shelves and furniture, such as a couch for reading great books (neatly displayed). There would be baskets filled with nature objects (seashells, rocks, twigs). There would be musical instruments, scarves for dress up, a few tried and true games, lots of blocks, water, sand and light tables, and windows looking out onto the seasons. There would be a variety of art materials for children to use independently for expressing their ideas and thoughts about the world. On the walls would be children's artwork and other types of art such as documentation of classroom projects, work by famous artists, cultural art from other countries, and pictures of nature.

Practice #6a: Provide time for children "to be" in beautiful spaces so they might further develop basic dispositions through wonderment.

Pathways to Practice

One year, after winter break, the children in my classroom returned to find that I had removed all the Disney dresses and all the plastic shovels and pails from the sand table. The children were puzzled for a minute or two, then I witnessed a quick transformation. The children were encouraged to see what they could do with the sand using just their own hands. When I added some rocks, the children began bringing in their own natural treasures. When I removed the dresses, I replaced them with fabric and scarves. The children became much more creative and collaborative in their play as they discovered that a scarf could do much more than a Disney dress. The scarves were first used to put on a play for parents of *Goldilocks and the Three Bears*. Witnessing this, I became a believer that children really thrive in beautiful spaces, where natural materials are used and where less is best.

Practice #6b: Provide Jewish children with moments that go beyond simple wonder to include moments of the sublime by using blessings from tradition or from the heart. Children have the capacity to feel the presence of God in others and in the world around them.

Pathways to Practice

After a couple of decades working in Jewish preschools, I moved into an urban educational setting. One day my interest in young children's spiritual development was peaked as a young child came up to me holding a worm in his hand—his face aglow as if he were Abbahu studying Torah. I quickly discovered that I did not respond to him with a traditional blessing or prayer because he was not Jewish. However, he still had spiritual needs, as do all children. I remember learning from a colleague how to create spontaneous blessings or prayers using your own words.[29] Giving voice to prayers of the heart provides the language marking unexpected moments as holy. In seeing a miracle of nature, we might say, *"Baruch atah Adonai, Eloheinu Melech haolam, oseh maaseh b'reishit"* (Blessed are you, Adonai our God, Ruler of the World, Who Makes all of Creation) and/or a prayer from the heart such as, "Thank you God for sharing such an amazing creature as this worm."

Spiritual Moments in Nature

Study participants spoke of spiritual moments in nature—time to play with natural objects, both indoors and out. Children wonder when they blow on the seed head of a dandelion. Adding a blessing marks the sacredness of the moment. By showing children how to walk carefully among the dandelions, children learn to act respectfully toward nature.

There are many articles and studies highlighting the importance of nature education for small children. A few studies, such as one by Kirmani and Kirmani, integrated nature with spiritual development.[30] A study by Taylor, Kuo, and Sullivan found that on average, concentration improved when children saw a green view from home.[31] Sullivan, Kuo, and DePooter's findings showed that green spaces are capable of bringing people together in relationships.[32] Taylor and Kuo conducted yet another study of children with ADHD that showed children were more focused and calmer after walking through a park.[33] Kuo conducted a study on forests and recreation to discover improved social, psychological, and physical well-being for those spending time out in nature.[34] Collectively, these studies demonstrate the potential for nurturing a relationship between children and nature that can help nurture children's love of the earth.[35]

Principle #7a: Provide children with outdoor time in nature.

Pathways to Practice

I am a collector of nature. I walk my dog twice a day and on every walk, I find something worthy of saving. Whatever I find, I bring into school. Over the years, I have learned how to display my treasures so that my students also begin to appreciate what I see. They begin to bring nature into the classroom and so do their parents. Some of what we find is beautiful (e.g., autumn leaves) and other things are not (e.g., a decaying bird). The children and I observe plants, flowers, and trees that grow both indoors and outdoors. We watch things blossom and sometimes die. There are pets to care for and feed. I have had rabbits, iguanas, guinea pigs, hamsters, frogs, fish, ants, worms, and snails. I remember once, my classroom went to the pet store and purchased a turtle. It turned out that the turtle startled every time a block structure tumbled. At the children's recommendation, we redesigned the classroom.

Jewish Perspective to Nature

Spiritual moments, as described by Heschel include many references to nature. He used nature to talk about God's relationship to people and people's relationship to God. Throughout his book, God in Search of Man, Heschel referred to a quote from Isaiah 40:26.[36] It reads, "Lift up your eyes on high and see. Who created these?"[37] For Heschel, God was the creator of all. Therefore, when he looked at nature he saw it as a process, part of organic life, "consisting of . . . birth, growth, maturity, and decay" that could lead ultimately to the profound unknown.[38] He also offered a belief that people explore nature in their continuous search for the meaning of the sublime to catch a glimpse into something of greater meaning than themselves.[39] His response to the beauty and splendor found in nature was prayer, blessing, song, and celebration.

Principle #8b: Connect young children's exploration of nature with Jewish rituals, including Jewish prayers, blessings, songs, celebrations, and ceremonies.

Pathways to Practice

Often, the school year begins just before Rosh HaShanah. The children and I take a Rosh HaShanah walk so we can reflect upon the meaning of "birthday of the world." On these walks, children get to know each other, and I have an opportunity to observe the children. Together, we are a new community of learners. We collect nature treasures that become part of the new classroom environment. Sometimes a caring parent comes into the classroom to clean up and invariably throws away one of our decaying treasures—the cycle of life missed by their lens. When left for children to witness, the decay of a potato or an old piece of bark can lead to big questions. Big questions are very important to a child's spiritual and religious life, as they create the spiritual moments capable of taking children beyond themselves.

Spiritual Moments with Big Questions: Taking Children beyond Themselves

Participants in my study expressed a belief that young children have a deep need to connect to something beyond themselves. Gardner labeled this propensity, existential intelligence, an "unambiguously cognitive strand of the spiritual."[40] Some participants believed that when children ask and explore deep questions about life and death, they create spiritual moments for themselves and others. One participant told the story of a little boy, not quite two years old, holding a dead fish in his hands. The participant wrote:

> The particular image comes to my mind as I try to think about . . . my grandson at around the age of two. We were at a little neighborhood beach together, splashing around at the edge of the lake, when a dead little fish about the size of my little finger was floating near him. He was gleefully splashing around in the water, and he stopped dead in his tracks. He was riveted to this floating fish…It was something totally different happening for him. He scooped the fish up. I just observed this. He looked at me for some kind of reassurance or guidance or permission—whatever—and I just smiled and stayed with him. And he goes to sit on the edge of our blanket and cupped this little tiny fish in his hands, and tries to blow air into it.
>
> I don't know how we separate all of these things out. Because when my grandson sees this tiny fish—he knows the word fish—he must know something about it being dead because of how it's behaving, and then we see how he responded to it. But how did he know something about breath and the giving of life and that realm of life? Is this cognitive or spiritual? And he had emotion around it. And he had physical affect around it. He knew just how to cup this fish in his hands. I mean for the entire time he just sat and cupped it. We were there for—I don't know—an hour and a half when his mom was coming to pick him up. He never even moved from sitting with it, and I don't even think he was quite two. He just sat there holding this fish. Looking at it and blowing on it, looking at it and blowing on it, looking with questioning eyes at me, and we would have some conversation, but minimal. The joy the boy had in the water, the splashing and moving, were set aside while he sat very still with this tiny fish in

his hand. So how do you tease apart . . . these aspects of development? They are so intertwined.

Practice #9: Never underestimate the depth of a child's present knowledge, capacity to know, and ability to think big questions.

Pathways to Practice

This powerful description of a young child reflects many of the previously stated principles. First, it is obvious that this grandmother loves her grandchild. She also understands the value of natural places of beauty. She allows her grandchild the time and space to choose how he might relate to this environment. She does not interfere in his moment of contemplation. In his own way, her grandchild is displaying a sense of responsibility to the fish. He may also be contemplating some very deep questions about life and death.

Remember that young children have that absorbent mind. What they experience on a certain day will stay with them for a very long time, possibly a lifetime. The grandmother knew something about what was necessary for her grandchild at the moment. He didn't need to talk. He needed her to respect his quiet and let him say and do what came naturally to him. Later he might return to that moment and ask questions when he is ready. This is simply the beginning of a lifetime discussion on life and death.

In response to this scenario, I would remind adults not to respond too quickly during such moments, as too many words could disrupt the child's natural spiritual moment. Buber would have seen the nonverbal relationship between the child and the dead fish as one of those inexplicable I-Thou relationships. Heschel might stop to offer a blessing or a prayer for the sacredness of life the young child felt, while also acknowledging the child's ability to be in touch with the cycle of life created by God. Such a blessing might be, "Blessed is this child who has capacity to experience awe and wonder."

Conclusion

It is my hope that the above images of young children, the principles, and pathways to practice offer a greater appreciation of the spiritual development of young children. I believe, as did the early childhood educators from my study and many scholars,[41] that the nurturing of a young child's spiritual development lays a foundation for children to develop social responsibility and a growing ability to make ethical and moral decisions. As children deepen self-awareness and connection, they come closer to experiencing the presence of God within and around them.

Notes

1. Lilian Katz, *Intellectual Emergencies—Some Reflections on Mothering and Teaching* (Louisville: Kaplan Press, 2009).
2. The guidelines of practices listed in this article are not simple prescriptions, but rather require deep reflection about one's relationships with children and the environments created for them.
3. Maria Montessori, *The Secret of Childhood* , trans. B. B. Carter (Bombay: Orient Longmans, 1963), 15.
4. David A. Teutsch, *Kol Haneshamah*: *Shabbat Vachagim* (Philadelphia: Reconstructionist Press, 1994), 272.
5. Maria Montessori, *The Absorbent Mind*, trans. Claude A. Claremont (New York: Dell Publishing, 1967), 31.
6. Kathleen I. Harris, "Re-Conceptualizing Spirituality in the Light of Educating Young Children," *International Journal of Children's Spirituality* 12, no. 3 (2006): 263–75; Brendan Hyde, *Children and Spirituality: Searching for Meaning and Connectedness* (London: Jessica Kingsley, 2008); D. D. Liston, "Possibilities of Joy In School Improvement Processes," Poster session at American Educational Research Association Conference (New York, 2008), 3–11; Elijah Mickel and Cecilia Hall, "Choosing to Love: The Essentials of Loving (Presents and Problems)," *International Journal of Reality Therapy* 27, no. 2 (2008): 30–33; Ann W. Mitchell, "4 Good Reasons Why ECE is Not Just Important, but Essential," *Advocacy Exchange* (May/June 2009): 8–11.
7. John Bowlby, *Attachment and Loss*, vol.1: *Attachment* (New York, Basic Books, 1969).
8. Andrew B. Newberg and Stephanie K. Newberg, "A Neuropsychological Perspective on Spiritual Development," in *The Handbook of Spiritual Development in Childhood and Adolescents*, ed. Eugene C. Roehlkepartain et al. (Thousand Oaks, CA: Sage Publications, 2006), 183–97.
9. Ibid., 188.
10. Maxine Handelman and Deborah L. Schein, What's Jewish about Butterflies? (Springfield, NJ: A.R.E. 2004), 240–50.
11. Ibid., 248, 249.
12. Montessori, Absorbent Mind, 7.

13. John J. Dewey, Democracy and Education: An Introduction to the Philosophy of Education (New York: Barnes and Noble, 1916/2005); Carolyn Edwards, Lella Gandini, and George Forman, eds., The Hundred Languages of Children (Westport, CT: Ablex, 1998); Lev S. Vygotsky, Thought and Language, ed. and trans. E. Hanfmann and G. Vakar (Cambridge: MIT Press, 1962).

14. Carlina Rinaldi, In Dialogue with Reggio Emilia (London: Routledge, 2006), 8.

15. Ibid., 83.

16. Deborah Schein, "Early Childhood Educators' Perceptions of Spiritual Development in Young Children: A Social Constructivist Grounded Theory Study" (ProQuest Dissertations, 2012).

17. Joseph Schwab, "The Practical: A Language for Curriculum," School Review 78, no. 1 (November 1969): 1–23.

18. Gandini, "Educational and Caring Spaces," in Hundred Languages , 161–78; Dewey, Democracy and Education.

19. Schwab, "Practical."

20. Gandini, "Educational and Caring Spaces," in Hundred Languages, 161–78. A big project occurs when children work together with the guidance of an art studio teacher using art to help children share their questions and constructed knowledge.

21. Project Zero, Making Learning Visible (Cambridge: Reggio Children, 2001).

22. Abraham Joshua Heschel, God in Search of Man: A Philosophy of Judaism (New York: Farrah, Straus, and Cudahy, 1955), 131.

23. Ibid.

24. Abraham Joshua Heschel, The Sabbath (New York: Farrah, Straus, and Cudahy, 1951), 3–10.

25. Ibid., 3.

26. Linda Gillespie and Sandra Petersen, "Rituals and Routines: Supporting Infants, Toddlers, and Their Families," Young Children (September 2012): 76–77.

27. Gratz College, Philadelphia, 2005.

28. Carolyn Edwards, Hundred Languages.

29. Handelman, Butterflies, xiii.

30. Mubina Hassanali Kirmani and Sanaullah Kirmani, "Recognition of Seven Spiritual Identities and Its Implications on Children," Journal of Children's Spirituality 14, no. 4 (November 2009): 369–82.

31. Andrea Faber Taylor, Frances E. Kuo, William C. Sullivan, "Views of Nature and Self-Discipline: Evidence From Inner City Children," Journal of Environmental Psychology 22 (2002): 49–63.

32. William C. Sullivan, Frances E. Kuo, and Stephen F. DePooter, "The Fruit of Urban Nature: Vital Neighborhood Spaces," Environment and Behavior 30, no. 5 (September 2004): 679–700.

33. Andrea Faber Taylor and Frances E. Kuo, "A Potential Natural Treatment for Attention-Deficit/Hyperactivity Disorder: Evidence From a National Study," American Journal of Public Health 94, no. 9 (September 2004): 1580–86.

34. Frances E. Kuo, "Parks and Other Green Environments: Essential Components of a Healthy Human Habitat" (National Recreation and Park Association, 2010), http://www.nrpa.org/uploaded-Files/nrpa.org/Publications_and_Research/Research/Papers/MingKuo-Summary.pdf.

35. Stephen R. Kellert, *Building for Life: Designing and Understanding the Human-Nature Connection* (Washington, DC: Island Press, 2005), 3.

36. Heschel, *God in Search*, 31.

37. Ibid.

38. Ibid., 210.

39. Ibid., 39.

40. Howard Gardner, Intelligence Reframed (New York: Basic Books, 1999), 60.

41. Amitai Etzioni, *Next: The Road to the Good Society* (New York: Basic Books, 2001); James Fowler, *Stages of Faith: The Psychology of Human Development and the Quest for Meaning* (San Francisco: Harper Collins, 1955); Howard Gardner et al., *Good Work: When Excellence and Ethics Meet* (New York: Basic Books, 2002); Parker Palmer, *The Courage to Teach* (San Francisco: Jossey Bass, 1998).

"I Knew That Within Me There Was God"—Teaching Spiritual Awareness to Children

Amy Scheinerman

What Is Spirituality?

"I'm spiritual, not religious." How many times have we heard that? We know that Jewish tradition is rich in conveying purpose and meaning, the heart and soul of spirituality. But sometimes the spiritual quality is lost among the knowledge and skills orientation of Jewish teaching for children.

Spirituality is not easily defined; consider what Justice Potter Stewart famously wrote concerning obscenity.[1] I understand spirituality as the awareness that, and experience of, being a part of something larger than and beyond ourselves. Albert Einstein expressed it this way:

> A human being is a part of the whole, called by us "Universe," a part limited in time and space. He experiences himself, his thoughts and feelings as something separated from the rest—a kind of optical delusion of his consciousness. This delusion is a kind of prison for us, restricting us to our personal desires and to affection for a few persons nearest to us. Our task must be to free ourselves from this prison.[2]

Rabbi Abraham Joshua Heschel understood spirituality as life lived in the continuous presence of the Divine. Spirituality is the conscious awareness that everything is a manifestation of God and that everything is inseparably connected in a tapestry of existence and meaning. Torah is the blueprint for the universe,[3] and a

RABBI AMY SCHEINERMAN (NY84) is a Jewish hospice chaplain, teacher, writer, and visiting scholar. She is the immediate past president of the Baltimore Board of Rabbis, current president of the Greater Carolinas Association of Rabbis, and a current member of the Board of Trustees of the CCAR.

spiritual approach to Torah guides us to the blueprint of our souls. For some of us, spiritual awareness is best evoked through prayer and meditation; for others through study, the natural world, engagement in social justice issues, or the experience of aesthetics such as art and music.

The Mountain and the Bush

Religion helps us cultivate and nurture spiritual mindfulness and act on the basis of it. Judaism offers a treasure trove of spiritual values, texts, and practices that inspire and train us in mindfulness. They are the rightful inheritance of every Jew. Teaching spirituality differs from teaching religion in that the latter focuses on the "nuts and bolts" of ritual skills, history, and ethical values, while the former focuses on the experience of the Divine in one's life *through* the "nuts and bolts." If we incorporate spiritual attunement in our teaching of young children—from their first moment of formal Jewish education—they will grow and learn in a spiritual mind-set.

Everything we teach and do with children can and should have a spiritual overlay in order to train children to always be open to the spiritual dimension of their life experiences. For children, this comes naturally. They live in a world of wonder. They want to know what things mean and what their place in the world is. Their minds are open to new ways to think and experience.

How then to proceed? We might begin with two teachings concerning Moses' earliest experiences of the Divine. In the first, "The Lord said to Moses, 'Come up to Me on the mountain and be there, and I will give you the stone tablets with the teachings and commandment which I have inscribed to instruct them'" (Exod. 24:12). There is an apparent redundancy in this verse. If Moses is to "come up," he will certainly "be there." After all, where else could he possibly be? Rashi, trying to make sense of the redundancy, adds the words "forty days" so that the verse can be understood, "Come up to Me on the mountain and be there forty days. . . ." But the Kotzker Rebbe[4] offers a insightful spiritual interpretation:

> But from this apparent redundancy we find proof that even one who strains himself to ascend onto a high mountaintop, and is indeed able to reach the summit, it is nevertheless possible that he is still not there. Even though he may be standing on the very peak itself, his head may be somewhere else.

God wants Moses to be not merely physically present, but fully present—mind and body—so that he can encounter God. It was the Kotzker Rebbe who famously taught: "Where is God found? Wherever you give God entry." The second teaching of Moses' encounter with the Divine comes from a midrash on the burning bush. Rabbi Yehoshua ben Korcha was asked, "Why did God choose a thorn bush from which to speak to Moses? Were it a carob tree or a sycamore tree, you would have asked the same question. But to dismiss you without any reply is not right, so I will tell you why. To teach you that no place is devoid of God's presence, not even a thorn bush."[5] The magic of Jewish spirituality is that it teaches us that through mindfulness we can find God even in a thorn bush.

Posters displaying Mt. Sinai and the Burning Bush in the classroom can serve as graphic spiritual reminders that the teacher can refer to at any point in a lesson. The Mountain reminds us to be mindful; the Bush reminds us to ask, "Where is God in this?" In this way, every lesson can be brought into the spiritual realm, and children learn to seek the spiritual dimension in their learning and in their lives.

Children learn through their physical senses; good teaching takes advantage of this. Howard Gardner pioneered the work in multiple intelligences in the early 1990s. He explained that we know the world through language, logical-mathematical analysis, spatial representation, musical thinking, bodily kinesthetic, an understanding of other individuals, and an understanding of ourselves. One of the implications of Gardner's research is the importance of providing opportunities for children to learn via multiple channels to be sure to reach their type(s) of intelligence. Each type of intelligence is a gateway to spirituality.

As one example: prayer can be taught and experienced through language (the poetry of the words), logic (understanding the order of prayers and the reason for the order), special representation (drawings inspired by prayers), music (melodies and *nusach*), bodily kinesthetic (the choreography of prayer), understanding others (what concerns of others do the prayers address?), and self-knowledge (how do the prayers speak to me?). Of prayer, the Israeli poet Rivka Miriam wrote:

And from time to time, I pray. I don't understand the words of prayer.
Everyone who understands the words cannot say them.

Therefore generations have opened their heavy prayerbooks
And in love erased the meaning of each word.[6]

While we help children and adults to understand what the words meant to the Sages who composed them, and generations of our people who uttered them, for Jews to have a spiritual relationship with the siddur, we must enable them to let the words wash through them so that they can make them their own. While teaching the "nuts and bolts" of a prayer, the teacher points to Mt. Sinai and asks the children to reflect on how the words of the prayer, or perhaps the choreography of prayer, helps us achieve mindfulness. Pointing to the Burning Bush, the teacher asks the children where God is in the prayer.

An Organizational Scheme for a Spiritual Curriculum

There are as many curricular organizing schemes as there are curricula. Each reflects a different priority and encourages a different emphasis: history, practice, values, etc. In truth, infusing children's education with spirituality can be an overlay on top of any existing curriculum—the Mountain and the Bush can help—but a spiritual orientation can also drive the organization. The "nuts and bolts" can be fit into an overarching spiritual approach to Jewish learning for our children.

However, if the goal is to design a curriculum around spirituality and fit the "nuts and bolts" appropriately and effectively into the curriculum, the curriculum might be organized around three general foci, components of an education that cultivates and nurtures children's spirituality: attitudinal *midot*, personal *midot* (character traits), and social and communal *midot*. We begin by working on ourselves and move outward in concentric circles of human experience: our relationships with other individuals and our relationship with community and humanity. Each of the three foci lends itself to lessons on history, practice, ethical values, and so on. What is more, the three foci interweave continually (as will occasionally be indicated below).

1. Attitudinal *Midot*: Foundation of Spirituality and Musar

Our attitude determines our mind-set. Four attitudes to cultivate in our children open them to thinking, apprehending, and acting spiritually: mystery, purpose, gratitude, and empowerment. Because our attitudes shape our perceptions, our thinking, and our behavior, I treat each at length.

1.1 Mystery

Children naturally see the world through spectacles of awe and wonder—what Abraham Joshua Heschel termed "radical amazement." It is, as Heschel reminds us, the gateway to spirituality (a gift adults do well to retain, or cultivate anew). For children, everything is new and amazing. They are apt to approach people as a mystery to unravel, not a biochemical factory to analyze. For children, the world is a place of wonders, not a machine operating according to the laws of physics. Heschel writes:

> The meaning of awe is to realize that life takes place under wide horizons, horizons that range beyond the span of an individual life or even the life of a nation, a generation, or an era. Awe enables us to perceive in the world intimations of the divine, to sense in small things the beginning of infinite significance, to sense the ultimate in the common and the simple.[7]

Outdoor activities work in parallel with children's natural spirituality. A park, a hike through the woods or out into the desert, or a family retreat in a natural setting make ideal educational venues for spiritual experiences in the world beyond the classroom. Below are several suggestions incorporating the wisdom of Gardner's multiple intelligences, as well as our standard categories of Jewish experience (prayer, study, mitzvot, ritual, and ethical values):

- In the context of a lesson on psalms, read Psalm 104 (a creation psalm). Listen to HaTeva's musical version of Psalm 104,[8] draw an interpretation of the psalm, discuss thoughts and feelings.
- Appreciation for the natural world (see Gratitude below) teaches us the obligation to protect it (see Social and Communal Values below). *Midrash Kohelet Rabbah* 7:13 tells us: "Upon creating the first human beings, God guided them around the Garden of Eden, saying, 'Look at My creations! See how beautiful and praiseworthy they are! I created everything for you. Make sure you don't ruin or destroy My world. If you

do, there will be no one after you to repair it.'" Is there a conflict between the world being created for our sake, and our
responsibility to see that it is not destroyed? How do we fulfill
this mandate? Study the mitzvot related to sustainability.

- Learn the blessing recited upon seeing wonders of nature
  (including sunrise, mountains, lightning, and shooting stars)
  and encourage students to use it.[9] Students can be encouraged
  to compose their own blessings in response to the experience
  of awe and wonder.
- Rebbe Nachman of Bratzlav's prayer[10] opens the door to seeing the entire world as a sanctuary. Take students into the
  woods to recite it and discuss the imagery. What do we learn
  about the world, God, and ourselves when we say this prayer?
- Invite children and their families to gather for the last hour of
  Shabbat to watch the sun set while learning about *Havdalah*
  (with its emphasis on the human physical senses—our gateway to perceiving and enjoying the world). Count the stars,
  and then make *Havdalah*. What does it mean to be part of the
  created world?
- Children are moved by the poetry of *Maariv Aravim*. Invite
  them to describe and draw the images it evokes in their imaginations, and then share them with their peers. Invite them to
  compose their own prayer reflecting their experience of sunrise and sunset.
- A lesson can be built around *Motzi*, whose peculiar phrasing
  ". . . Who brings forth bread from the earth" begs us to ask:
  given that baked loaves of bread do not spring forth from
  the earth, what can the blessing mean? When children learn
  that bread requires the efforts, inventions, and cooperation of
  many people, they begin to see how civilization is built. Bread
  can also be seen as a metaphor for the human-Divine partner-
  ship. How else do we partner with God?

1. 2 Purpose

It is said that one day Rabbi Moshe Leib of Sassov told his students, "There is no quality or human ability that was created to no
purpose. Even what you think are base and corrupt qualities can
be uplifted to serve God." One skeptical student asked, "Rabbi, to
what end can the denial of God have been created? Surely there is

no purpose to atheism." Rabbi Moshe paused but a moment before replying, "This too can be uplifted through deeds of *tzedakah*. For if someone comes to you and asks your help, you shall not turn him away with pious words, saying: 'Have faith and take your troubles to God!' You will act as if there were no God, as if there were only one person in all the world who could help this person—and that one person is you."

Children behave better and treat others with greater kindness when they have a sense of purpose in the world. The most powerful way to promote a sense of purpose is for children to help others: visit elderly people in nursing homes, tutor peers in Hebrew, visit a sick classmate, help out more at home, pursue social justice. Teens can arrange a Purim carnival for younger children. Young children can make and sell craft items to earn money for *tzedakah*.

Lessons concerning the stories of Genesis, the concept of Chosenness, the Prophets, and social justice, are but four examples of topics that lend themselves to the spiritual dimension of purpose.

1.3 Gratitude

To be grateful is to know you are blessed—*that* is a spiritual experience. What is more, appreciation is the quickest and most direct route to happiness. Dr. Martin Seligman, professor of psychology at the University of Pennsylvania, is known as the father of Positive Psychology—a branch of psychology that asks, "What makes us genuinely happy?" Seligman and his colleagues work with people who suffer depression and helplessness. Their extensive, data-driven research confirms that happiness is not related to what we *have*. It is about our *attitude* toward what we have. Seligman's research has demonstrated that the optimism born of gratitude is associated with better physical health, less depression and mental illness, and longer life.

Children can learn to be consciously grateful for the blessings of life and their ability to enjoy them. "The whole world is full of God. The Earth is the Lord's and the fullness thereof" (Ps. 24:1).

Gratitude should infuse our Jewish teaching and learning as it does our lives. Chanukah teaches us to be grateful for religious freedom and view ourselves as obligated to ensure it for others (purpose); *Sim Shalom* inspires us to be grateful for peace and on that basis pursue it (empowerment). The blessings for food, as well as special occasions and experiences in our lives, are spiritual tools for cultivating mindfulness.[11] Learning these blessings, and having a list of them at ready access at home, encourages children to think in positive, grateful terms. Children might keep a journal, in which they write each day something they appreciate, together with a traditional blessing or one that they compose.

1.4 Empowerment

We all wonder how powerful we are. Children, no less than adults, and perhaps more because their power is often untried, think about their abilities and their limits. When they are young, we can help them to think broadly about the meaning of power. In *Pirkei Avot* 4:1, Ben Zoma taught, "Who is mighty? Those who conquer their evil impulse, as it is written, *One who is slow to anger is better than the mighty, and one who rules over his spirit, than one who conquers a city* [Prov. 16:32]." The prophet Zechariah warned the Jewish people not to mistake physical power for spiritual power: "Not by might, and not by power, but by My spirit—said the Lord of Hosts" (Zech. 4:6). Children can examine the implications of these teachings for their own lives in the religious school classroom. Jewish ethics is based on the belief that we have free will and govern our own behavior.

Spirituality is empowering. It is often through our spiritual lives that we reveal our potential and discover our capacity to imbue our lives with purpose. Spiritual consciousness, by its nature, affirms the value and importance of each person. Coupled with Jewish social and ethical values, spirituality helps children to find direction for living their lives and criteria by which to make difficult decisions. In the life of a child, some of the most difficult decisions are made on the playground or playing field, in the cafeteria or classroom, or around the family dinner table. It is in these places that personality is shaped and children forge their personal value systems. By evoking the Mountain and the Bush, we teach children that their decisions have an impact far beyond what they might have thought because they are part of something greater than themselves.

Children are inspired by the stories of other children who exhibited courage, moral conscience, and compassion. Such stories are spiritual in nature because they touch the inner core where our sense of whom we *might be* dwells. The stories can incorporate elements of the "nuts and bolts" curriculum, demonstrating that *everything* has a spiritual dimension. Sharing and discussing stories of this nature encourages children to envision themselves as the "hero."[12]

As just one example of a lesson integrating many facets of a spiritual curriculum, *Asher Yatzar* captures many facets of spirituality: the body-mind connection (the Mountain and the Bush); the importance of our physical bodies as vessels for holiness (Jewish practices); and gratitude. Children can learn *Asher Yatzar* and be encouraged to recite it every morning before getting dressed, reminding themselves that each new day before them provides new opportunities to fulfill their purpose, bring meaning to their lives, and make a positive difference in the lives of others.

Religious education that includes a strong spiritual component empowers children to use their strengths for good (purpose), understanding that their lives are integrally connected to the lives of others (interpersonal skills), their communities (social and communal values) and, indeed, the entire universe.

2. Personal *Midot*

In his marvelous little book, *Haikus for Jews*,[13] David M. Bader offers this gem:

> Is one Nobel prize
> So much to ask from a child
> After all I've done?

Humor aside, what we *truly* want is for our children to become menschen. Rabbi Israel Salanter,[14] the acknowledged master of the modern Musar movement,[15] wrote: "The Maharal of Prague[16] created a golem, and this was a great wonder. But how much more wonderful is it to transform a corporeal human being into a mensch!" In the words of the Mussar Institute:

> Mussar is a path of contemplative practices and exercises that have evolved over the past thousand years to help an individual soul to pinpoint and then to break through the barriers that surround and obstruct the flow of inner light in our lives. Mussar is a treasury of techniques and understandings that offers immensely valuable guidance for the journey of our lives . . . The goal of Mussar practice is to release the light of holiness that lives within the soul. The roots of all of our thoughts and actions can be traced to the depths of the soul, beyond the reach of the light of con-

sciousness, and so the methods Mussar provides include meditations, guided contemplations, exercises and chants that are all
intended to penetrate down to the darkness of the subconscious,
to bring about change right at the root of our nature.[17]

Spirituality that is "all about me and my soul" is narcissism. Genuine spirituality connects us with what is beyond us (people, community, the world, and the universe) as well as God within. Spirituality
enables us to see ourselves as significant strings in a vast lyre whose
music is so exquisite and wondrous that we are inspired to live so
that our string vibrates at high frequency. Developing *midot* is a crucial part of the enterprise. For some, private meditative practices are
the best way to learn *midot*, but for many others, more traditional
group learning modalities are effective and have the side benefit of
building community among the learners.[18] We can teach the *midot*
through story, discussion, journaling, and role-playing.[19]

Rich resources exist for the study of *midot*.[20] There are traditional
lists of *midot*,[21] but they are far from canonized. Your list can be
flexible and expandable. For me, compassion, humility, patience,
and honesty are core traits because they touch so many of our decisions and behaviors every day and can have a transformative
effect on the quality of our relationships.

Space precludes discussing each at length, so I will expand upon
compassion as a model. Compassion, acting on the feeling of empathy for another, is the foundation for ethics. In a letter to Rabbi
Robert S. Marcus, quoted above (dated February 12, 1950), Albert
Einstein wrote that our experience of ourselves as separate from the
universe is an "optical delusion of . . . consciousness." He continues:

> This delusion is a kind of prison for us, restricting us to our per
> sonal desires and to affection for a few persons nearest to us. *Our*
> *task must be to free ourselves from this prison by widening our circle of*
> *compassion to embrace all living creatures and the whole of nature in*
> *its beauty.* Nobody is able to achieve this completely, but the striv
> ing for such achievement is in itself a part of the liberation and a
> foundation for inner security.[22]

Our textual tradition abounds with magnificent stories that illustrate and nurture the development of compassion: from Torah,
Abraham and Sarah's oasis of compassion and hospitality in the
desert (Gen.18:1–8); from Talmud, Rabbi Y'hudah HaNasi, whose

lack of compassion brought on his own suffering, and whose subsequent compassion dissipated it.[23]

Lessons can be built around *midot*, or teaching *midot* can be
folded into existing lessons. Three suggestions follow:

- Rabbi Nachman of Bratzlav, in *K'dushat Levi*, writing about,
  "The Lord! The Lord! A God compassionate and gracious, slow
  to anger, abounding in kindness and faithfulness . . ." (Exod.
  34:6), tells us there is nothing about *g'milut chasadim* (loving-
  kindness) that in itself compels God's kindness toward his creation. It is rather compassion that "evokes something in a person, in their innermost being, so they are not able to bear to see
  (God forbid) bad things [happening to] their fellow."[24] In fact,
  the Bratzlaver suggests, the *shefa*[25] is God's compassion continually flowing into the world. The implications of this teaching are enormous: Compassion fuels goodness in the world,
  and compassion is attained through spiritual seeking and encounter with God. When God's compassion flows through us,
  g'milut chasadim naturally emanates from us. This teaching can
  launch a discussion about deeds we do that come from the Divine within us, rather than the pressures of the world around
  us. In the context of lessons on the High Holy Days, the Bratzlaver's teaching adds a spiritual dimension to liturgy (Torah
  service, confessional) and *t'shuvah*. Also in connection with the
  High Holy Days, the haftarah for Yom Kippur morning, particularly Isaiah 58:5–8, rails against social injustices. What are
  the implications of this haftarah for us?
- The *Zohar*, commenting on Leviticus 22:26–28,[26] teaches:

  If a man does kindness on earth, he awakens loving-kindness
  above, and it rests upon that day which is crowned therewith
  through him. Similarly, if he performs a deed of mercy, he
  crowns that day with mercy and it becomes his protector in
  the hour of need. So, too, if he performs a cruel action, he has
  a corresponding effect on that day and impairs it, so that sub-
  sequently it becomes cruel to him and tries to destroy him, giving him measure for measure. The people of Israel are withheld
  from cruelty more than all other peoples, and must not manifest
  any deed of the kind, since many watchful eyes are upon them.[27]

  The *Zohar* tells us that each act we perform—kind or cruel—
  has repercussions far beyond us. There is a ripple effect that

reaches out into the world. The text suggests, as well, that the good we do will return to us, as will the harm. When teaching about the concept of mitzvot, and specifically about the dichotomy between *mitzvot bein adam LaMakom* and *mitzvot bein adam lachaveiro*, the *Zohar* reminds us to think in terms of personal relationships. The passage fits well in a discussion of Jewish God concepts and beliefs. Historically, the *Zohar's* concern about the place of the Jewish people in the world is insightful, as well.

- When learning about Shabbat, children can be taught *hidur mitzvah*, and the value of setting a beautiful table for Shabbat dinner. The Chasidim tell the story of a man who was to host an important rabbi in his home for Shabbat dinner. His wife's diligent efforts to prepare a perfect Shabbat dinner met with his anger and ridicule when he noticed she had neglected to cover the challot. The rabbi reminded his host that we cover the challot while we make *Kiddush* over the wine to save them from embarrassment. If we have compassion for the feelings of mere loaves of bread—which are, after all, inanimate objects—how much more so should we have compassion for people, who have real feelings? This story teaches educators and listeners a trenchant lesson: our rituals and practices can be signposts to Jewish values and ethics, and reinforce ethical *midot*.

3. Social and Communal *Midot*

Mark Zborowski's classic work about Eastern European Jews made the phrase "life is with people"[28] synonymous with Jewish culture. From a spiritual perspective, insight, serenity, and peace require good relationships and constructive interpersonal skills. Jewish life is inconceivable without family and community, and a full and satisfying life cannot be achieved in a silo.

Jewish tradition is replete with communal spiritual values: human dignity, justice, *g'milut chasadim*, environmental sensitivity, and concern for the suffering of animals are but a few that resonate strongly with children. Ample material exists to construct lessons around these values. The spirituality link is just that: we are all linked. When we understand that we are not separate beings, but part of a larger whole, Jewish communal values take on new resonance. Working on behalf of social justice can be experienced as a spiritual practice. The Mountain and the Bush can help direct lessons and discussions toward spiritual considerations.

Among the spiritual values most resonant with Jewish social and interpersonal values are the *midot* of listening, choosing our words carefully (*lashon hara*), controlling anger, and *dan l'chaf z'chut* (judging others for merit; giving them the benefit of the doubt).

I provide two illustrations of the possibilities for teaching anger management and *dan l'chaf z'chut*:

- In the imagination of the Rabbis, even God struggles to control his anger and reserve harsh judgment. God consults Rabbi Yishmael ben Elisha in the Holy of Holies, who gives God a blessing: "May it be Your will that Your mercy may suppress Your anger and Your mercy may prevail over Your other attributes, so that You judge Your children according to the attribute of mercy and may, on their behalf, stop short of the limit of strict justice!"[29] Individually, or as a class, children can pen their own version of this prayer to recite each morning.[30] This lesson dovetails nicely with lessons on God concepts and beliefs, prayer (in general), and Talmud.

- Yehoshua ben Perachia taught, "Judge every person favorably."[31] This is a challenging standard to meet. Children can easily recount examples from their lives when they have followed this advice, or failed to follow it, and identify the consequences. Talmud tells the story of an employer who seemingly had reason to distrust his employer, yet time and again gave him the benefit of the doubt, to eventually be proven righteous in his patience and reservation of judgment.[32] (The teachings of Rambam, the Chafetz Chaim, and Rabbi Nachman of Bratzlav provide excellent fodder for group discussions on the challenges and limits of reserving judgment.) In the context of a lesson on prayer or the High Holy Days (particularly the notion of *Yom Din*) this adds a spiritual dimension, particularly when children are taught that the obligation of *t'shuvah* entails judging themselves, not others.

Beginnings and Endings

Socrates taught that one's primary duty is "to know thyself." Polonius's last words of advice to his son Laertes are: "This above all: to thine own self be true, And it must follow, as the night the day, Thou canst not then be false to any man. Farewell, my blessing season this in thee!"[33] Polonius intends to warn Laertes against engaging in foolish and damaging behaviors that would harm his image, but we might tend today to hear his words as wisdom for spiritual living. For Howard Gardner, self-knowledge is a type of intelligence. For many, self-knowledge is the ultimate goal of spirituality. For others, it is the outcome. Most likely, it is in some ways both—the beginning and the culmination. Viewing the world through a spiritual Torah lens helps us see the blueprint of our souls.

"Source of My Being" by Rabbi Moshe ben Yaakov ibn Ezra[34] tells us that when we come to truly understand God, we see that God is within us, kindling a sacred lamp that allows God's glory to shine brightly in the world through us—we, who are images of the Divine.

A vision of the Almighty took hold of my mind,
And I knew that within me there was God.
His magnificent splendour was hidden,
But he was revealed in deed before the eyes of thought.
In my body he has kindled a lamp from his glory;
It tells me of the paths of the wise.
It is the light which shines in the days
Of youth, and grows brighter in old age.
Were it not derived from the mystery of his light
It would fail with my strength and my years.
With it I search out of the chamber of wisdom,
And I climb with no ladder to the garden of delights.[35]

Our children can come to know, and experience, God within.

Notes

1. Justice Potter was speaking about the threshold for obscenity in the public square. Stewart famously wrote: "I shall not today attempt further to define the kinds of material I understand to be embraced within that shorthand description, and perhaps I could never succeed in intelligibly doing so. But I kno it when I see it."
2. Howard W. Eves, *Mathematical Circles Adieu* (Washington, DC: Mathematical Association of America, 2002), 60 n.119. In a draft of the letter Einstein wrote, "The striving to free oneself from this [optical] delusion [of consciousness] is in the one issue of true religion." The draft letter is located in the Albert Einstein Archives of the Hebrew University of Jerusalem. It can be viewed at http://

www.flickr.com/photos/speakingoffaith/4090564390/ (viewed December 27, 2012).

3. *Genesis Rabbah* 1:1.

4. Menachem Mendel Morgensztern of Kotzk (1787–1859), considered to be the founder of the Ger dynasty. He was the student of Rabbi Simcha Bunim Bonhart of Peshischa, one of the most important Chasidic leaders in Poland in the late eighteenth and early nineteenth centuries.

5. *Midrash Exodus Rabbah* 2:5.

6. Rivka Miriam, "And From Time to Time, I Pray," in *My Father Commanded Me Not to Die* (*Avi Tzivani Lo La-mut*) (Jerusalem: Carmel Press, 2007) (translation provided by Rabbi Steven Sager).

7. Abraham Joshua Heschel, *God in Search of Man: A Philosophy of Judaism* (New York: Farrar, Straus and Giroux, 1976), 75.

8. The name of the album is *Skin of God* (track 11). HaTeva's Psalm 104 beautifully conveys the wonder of the created world.

9. *Baruch atah Adonai, Eloheinu Melech haolam, oseh maaseh b'reishit.* (Blessed are You, Lord our God, ruler of the universe, source of creation.)

10. The prayer can be found on many websites, including: http://jewishappleseed.org/apple/spiritp.htm (viewed December 27, 2012).

11. For example, upon smelling fragrant spices, trees, or fruit; upon seeing lightning, shooting stars, mountains, deserts, or a sunrise; upon hearing thunder or seeing a rainbow; upon receiving bad news; for wearing new clothing the first time; upon meeting a wise person.

12. Teens are equally inspired by such stories, particularly when they are about other teens.

13. David M. Bader, *Haikus for Jews* (New York: Harmony, 1999).

14. Rabbi Israel Lipkin Salanter (1810–1883) launched the nineteenth-century Musar movement in response to social changes brought about by the European Enlightenment, and the corresponding Haskalah in the Jewish world.

15. The Musar movement, which developed in the nineteenth century in Eastern Europe, focused on Jewish ethics. The term *musar* derives from Proverbs 1:2, where it connotes moral conduct, discipline, or teaching. While there is earlier classical Jewish ethical literature, including *M'silat Y'sharim* (The Path of the Just) by Moshe Chaim Luzzatto and *Cheshbon HaNefesh* by Menachem Mendel of Satanov, the Musar movement initiated by Israel Salanter (1810–1883) shaped a vigorous spiritual and intellectual discipline.

16. Rabbi Judah Loew ben Bezalel (1520–1609).

17. http://www.mussarinstitute.org/wisdom-way.htm (viewed November 30, 2012).

18. For congregations that choose a yearly theme and plan programming around it, *midot* would serve as an excellent theme.

19. Role-playing is especially efficacious for children because *midot* require practice to develop.

20. Traditional resources include *Cheshbon HaNefesh* by Menachem Mendel of Satanov, *M'silat Y'sharim* by Moshe Chaim Luzzato, and *Chovot HaLevavot* (Duties of the Heart) by Rabbi Bachya ben Yosef ibn Paquda. All three are published in facing Hebrew-English by Feldheim Publishers. Alan Morinis's *Every Holiness: The Jewish Spiritual Path of Mussar* (Boston: Trumpeter Books, 2007) is an excellent teaching book for adults and many teens.

21. Among the best-known compilations of *midot* are those of Rabbi Mendel of Satanov in *Cheshbon HaNefesh*, and Rabbi Moshe Chaim Luzzatto in *M'silat Y'sharim*.

22. Eves, *Mathematical Circles*, 60 n.119. (Emphasis mine.)

23. BT *Bava M'tzia* 85a.

24. *K'dushat Levi* 92b. My thanks to Rabbi Louis Rieser for bringing this passage to my attention.

25. Literally, "abundance." The term *shefa* in Kabbalistic thinking refers to the continuous divine flow of goodness between heaven and earth.

26. "The Lord spoke to Moses, saying: When an ox or a sheep or a goat is born, it shall stay seven days with its mother, and from the eighth day on it shall be acceptable as an offering by fire to the Lord. However, no animal from the herd or from the flock shall be slaughtered on the same day with its young." Lev. 22:26–28. The *Zohar*, as have other commentators, understand these mitzvot to require compassion for animals (*tzaar baalei chayim*).

27. *Zohar*, iii, 92b.

28. Mark Zborowski's *Life is with People* was co-authored with Elizabeth Herzog and first published in 1952.

29. BT *B'rachot* 7a.

30. For example, Help me, God, to find the strength and courage to be compassionate today, so that I don't get angry, and so that I treat others with kindness.

31. *Pirkei Avot* 1:6.

32. BT *Shabbat* 127b.

33. William Shakespeare, *Hamlet*, act 1, scene 3, 78–82.

34. Jewish Spanish poet and philosopher of the eleventh and twelfth centuries.

35. David Goldstein, trans., *The Jewish Poets of Spain 900–1250* (New York: Penguin Books, 1965), 107. (Emphasis mine.)

Section Three: Jewish Spiritual Guidance and Formation

The Quest for Meaning: Insights on Nurturing Adult Spiritual Development

Roberta Louis Goodman

I have to admit that there is a way in which I like going to funerals. I don't like it that people have died, but I do like hearing the eulogies, with clergy, family members, and friends sharing their thoughts and feelings about the deceased. I appreciate getting to know these individuals in a deeper way through hearing their life story, in a way that reveals who and what gave their life meaning. These eulogies capture the person's essence, a glimpse into his/her inner self, a look at his/her soul.

I currently am the education director in a large Reform congregation. I wonder what brings each of our congregants to our particular synagogue. In today's world, why are they here at all? What do they find compelling about what we are doing? With whom do they connect: clergy, staff, friends, families, and others at the congregation? Why do they come to this event and not that? What are they seeking? Why is one interested in study, another in prayer, and another in *tikkun olam*? Where are God, Torah, and Israel in their lives? What else are they involved in Jewishly and in the larger world? What do they get out of that involvement? How does their background and life experiences affect their relationship to the congregation? I also wonder about them as a "whole people" and not just for their connection

DR. ROBERTA LOUIS GOODMAN is the education director at North Shore Congregation Israel, Glencoe, Illinois, and a consultant specializing in research and evaluation. She graduated from HUC-JIR's Rhea Hirsch School of Education in 1981, studied with Dr. James Fowler at Emory University, and completed her doctoral studies at Teachers College/Columbia University, having studied with Drs. Jack Mezirow and Stephen Brookfield.

to our congregation or their Jewish identity; I wonder what makes them tick? About what are they passionate? Who or what inspires them? What ideas, books, or people have influenced who they are? Who do they care about and who cares for them?

Anytime I teach a group of adults, I wonder what brings them to class. Why now? Why here? What do they get out of it? How does it connect to who they are and what they hope to get out of life? What experiences and baggage as well as knowledge and skills are they bringing to the group learning experience? What questions about their lives are they coming with that will help them dig deeper? What will inspire or challenge them? What will keep them coming back to examine their lives in relation to Jewish ideas and texts? What will turn them off?

What these questions share is that they all explore a person's quest for meaning. As a student of James W. Fowler, I too believe that what characterizes us as humans is that we are meaning makers. Fowler calls this quest for meaning, faith development. All people, agnostic or monotheist, a member of a religious group or a secular humanist, a God believer or worshiper of fame and fortune, seek meaning about their world and their place in it. For some their understanding of and relationship to God informs who they are and the values by which they live. For others, the experience of what is transcendent in life comes from other sources. Call it faith, meaning, or spirituality—it is part of every human beings' existence. Part of the brilliance of Fowler's understanding of faith is that he overcomes the Western, Enlightenment notion that splits the world into the religious and the secular, marking spirituality, meaning making, into something associated solely with religion. Rather, he recognizes faith as something common to all human beings.

The purpose of this article is to share some insights from research on the spiritual development of adults in order to aid the work of those who desire to nurture people's quest for meaning. This article draws on theorists from the fields of human development and adult education who inform my thinking about how best to nurture adult spirituality.

Assumptions

The following assumptions are based on theories of spiritual development combined with my own experience.

- *All people are seekers.* They are constantly making sense of the world, seeking answers to life's significant questions, and crafting and recrafting their own stories of purpose.[1] Candle lighting, Jewish friends, support of Israel, and giving *tzedakah* are outward Jewish manifestations that often do not fully capture the ways in which Jews are finding meaning in being Jewish. What are the rituals and celebrations that make people's lives holy and how, if at all, do they connect that to being Jewish?

- *People are seekers in different ways.* For some the path is through institutionalized religion. For others, it is through *tikkun olam* (repairing the world), caring for family members, exploring nature, yoga, meditation, and more. We cannot afford to think that the conventions of the past will meet the needs of today's seekers. We live in a global society, in a multicultural world where spiritual direction comes in many forms and sources. We need to be open to new experiences within the established Jewish institutions. We need to figure out how to capture the energy and potential of these ideas and bring them into conversation with Judaism.

- *The content of people's faith, meaning making, changes over time.* Just as people grow physically, cognitively, and emotionally, so too do people grow and change spiritually. What gives their lives meaning and purpose, their views of God, and the sacred and their connection to symbols and customs change. We can speak of and analyze their faith or spiritual development as readily as we can their intellectual ability. We know of people who get stuck on a childhood image of God as an old man with a beard, but most people's ideas about God hopefully evolve and deepen.

- *We as Jewish professionals need to intentionally nurture people's spirituality.* People are walking philosophers and theologians whether or not we as Jewish professionals enter into the conversation with them. If we as Jewish professionals do not intentionally explore with them life questions, their purpose in this world, how they relate to others, and even where God is in their lives, then they will find us to be irrelevant. We will have marginalized or limited ourselves to liturgy, life cycles, and study, but not to the fullness of what is important to those we serve.

- *We need to foster spiritual development from the "outside in."* This is Franz Ròsenzweig's understanding of how we bring most Jewish adults in an acculturated or assimilated world into understanding their life through a Jewish framework.[2] We need to start with the seekers' experiences and interests, their spiritual paths, and from there, move towards what Judaism has to offer to the questions and quests that they pursue. For some, working from the "inside," the core of Jewish texts will stimulate their spiritual quest. For others, if not most, we need to understand the questions they are asking, their roles—as parents, spouses, adult children taking care of aging parents, professionals, lay leaders—that matter to them, and then introduce content-rich Jewish learning and experiences. We need to give them skills so that they are just as confident, comfortable, and capable as they are in the other areas of their lives.

Faith Development: Insights from Fowler and Parks

James W. Fowler, a Protestant minister, studied for his doctorate at Harvard when Lawrence Kohlberg, the famous theorist of moral development, taught his theory of moral reasoning. Kohlberg encouraged Fowler to take his notions about faith and people's life journeys and test them out empirically. He did this by interviewing people of different ages, genders, socioeconomic backgrounds, and religions (including Jews), who had different views about God and various relationships to organized religion. These interviews were analyzed for the patterns of how individuals construct meaning. This led to his creation of stages of faith.

Fowler's stages are similar to other developmental theories like Piaget's cognitive development and Kohlberg's moral development. These linear, hierarchical, and invariant theories claim to be descriptive of all human beings. Feminists and people from more traditional cultures question this way of describing human behavior. Still, Fowler's underlying principles and ideas about how people make meaning out of life are valuable for our conversation.

Seven Aspects of Faith

Fowler identified seven aspects of faith that give us a more textured understanding of what constitutes people's faith structures. Foremost, these seven aspects suggest that meaning making is about the whole person and not limited to what a person feels, or even what he/she knows. I present the seven aspects by providing questions that describe the essence of these stages:

1. *Form of logic*. What is my reasoning process? How does what I know and what I am passionate about affect my views?
2. *Perspective taking*. In what ways am I able to consider the viewpoint of others?
3. *Form of moral judgment*. How do I make moral decisions? How do my views of right and wrong, good and evil affect my attitudes and behavior?
4. *Bounds of social awareness*. Who do I see as part of my group? Who do I care about? How do I feel about people who are different than I am?
5. *Locus of authority*. Who or what influences my life choices?
6. *Form of world coherence*. How do I make sense of the world? Do I experience the world in an episodic or systematic way? Do I have a single understanding or is my view more like Swiss Cheese: with lots of holes and multi-systemed?
7. *Symbolic function*. What are the symbols, rituals, and customs that inspire me; connect me to others; embody who and what I believe in?

These seven aspects give us some idea of what constitutes faith. The questions themselves are theological and teleological in nature.

Definition and Description of Faith

Fowler defines faith as the "process by which a person finds and makes meaning of life's significant questions and issues, adheres to this meaning, and acts it out in his or her life."[3] Faith links questioning, seeking, and believing with action. Fowler describes faith in terms of a triadic interplay of self, other(s), and shared centers of value and power. Imagine a triangle with "self" in the lower left-hand corner, "others" in the lower right-hand corner, and "shared centers of value and power" on top. While faith development is a theory about individuals, faith is formed in relation to others: individuals; groups of people like one's co-workers, family, or synagogue community; or even society as a whole. What mediates this relationship between one's self and others are what Fowler calls "shared centers of value and power," which include everything from honesty and kindness to fame and fortune to holiness and God. A shared center of value and power is not necessarily something positive; it can be revenge, hatred, or greed. This relationship between the self and others, built around the shared centers of value and power, may lead to a sense of trust and loyalty, to something that becomes covenantal.

This triadic nature of faith has a narrative quality. We are constantly creating and re-creating stories about who we are and what is important in our lives. These stories help reveal to us and others what guides our lives, who we want to become, and how and with whom we want to spend our time.

What is powerful here is that meaning making is formed in relationship to others. When you and I share any kind of experience—reading a book, attending a concert, traveling to Israel—our stories become connected; we have a collective experience. They become part of our story in small or large ways.

Studying narratives from Torah and other Jewish texts are powerful vehicles that can challenge and shape our shared centers of value and power, our sense of self and views of others. How much more palatable, compelling, and memorable are "lessons," conveying ideas when they are presented in the form of a story.

Hearing stories of others and of our people helps to shape our own story just as our personal story shapes our people's story. It is through the stories of our lives that the content of our faith becomes visible.

Big Questions and Imagination

Sharon Parks, who was at Harvard when Fowler did his doctoral work, studied emerging adults—primarily twentysomethings. She highlights the importance of asking big questions and the role of imagination to enrich one's faithing process. She expresses the concern that

> too many emerging adults are not being encouraged to ask the big questions that awaken critical thought in the first place. Swept up in religious assumptions that remain unexamined (and economic and political assumptions that function religiously), they may easily become vulnerable to conventional assumptions and miss being invited to their own authentic and worthy dreams.[4]

Parks connects asking big questions to fostering imagination, an activity fundamental to a person forming meaning and purpose.

Imagination is a process, "the power to give form to our knowing—the power of naming—the content of feeling and thought."[5] That process gives rise to the way we act in the world. "Human beings participate in the ongoing creation of life itself, for better and for worse, continually birthing our shared reality."[6] This too can this be said of stories.

Influenced by Sharon Parks's work, Rabbi Josh Feigelson, while director of the Hillel at Northwestern University, started the Ask Big Questions project, where undergraduate and graduate students discuss questions like: Where do you feel at home? What could we sacrifice to repair the world? Now he has taken this project to universities and other settings across the United States to help a wide range of Jewish emerging adults examine what gives their lives meaning and purpose. How many of us as Jewish professionals are providing opportunities for our adults, emerging or otherwise, to ask big questions and examine our assumptions within a Jewish framework? We are all well advised to cultivate these conversations so that images and narratives from the larger culture do not overshadow the images and stories of the Jewish people. We want our adults to believe that what we are doing, what Judaism has to offer, has something to do with the significant questions about life that they are asking on their own.

A significant "take away" from examining Fowler's theory of faith development and Parks's work related to his theory is that meaning is individually and socially constructed. We may grow up and live in a particular culture, historical period, household, and tradition; we may be surrounded by certain symbols and rituals, immersed in particular stories, values, and way of seeing the world, but ultimately, we choose what is meaningful to us. This is true even if we are choosing which authority helps us to decide what gives life meaning. In many ways, the shift from adolescence to adulthood involves challenging, if not shedding, the meaning-making structure that we grew up with, in order to create and choose our own. In the next section, I review some adult developmental and learning theories that help us understand this process.

Brookfield and Mezirow on Adult Development[7]

Leaving home, going to college, entering the military, or beginning to work for a living contribute to the emergence of adulthood (defined as taking responsibility for one's own well-being and that of others). What these transitions share is that they put us in relationship and dialogue with others, some of whom share our background, worldview, and values and others who do not. This contact with others broadens our perspective, challenging what we think, know, and believe about the world and ourselves. Those tacit, unexamined assumptions about the world that we grew up with are suddenly vulnerable, being tested by exposure to new ideas, attitudes, and values.

Critical Thinking

The process of uncovering and examining our assumptions and then deciding whether to hold onto or replace them is called "critical thinking" or "critical reflection." It is what distinguishes adulthood from childhood. Assumptions are "taken-for-granted beliefs about the world and our place within it that seem so obvious to us as not to need stating explicitly."[8] The examination of our assumptions is a lifelong, usually generative process. It adds depth and richness to our lives. It involves emotion as well as intellect. The process is precipitated by positive and negative events.[9]

In many ways, Harold Kushner's book *When Bad Things Happen to Good People* debunks a set of assumptions that often surfaces with people's experiences. Kushner challenges the belief that in order to be a good Jew or a good Christian, we must believe in an omnipotent God who rewards the good and punishes the bad. Those ideas are repeated in biblical texts. Is it true when someone develops cancer? Is God really punishing that person? Is God really omnipotent giving a person cancer? A crisis of faith can emerge when we are stuck with this belief; when we are unaware that Judaism offers other views of God or other ways of thinking about theodicy.

Perspective Transformation

Jack Mezirow, former adult education professor at Teachers College/Columbia University, takes critical thinking, the challenging of assumptions, one step further, introducing the concept of "perspective transformation." Perspective transformation, in contrast to critical thinking, comes when our deepest assumptions collapse, leading to radical changes in one's worldview and identity. For some, transformation is precipitated by changes in roles, life-cycle events, or transitions: becoming a parent or grandparent, entering retirement, confronting adversity, seeking consolation during difficult times. It may come from learning more about one's roots, one's family, or one's self. Intensive learning or immersion experiences, Jewish or otherwise, can on their own, or in combination with these life factors, lead to transformation.

I know a man who started his career as a lawyer. When his family and community were devastated by a powerful hurricane, not only did he move his residence, he refocused his personal and professional life on Jewish living and learning. For him, studying Musar has been a transformative learning experience, reorienting the way he interacts with others, helping him through his crisis, and satisfying his soul. All of this has led to major changes in assumptions about himself and the world; it has reordered his priorities and shifted the focus of his activities from what he was doing before. We cannot underestimate the significance of the readiness and openness of Jewish professionals to facilitate experiences and learning for seekers like this man.

My assumption is that we, as Jewish professionals, are interested in facilitating meaning making and critical thinking and fostering transformation to strengthen people's lives, the Jewish community, and our society and world. If indeed these are our goals, then we need to consider how to nurture meaning making. The next section shares some ideas about how to do this.

Nurturing Meaning Making

I present two approaches to nurturing the meaning-making activities of adults: (1) helping adults identify their assumptions in order to facilitate meaning making, and (2) educating the spirit. Using narratives to facilitate spiritual growth is another effective approach that is addressed in the article by Peninnah Schram in this issue and by Sandy Sasso[10] in other resources.

Brookfield on Examining our Assumptions

There may be something that seems inherently contradictory between facilitating critical thinking and strengthening one's connection to a religious tradition. Yet, we know that many people carry baggage about God, Hebrew school, or prayer services that would benefit from a healthy dose of examining assumptions. Fowler advised that when a person states "I don't believe in God" the best response is "Which view of God is it that you have rejected?" This explicitly challenges the assumption that there is a singular understanding of God that is accepted in a particular religious tradition. The book that Rabbis Rifat Sonsino and Danny Syme wrote, *Finding God*, presents ten different views of God from famous Jewish theologians and philosophers that can guide individuals to expand their ideas about God. In our fast-paced, constantly changing global world, our ideas, beliefs, values, and ways of doing things are constantly being challenged. Being able to identify and reflect on our assumptions can help us respond to these challenges, deciding when to hold fast and when to change.

Brookfield has many different ideas about how to foster critical thinking. At the core of the techniques he presents is the importance of critical questioning that is designed to prompt reflective analysis more so than to elicit information.[11]

One technique that he describes to help uncover our assumptions is the use of a critical incident, a concrete example that comes from a person's experience. Individuals are asked to write two paragraphs or bullet points that describe the who, what, when, and where of an actual event that relates to an issue, value, or item: a time they experienced joy or doubt, a positive or negative synagogue encounter, an interaction with a person where they felt respected or ignored, etc. Through the sharing of a critical incident, other participants raise questions, contribute their perspectives, and aid the person in helping to draw out the buried assumptions. Because the person is focusing on something that happened, there is observable evidence to reflect upon that helps make the implicit visible, helping to move the conversation from the specifics to more general ideas or concepts. This technique gives us a way of unpacking baggage, figuring out what stands in our way of growing spirituality. This process can create a void, exposing a sense of emptiness; hopefully this is followed by the individual wanting to explore new ideas or experiences.

Imagine the potential energy that could be released by gathering a group of parents of third graders with children in the religious school—a time when many people are first coming to congregations as adult members—to talk to them about what matters to them. What are the questions that you have about life? What compels you as an individual? What are you seeking? For some it may start with a conversation about their role as parent, their vision of family, and of what they are hoping to provide their children through Jewish schooling and bar/bat mitzvah. For others, it may start with sorting through the ideas and beliefs they grew up with about religion or God that they question. Combine this with exploring Jewish texts, values, and ideas related to their questions and assumptions, and this could deepen their worldview.

Shire on Educating for Religiosity

Michael Shire's approach to educating for religiosity comes from his empirical study of teenagers in formal and supplementary school settings and in informal settings such as Jewish overnight camp and Israel experiences. Although he focuses on youth, his theory is worthy of consideration of those working with adults. Through an analysis of Jewish texts and philosophers, Shire chooses to speak of "religiosity" instead of "spirituality" or "meaning making" as the term best described what he was trying to capture, a sense of spiritual awareness and an explicit religious expression such as performing mitzvot. Quoting Arthur Green, Shire defines religiosity as "striving for the presence of God and fashioning a life of holiness appropriate to such striving."[12] Shire examines religiosity in Jewish education programs and institutions and develops an approach for fostering it. He observes that the contemplative, inner self and soul, the God relationship, and the sense of the holy are ignored or minimized in Jewish settings.

Shire describes three parts in his approach: encounter, reflection, and instruction for religiosity. Encounter is a feeling of spiritual awareness.[13] It involves "evoking intense feelings of contemplation, peacefulness, wonderment, and concentration."[14] It comes from things like walking up Masada, visiting holy sites in Israel, celebrating *Havdalah* at a summer camp by a lake, or praying in the woods.

Reflection is linked to encounter in particular. Reflection is the opportunity and ability to contemplate and deliberate on religious encounters.[15] Religious experiences can occur outside of an educational setting, as life "happens," in our homes, community, and the larger world. Writing and discussing are reflective activities that can occur after some "encounter." The more powerful the encounter the deeper and more compelling are the writings or conversations.

Instruction for religiosity "provides the theoretical underpinnings for students' spiritual experiences."[16] Teaching knowledge and skills that assist one in interpreting Jewish texts, working on prayer mastery, exploring the various names of God, or teaching the history and order of the prayer book are all examples of instruction for religiosity.

Shire argues that all three parts—encounter, reflection, and instruction for religiosity—are needed for a strong sense of religiosity. Typically too much of adult learning in our institutions focuses on instruction. The goal is to strive for balance and connection among these three parts. There are several challenges in applying Shire's approach to fostering religiosity among adults. Think of adult experiences aimed at facilitating spirituality: a weekly Torah study and a yoga Shabbat.

In the classroom, how do we foster a sense of intimacy and safety that leads to a deeper examination of those life significant questions that go beyond information? How do you create moments of "encounter"—moments that stand out as being special or holy? How can this be done by using different space, light(s), rituals, and objects? What effect does changing the format, telling our stories, using drama games, setting up a debate, sharing of encounter experiences, and journaling have on the individual's search for meaning? How is reflection used as a tool for deepening the impact of the instruction? How might we bring yoga or other spiritual traditions like meditation into a mainstream prayer so that they bring deepened meaning to the experience?

All three of these types of learning have the potential for reaching adults—stretching their imaginations and enriching their souls. On the one hand, adults have more resources, a greater ability to navigate their communities and world. On the other hand, adults don't have to enter our sphere of influence as youth are required. Adults can and often do choose options that have little if anything to do with seeking experiences within a Jewish framework. The problem that led Shire to create a Jewish educational approach to religiosity for adolescents may even be of greater value for adults. What is going to compel adults to go on this journey with us? What opportunities are offered to Jewish adults that foster religious experience? Are these offerings in any way connected to the main institutions of the Jewish community (e.g., the synagogue)? Are we adapting to the ideas and values, ways of being, and worldview of the younger adults? How do we reach adults who are not a homogenous group and represent many generations?

Conclusion

We must concern ourselves with adult spiritual or faith development. Our adults are already engrossed in meaning-making processes. Many are seeking avenues to further their spiritual growth outside of the Jewish community. Our job is to try to connect their exploration within a Jewish framework and community to help them see how Judaism enriches their lives and souls. It is possible to nurture spiritual and faith development. I have presented some of the theorists that help us think about how adults develop and how we can nurture their faith. We have to figure out what are the issues that speak to each generation, to people's different roles, to the various phases of one's life, and connect these to the learning opportunities that we offer. We need to be open to shaping different types of experiences as not all seekers do their seeking in the same way. We cannot limit ourselves to conventional adult education classes; we have to be bold and adventuresome. Remember, it is not ours to complete the task, but neither can we desist from it as the "Master" is impatient as are the Eternal's people.

Notes

1. James W. Fowler, *Stages of Faith* (San Francisco: Jossey-Bass Publishers, 1981).
2. Franz Rosenzweig, *On Jewish Learning* (Madison, WI: University of Wisconsin Press, 2002).
3. Roberta Louis Goodman, "Developmental Psychology," in *The Ultimate Jewish Teachers Handbook*, ed. Nachama Skolnik Moskowitz (Denver: A.R.E. Publishing, Inc., 2003), 85–108.
4. Sharon Daloz Parks, *Big Questions, Worthy Dreams* (San Francisco: Jossey-Bass, 2011), xi.
5. Ibid., 139.
6. Ibid., 140.
7. For a more detailed discussion of these theorists and their implications for Jewish settings, see Roberta Louis Goodman and Betsy Dolgin Katz, *The Adult Jewish Education Handbook* (Denver: A.R.E. Publishing, Inc., 2004), 77–121.

8. Stephen Brookfield, *Becoming a Critically Reflective Teacher* (San Francisco: Jossey-Bass Publishers, 1985), 2.

9. Stephen Brookfield, *Developing Critical Thinkers* (San Francisco: Jossey-Bass Publishers, 1987).

10. Sandy Sasso, "Children, Adults, and Shared Responsibilities," in *Children's Spirituality in the Jewish Narrative Tradition*, ed. Marcia J. Bunge (London: Cambridge University Press, 2012); Sandy Sasso, "Tell Me a Story about God," in *Teaching about God and Spirituality*, ed. Roberta Louis Goodman and Sherry H. Blumberg (Denver: A.R.E. Publishing, Inc., 2002), 180–88.

11. Brookfield, *Developing Critical Thinkers*, 93.

12. Michael Shire, "Educating the Spirit," in *Teaching about God and Spirituality*, 120.

13. Ibid., 121.

14. Ibid., 121.

15. Ibid., 123.

16. Ibid., 125.

Jewish Spiritual Direction: Developing a Vocabulary for the Experiences of Our Inner Lives

Jacob J. Staub

In the summer of 2002, I happened to be chatting with a member of a congregation affiliated with the Jewish Reconstructionist Federation who had served that year on his synagogue's rabbinic search committee. I asked him about that experience. "It was inspiring!" he replied. "We were interviewing X, proceeding through the list of questions we had agreed upon, and we asked him to describe his prayer life. We expected the standard account of how often he attended services, which kind of services he preferred, and so on. Instead, he began to speak about what happens for him when he engages in prayer! The whole committee sat entranced, listening for over twenty minutes. We had never heard a rabbi talk like that! We never got to half the questions on our list, but we offered him the position."

It was a memorable moment for me. Rabbi X had just completed the RRC rabbinical program and was in the first class to have sat with one of our spiritual directors for four years. He is not particularly the praying type. He is a social activist who decided to become a rabbi after years of political organizing. He was competing for this congregational position with a number of more experienced and accomplished colleagues. And he had been offered the job because of his prayer life and his ability to speak compellingly about it. A decade ago, members of Reconstructionist congregations still had the reputation of being rationalist non-supernaturalists, interested more in social justice work than in God. Yet it turns out that even people who find it more spiritually uplifting to spend

RABBI JACOB J. STAUB (RRC77) is professor of Jewish Philosophy and Spirituality at the Reconstructionist Rabbinical College. He was instrumental in founding its Jewish Spiritual Direction program in 1998 and continues to direct it.

Shabbat working in a soup kitchen than sitting in the synagogue sanctuary also yearn to have fully developed prayer lives.

Perhaps the most effective way to promote spiritual awareness in those with whom we work is to embody, exemplify, and articulate living a life of the spirit, so that rabbis, educators, congregational officers, and parents can serve as models to be emulated. And Jewish spiritual direction is an effective means to lead our communities towards this objective.

Definitions

I use the term "spiritual" to describe that aspect of one's internal life in which one reaches upward and inward to deepen awareness of the unseen transcendent and immanent dimensions of life, so that one develops a deeper sense of one's place in the universe and of the sanctity of all existence, particularly as it infuses all of one's actions. Note that according to this definition, spirituality need not include any reference to God or any traditional practice of prayer or ritual practice, though, of course, these elements are often central to a person's spiritual life.

I use the term "prayer" to refer to the traditional verbal expressions of petition, praise, yearning, and gratitude that are found in the siddur, but also to a state of consciousness that need not be expressed in words or concepts at all. That is, prayer is not only the words of our prayers; it is also the states of heart and spirit that those words seek to describe. The *Sh'ma*'s declaration of God's unity might point to the transformational intuition of the interrelatedness of all reality. That intuition itself is a state of prayer. The words of gratitude in the *Modim Anachnu* section of the *Amidah*, "for all of your wonders, at every moment, evening, morning, and afternoon," become "prayerful" when the worshiper comes to see the wondrousness of every moment. Reciting the fixed words of the *matbea* in the siddur on a daily or weekly or occasional basis is a spiritual practice that acculturates us to these perspectives, so that we can have ever deepening prayerful experiences.

Jewish Spiritual Direction

The practice of spiritual direction (SD) generally takes place when two people sit prayerfully and reverentially in the presence of the Holy—most often for one hour each month. Since a central principle of SD is that the terms of the conversation are defined by the directee/seeker, the two may sit in the presence of God—however the seeker images God—or in the presence of the Holy, or of the Mystery, or of the Infinite, or of the Process. The director witnesses nonjudgmentally the journey of the seeker, listening openly and compassionately, noticing when "the divine light" may be shining through the seeker's narrative, inquiring about the invitation or opportunity that the seeker discerns in this or that experience.[1]

The director is primarily a witness and a companion on the seeker's journey towards discernment. Beyond this, she has no agenda of her own. She often sits in silence for most of the hour; sometimes they both do, listening for the Holy. When the seeker is open to it, the director may invite him to imagine what he himself looks like from God's point of view; to welcome God into whatever situation he is experiencing in order to see if that awareness of the Divine Presence changes anything; to a practice of cultivating self-compassion, for example, or gratitude, or forgiveness, or imagining himself in the comforting arms of God; or to a daily practice of cataloguing blessings for which he is grateful. The director, however, does not arrive with a program or a prescription. She listens contemplatively and responds as she witnesses the movement of the spirit in the seeker.

Unlike what happens in therapy or pastoral counseling, spiritual direction is not about solving problems. If the seeker is experiencing a marriage that is dissolving, for example, the director might refer her to a marriage counselor, but he himself will not take on the challenge of helping the seeker to repair what is broken. Instead, the director will remain present to the seeker's pain and anger, probing for where the divine invitation may be found in the experience. Sitting with a seeker who is mourning the death of a relative or friend, the director may offer silent companionship while the seeker grieves, waiting however long it takes for the seeker to heal sufficiently to receive comfort.

Group spiritual direction is another mode of this discernment practice. Typically three or four seekers meet for two hours, and a fraction of the time is allotted for each of them to speak and to hear the contemplative responses of the other participants. While such groups often begin with a facilitator, after group members become accustomed to the practice, they can often continue without a facilitator. Yet another mode is the practice of spiritual *chevruta*, in which two peers meet regularly for an hour, splitting the time between them, each witnessing the journey of the other in supportive silence. Like one-on-one SD with a director, both of these modes is not about analyzing causes of problems or seeking solutions to them, but is rather about creating a communal sense of the sacred and finding ways to discern and develop a common vocabulary for describing that sense.[2]

The practice of discernment that is the ultimate goal in spiritual direction is related to the traditional Jewish practice of reciting at least one hundred *b'rachot* each day—finding innumerable opportunities to give thanks for our blessings. There is a subtle difference, however, between giving thanks for blessings that may come from a divine source and noticing the way that the Divine Presence permeates all aspects of our everyday lives—including those aspects that are painful and over which we would not ordinarily be inclined to recite a *b'rachah*. The set formula of the *b'rachah* provides us with the words to express our feelings, but it can also serve as a barrier to a feeling of intimacy with the Divine Presence. Spiritual direction seeks to cultivate that feeling, so that the *b'rachah* is truly a vehicle for its expression, rather than an obligation to be discharged or a tradition to be recited. The key to enhancing the spiritual life of the members of our communities is to cultivate their ability to maintain their "spiritual awareness" when they are not formally engaged in *t'filah*. Where is God (or the Mystery, etc.) when I am in a traffic jam? Arguing with my child? Weeding my garden?

Spiritual Types

It is axiomatic in the literature of SD that not everybody is spiritual in the same way, and that it is not a matter of who is more spiritual and who is less spiritual. There are many different typologies of the differing spiritual types. Tilden Edwards offers one of the simplest, describing four types:

1. *Cognitive*—those people who seek the Mystery through intellectual means, by reasoning, through argumentation; for example, the spiritual fire generated in intense Talmudic study.
2. *Devotional*—those people who are best elevated emotionally through prayer, song, chant, or ritual; for example, the transcendent feeling of group singing.
3. *Activist*—those people who feel most connected to the universe when they are engaged in the work of *tikkun olam* and

or *g'milut chasadim*; for example, the transformational power of an American Jewish World Service trip to the Third World.

4. *Iconoclastic*—those people who are single-mindedly devoted to showing that all belief claims are baseless, idolatrous attempts to express the ineffable; for example, Abraham smashing his father's idols.[3]

None of us is a pure type; we are all mixes in combinations that vary through the journeys of our lives. Moreover, the list of types might be much longer: aesthetic, creative, familial, and so on. The primary point, however, is that there is a wide variety of ways to reach upward and inward to the transcendent and immanent dimensions of reality. We probably all need to be careful not to assume that the most spiritual among us are Type 2 (devotional). And any successful strategy designed to promote spiritual formation will anticipate that different people are inclined to be spiritual in different ways.

The Power of a Discernment Practice

At its best, SD will facilitate a transformation in a seeker's outlook. The simple practice of sitting for an hour each month with someone who is expressly listening for divine footsteps will gradually help the seeker to acclimate to the possibility that there are divine footsteps and that they can be discerned if we quiet the mind and open the heart. There have been many surveys of Americans that reveal that the majority of people have intuitions of the Mystery but have never spoken to anyone about their experiences because there is neither a shared vocabulary nor the assurance that you won't be shunned as weird or worse. Spiritual direction provides that safety, as well as the opportunity to develop one's own vocabulary. Initially, if you ask most Jews, "Where is God in this experience?" they are likely to shut down. But if they are asked, "What is the invitation/opportunity in this experience?" they can discern meaning without labeling it as divine, and that is an important first step in the discernment process.

Given the secularized discourse in which so many of us live, SD's most important attribute is that it requires no belief in a God who hears my prayers or is even aware of my existence. Whether or not I believe in a God who is aware of me, however, my relationship with God is something that I need to cultivate as I cultivate relationships with other people. It is not enough to believe in God or in the unity of the cosmos; a practice of awareness builds the relationship. And it turns out that it is possible to build a personal relationship with a non-personal God.[4]

The journey of each seeker is unique, but some trends emerge. A discernment practice helps people to slow down and "smell the flowers." The seeker notices not only sunsets and the first buds of spring, but also is less likely to take for granted moments of wonder in his interactions with others, moments of grace (chen). He frequently develops self-compassion and is then better able to be compassionate to others and to receive compassion from them. He realizes that is he not as in control of outcomes in his life as he had imagined and therefore is more self-forgiving and forgiving of others. She is able to relinquish the deeply felt belief that she must be self-reliant, that it is all up to her, and so is able to ask for help, or at least to acknowledge that she cannot do it alone. She recognizes the uncertainty and fragility of our lives and is better able to face that uncertainty and embrace the journey without knowing where she is headed. She is better able to remain open-hearted.

All of this occurs whether or not the seeker professes a belief in God or attends worship services. It is possible to plan and lead "spirituality" programs without assuming either of these.

Strategies for Sacred Teaching

Spiritual direction cannot be imposed or required in any kind of coercive way. When it is transformative, it works through the free and unconstrained movement of the spirit. A seeker must be seeking something; the first question a director asks is "What are you seeking?" Whatever resistances the directee has to discernment, one of them is not whether to be in SD. Thus, programs must be offered without the expectation that people will respond.[5]

Professional Leaders

Returning to Rabbi X in my opening anecdote, I would argue that rabbis and educators who are interested in helping people to enrich their spiritual lives would do well to begin with themselves so that we can model, embody, and articulate a life of the spirit, and that an excellent way to do so is to find your own spiritual director. The Jewish Spiritual Directors listserv now has several hundred members, and Sandy Jardine maintains an up-to-date list (sandyjardine@cox.net). On its website (sdiworld.org/Seek-and-Find), Spiritual Directors International posts a Seek and Find guide that lists all of its members geographically, noting their religious denominations. While in-person SD is preferable, I have had wonderful experiences with seekers with whom I have met via Skype. Also, the Institute for Jewish Spirituality (ijs-online.org) offers two-year programs for rabbis and lay leaders that include SD work as well as a variety of modes of spiritual enrichment.

For those interested in becoming a spiritual director, there are currently two Jewish SD training programs: the Morei Derekh Program of the Yedidya Center, directed by Dr. Linda Thal and Rabbi Ruth Sohn (www.yedidyacenter.org/the-morei-derekh-program), and Lev Shomea, directed by Rabbi Avruhm Addison and Barbara Breitman (www.isabellafriedman.org/levshomea). Each of the cohorts of these programs generally include rabbis and Jewish educators. There are also excellent training programs that are not under Jewish auspices.[6]

Synagogue professionals cannot serve as spiritual directors for congregational members without encountering significant complications related to boundaries and dual roles. How can you provide absolute safety and confidentiality to someone who may serve on the committee that decides whether to renew your contract? How do you balance your role as a pastoral counselor, in which you may need to be directive in helping a congregant to address a problem, with your role as spiritual director, in which you are nondirective and nonjudgmental; perhaps the invitation is to leave the marriage, for example, and not to work to save it! But a rabbi or educational director who is himself in SD or trained as a spiritual director can share his journey and experiences with congregants, breaking the secular silence that makes it taboo to talk about intuitions of the spirit.

In locations where there are multiple synagogues in reasonable proximity to one another, the rabbi of one synagogue can serve as the spiritual director of the members of another congregation, or lead a group SD there. Or a congregation can provide access for members to one or more trained spiritual directors in the area—perhaps even members of the congregation—subsidizing the cost of such meetings as a way to signal the value it places on such experiences.

The rabbi or educational director can also lead groups of other staff. If we want our teachers to address the spiritual development of their students, what better way is there to do so than devoting teacher in-services and other professional development opportunities to an exploration of the range of teacher's own spiritual experiences? If they can speak about unitive peak experiences and dream revelations, for example, with one another, then they have the permission and encouragement to open up opportunities for their students to share their own intuitions and experiences with one another in a safe atmosphere.

Lay Leaders

Imagine a self-selected group of congregational board members (perhaps as few as three or four) who respond to an invitation to form a monthly SD group in which they share their spiritual journeys in the mode of group SD described above and thus bring a different sensibility to board and other committee meetings. How might their joint perspective alter the meeting discussions when priorities are being set or controversial decisions are discussed? How might the entire congregation be affected by a collective awareness that some board members are devoting themselves to their own spiritual development?

Small Groups

An invitation to join a monthly SD group to witness one another's spiritual journeys in a congregation of several hundred or more is likely to evoke a positive response from at least a handful of members who will rejoice that their needs are being met. A response of four or eight members should not be regarded as signifying failure. After a few months, even a group of four people that meets monthly for two hours will begin to have an impact on the entire community. They will be speaking to friends about the experience, encouraging them to join. In *d'var Torah* discussions or adult education classes, members of the group may raise questions about the spiritual experiences of biblical characters or the insights that can be gleaned from the text being studied for our own encounter with the sacred. Every such comment moves the community a little bit closer to being a sacred congregation in which it is appropriate to give voice to one's inner yearnings.

Tikkun Olam Groups

When social action committees frame their work as spiritual, the spiritual needs of Type 3 (activist spirituality) are better met. One group that was devoted for the year to changing the predatory lending practices of banks would meet themselves before meeting with city council members or bank officials to recite a *b'rachah* (*laasok b'tzorchei tzibur* [to engage in the needs of the community]) and express their *kavanah* (sacred, prayerful intention). After doing their lobbying work or collecting signatures on petition, they would meet in contemplative silence and discern where the divine face peeked through the mundane work of the day. This spiritual framework transformed their commitment to social justice into an experience of the mystery and sanctity of the universe.

Spiritual Interest Groups

We are all familiar with the importance of congregational support system networks: parents of teens with drug-use issues, children caring for elderly parents, people who have lost their jobs, retirees, relatives of people undergoing chemotherapy. Congregational support systems can connect members with others facing similar challenges, and they can mobilize the larger community to help out—finding the best rehab resources or geriatricians, networking to help with a job search, driving people to and from the hospital. When support groups add the element of spiritual direction, however, new and wonderful things can happen. A group of parents with children who have developmental challenges meets monthly and together seek the invitation and opportunity presented by their shared experience. Their isolation is mitigated not only by others in similar situations, but also by a shared sense of how they can each open their hearts to divine strength and comfort and to the extraordinary lessons they learn from their children.

Contemplative Reading Groups

Sometimes, people are more comfortable gathering in sacred contemplation around a text. It doesn't matter which texts are chosen. Contemplative reading differs in a number of significant ways from the way we usually read. The group sits in silence and then someone reads the first line or sentence. The group members then contemplate the words, without feeling bound by their literal meaning. The text serves as a vehicle that evokes our responses, often nonlinearly, a portal to new revelatory interpretations. One may respond to a word, a sound, a letter. She may free associate to an experience that she is undergoing; she may gain a new perspective through her contemplation of the text. Or one may reflect on the literal meaning of the words of the text. The only rules are that there is a bit of silence after each person speaks, in order to discourage cross conversation, and that no response or interpretation may be ruled incorrect on any grounds. The text is a focal point for contemplative awareness, functioning in a way that is similar to the words of a chant or the breath in meditation. The point is to notice what arises through the practice. And when one of the group members decides that the group has been silent for long enough, he then reads the next line aloud.

Focusing the group contemplation on a sacred Jewish text can ground the experience in the chain of textual interpretations over the many centuries. One often hears that Jews never read sacred Scripture directly, without the commentaries of prior generations. That is a relatively new circumstance, however, that began with the printing press in the fifteenth century, when typesetters surrounded the biblical text with commentaries. Prior to that moment, commentators were free to interpret the text in ever new and startling ways, regarding the text as divinely revealed and thus embedded with an infinite number of meanings. This practice of contemplative reading follows in that tradition and allows participants to experience the sanctity of Scripture, thus discerning God in its words.[7]

A variation of this practice has participants read the text with compassion, forgiveness, or love. The group members engage first in a practice of cultivating a compassionate heart, for example, and then read the text compassionately—towards the characters in the text, towards the author of the text who may have discerned the Divine as manifest in values that the reader may find offensive, or towards oneself, for the pain that the text has caused the reader. What arises is often moving and always unpredictable. In one group, a member read Genesis 3 with a compassionate heart; identified with Eve, who is blamed just as this reader was blamed by her ex-husband for their divorce eight years before; and in sending compassion to Adam, was able to feel compassion for her ex-husband for the first time. Another member read God's blustery response to Job in Job 40 and felt compassion for God who has no good answer for Job and instead makes a lot of noise—just as her authoritarian father did throughout her childhood. Reading the text compassionately led her to a shift in her attitude toward her long-dead father. As each participant shares his response to the text, the others are affected and may be moved by the spirit in new ways. The experience of revelatory insights generated by the contemplation of a sacred text may change members' attitudes about the possibility of spiritual renewal through traditional forms.

Jewish Authenticity

If these practices are modifications of practices from other traditions, can they be authentically Jewish?[8] It is my conviction that all Jewish beliefs and practices were borrowed from some aspect of the contemporary cultural milieu and translated into Jewish language, idioms, and values. Even the Decalogue appears to be an adaptation of contemporary suzerainty treaties. After a while— often a very short while—the borrowing comes to feel authentic and may be assumed to date back to Sinai. Most such experimental borrowings, I suspect, don't meet authentic Jewish needs and disappear, out of our memory.

My *Bubbe* Yussy, my mother's mother who arrived alone in the United States from the Ukraine at age seventeen, lived every moment of her life in conversation with a God who was close enough to hear her. The challenge that we face today is to restore our own awareness of God, the Ineffable, the Infinite, the Mystery, the Presence, the Compassionate One, to the warp and woof of our daily lives, despite the theological, cultural, and sociological distance that we have traveled from my grandmother. *Bubbe* Yussy's beliefs were not Sinaitic; neither Rabbi Akiva nor Maimonides would have found them familiar. She was raised in Nevardok, by a *melamed* father himself shaped by the surrounding culture. It is our responsibility to adapt whatever we can to deepen an awareness of the part of reality that cannot be accessed or measured materially.

We are each spiritual in a unique combination of ways. We use our human faculties to perceive that which is beyond our ability to conceive in our limited categories of thinking. The practice of discernment may be able to move many of us to richer realms of spiritual awareness.

Notes

1. For a description of Jewish spiritual direction, see Howard Avruhm Addison and Barbara Eve Breitman, eds., *Jewish Spiritual*

Direction: An Innovative Guide from Tradition and Contemporary Sources (Woodstock, VT: Jewish Lights, 2006). For an introduction to spiritual direction, see Margaret Guenther, *Holy Listening: The Art of Spiritual Direction* (London: Darton Longman and Todd, 1992).

2. See Ann Kline, "*Chavurat Ruach* (A Fellowship of Spirit): Community for Spiritual Direction," in Addison and Breitman, *Jewish Spiritual Direction*, 154–68; Rose Mary Dougherty, *Group Spiritual Direction: Community for Discernment* (New York: Paulist Press, 1995); and Monica Maxon, Lynne Smith, and Rose Mary Dougherty, *The Lived Experience of Group Spiritual Direction* (New York: Paulist Press, 2003).

3. Tilden Edwards, *Spiritual Friend* (New York: Paulist Press, 1979), 90–104.

4. See my article, "Worship for Agnostics: Building a Personal Relationship with a Non-Personal God," in *Zeek* (Fall 2010), 57–61, http://zeek.forward.com/articles/116966/.

5. In his book, *A Quiet Pentecost: Inviting the Spirit into Congregational Life* (Nashville: Upper Room Books, 2013), Dwight H. Judy explores a host of ways that Christian churches are now engaged in this work. Some of the programs described could be adapted to synagogue life with some adjustments.

6. Two excellent programs are The Shalem Institute for Spiritual Formation in Washington, D.C. (www.shalem.org) and The Mercy Center in Burlingame, California (http://www.mercy-center.org/ProgramsSD/SpiritualDirection.html).

7. The Christian practice that this resembles is called *Lectio Divina*, the reading of divinely revealed texts, and is commonly focused on the Book of Psalms.

8. I address this question at greater length in my essay, "Jewish Theologies and Jewish Spiritual Direction," in Addison and Breitman, *Jewish Spiritual Direction*, 3–20.

The Practice of Teaching
Jewish Spirituality:
Some Lessons I Have Learned

Sheila Peltz Weinberg

I teach at the Institute for Jewish Spirituality, which is a nonde-nominational organization that supports and strengthens the spiritual lives of Jewish leaders: rabbis, cantors, educators, lay leaders, and social justice activists. We use a variety of modalities including retreats where we teach and practice prayer, meditation, yoga, spiritual direction, and text study. We endeavor to mine Chasidic and other Jewish sources that emphasize the inner life and provide a language for sharing our journeys and struggles with each other.

When I tell people the name of the organization, they react in ways that reflect their understanding of the word "spirituality." Many Jews feel relieved that Judaism cares about the inner life. Others feel uncomfortable and avert their eyes. Then there are those who start talking about angels, strange experiences, or visions. Some are anxious that we are turning our backs on activism in favor of navel gazing. Others just sigh wistfully.

To me, spirituality is not weird and it not self-centered or passive. Spirituality is, as the Kotzker Rebbe defined Chasidism, *arbeit auf zich* (work on oneself). It is the work of growing awareness. Its purpose is to reveal the hidden fears, desires, obstacles, and barriers to living lives of gratitude, generosity, and service. Since we live in relationship with others in all dimensions of time and space, our human development is nurtured by others and nurtures them. We aim to establish conditions in our families, synagogues,

SHEILA PELTZ WEINBERG (RRC86) served for seventeen years as a congregational rabbi. She is one of the founders of the Institute for Jewish Spirituality (jewishspirituality.org), where she has taught mindfulness, embodied practice, and offered spiritual direction. She is the author of *Surprisingly Happy: An Atypical Religious Memoir,* and for the last two years she has served as an adjunct faculty member of HUC-JIR in New York and the URJ.

communities, and nations to foster awareness, wise choices, and loving relationships in the service of our sacred values: peace, justice, and love. These values are known to us because we are in relationship with something greater than our fragmented selves, greater than our limitations. We call that greatness, God.

Mindfulness and Honesty

I have been deeply influenced by the work of Dr. Mordecai Kaplan. I believe that he has had one of the most profound impacts on all branches of liberal Judaism. Permeating everything that Kaplan wrote and taught is a fearless willingness to tell the truth. He was the one to say let's face it, this is what we really believe, so let's start admitting it to each other. His notion of spirituality was an articulation of values and a creation of conditions both internally and externally to integrate those values into our personal and collective lives.

The ability to know what is true takes effort and practice. We become scientists of our own experience and learn how things work, what choices we have, how we suffer and cause harm, and how we become free. We learn about what separates us and what brings us closer. It is not theoretical. It is practical, based on our own experience. We learn what is of abiding significance and what is a chimera, a habit, or a confused idea. Mindfulness is moment-to-moment awareness of our experience without judgment. It is learning to be with what is and relaxing in that awareness before we set out to strategize, fix, change, and save.

I teach mindfulness to Jews though the language of Torah and Jewish tradition. Mindfulness is most of all about telling the truth to ourselves again and again. The formal practice (which is a big part of what I teach) may involve eliminating other distractions in order to pay attention to a simple and unified focus. It might be the breath as it rises and falls, the sounds that are filling the room, or the sensation of a step on the bottom of one's foot. We practice knowing what we feel in our bodies as a way of getting closer to the truth of our experience. Very soon, mental proliferation begins. Wild stories and thoughts float through the mind. When we notice them, we see they have only passing substance. Space opens up around the thinking process itself. Thoughts loosen their grip upon us. In time, we mostly see the truth of how temporary is all experience. We also see the infinity of awareness itself and the interconnection between this and that—this sound and this thought, this thought and this desire and this story. We see how inseparable we are from each other and from all life, which holds and sustains us moment to moment.

Spiritual Practice

The capacity to be present in a mindful way is a spiritual practice in itself and it is the baseline for all other practices. Without this fundamental and experiential honesty we are in the realm of the supernatural, a realm of conjecture, fantasy, or magic. It makes sense to me that the purpose of religion is to humanize humanity, to live into our highest potential as created in the divine image. In order to do that, people need to work on themselves. We need to tell the truth. We need to set conscious intentions. We need to confront our distractions, our fears, and the places where we cause and endure suffering. We need to learn to live with constant change and still make wise and loving choices.

Practice in community is the path to develop human qualities that we identify as divine—because they lead to happiness, equanimity, fulfillment, aliveness, and wisdom. These are wholesome qualities like generosity, gratitude, patience, and joy. We learn to see the factors that lead to suffering and harm such as greed, hatred, delusion, disconnection, resentment, and blame. We experience what invites freedom and release from the old patterns of hurt that manifest as self-centered fear. We need time and space for this. That is why we have dedicated periods in the life of a Jew to practice, to perform mitzvot.

For Jews, spirituality is cultivated through practices that we share with our people in time and space. We recognize that for many modern Jews, the idea of a supernatural God who commands obedience is not a realistic motivator. Yet, we understand that religion without practice is disembodied, theoretical, and abstract. Mindfulness practice is a way to return to spiritual practice for liberal Jews. In the simplicity of making a commitment to pay attention to each in-breath and each out-breath, we have a rubric for many other practices. Whether it is Sabbath observance, kashrut, *sh'mirat halashon*, *tzedakah*, or *lulav*, we must set an intention. As soon as we do that, we are faced with distraction and resistance. We then need to be very clear why we are practicing and how to work with the resistance. We find support in sustaining our practice in community with others who share a common motivation, experience, and language.

Setting Up Conditions to Allow the Soul to Appear

What kind of community nourishes the Divine within? In most situations in life we are ranked, compared, and judged on a multitude of external measuring sticks. The inner light, the soul, spirit, still point of consciousness shrinks back from these pressures. It needs other conditions. It needs quiet, acceptance, safety, support, and inspiration. This is the task of religious community. I believe it is a challenge for all of us. To teach spirituality we learn how to create these conditions. We set up safe spaces and times where there is no fixing or saving or proving each other wrong. There is a lot of listening. It is not a place of attainment. It is a place of revelation of soul. It is not about proving the existence of God. It is about sharing my experience of God. Rather than attempt to master material, the emphasis is on a meeting of hearts in common pain and shared meaning. We find that most people learn to trust when we feel we will not be judged.

I believe that our future depends upon creating communities of deep honesty and trust, places where people can be safe enough to tap their potential as human beings created in the divine image and name the places of common concern and action. I think this is what we all crave. We have despaired of the false promises of the marketplace. We are frustrated by the unfulfilled rhetoric and the weaknesses of our leaders. We yearn for the satisfaction of simplicity, stillness, sincerity, spaciousness, and peace. It is the job of teachers to provide that for others. They can only do so, of course, if they take the time to bring compassion to their own hurting places and renew their purpose, sense of awe, and inner light.

We live bombarded by external messages that tell us that safety— salvation—is found in more guns and more money. Our message is the opposite. Safety—salvation—is found in being present, in relationship, in working to improve the structures that sustain basic human needs, in opportunities for creativity and connection.

Safety or salvation is not found in the pursuit of perfection. It is found in embracing change. The name of the Divine is *Ehyeh* (Ever

Becoming). The constant of change is the most profound truth of all. It is the nature of life itself. When we sit in stillness and in silence something amazing happens. We recognize that there is no stillness and there is no silence. We are actually part of an infinite living organism. We live saturated with life, filled with life, and immersed in life. As the Chasidim understood the meaning of the verse, *M'lo kol haaretz, k'vodo,* we are part of God as God is part of us. When we cultivate our awareness, we develop a place to rest in the midst of all the change. It is a seat of safety. It is a point of connection. It is a place of freedom and unlimited possibility. Awareness is eternal and ever flowing, but it is only ours in the moment. This is true of all the divine qualities. There is only this moment to know joy or patience or love.

Living deeply on the inside we can afford to live with less material stuff. We know a deeper satisfaction. Our fulfillment comes from working toward greater equality and justice. This is what I think it means to be a spiritual Jew. It is radical, hard, fun, inspiring, and relevant. It is not a quick fix and is probably not likely to become a fad. As Dr. Mordecai Kaplan taught us, "We must, therefore, base Jewish religion of tomorrow not on what our ancestors have told of their experience with God, but on our own experience with God."[1]

The Great Jewish Manual for Teaching Spirituality

When I think about discussing my own experiences as a teacher of Jewish spirituality, it helps me to frame these experiences in the wisdom of *Pirkei Avot* (*Ethics of the Ancestors*), the great Jewish manual for teaching Jewish spirituality. It is a nearly two-thousand-year-old compilation of statements designed to inspire and orient the teacher/rabbi creating a new paradigm of spiritual work based on learning Torah. In our time of paradigm shift, infinite digitized knowledge abides next to intractable conflicts and scenarios of devastation. The old forms are suspect. We find solace in this book of wisdom and guidance because it deals with the inner life. It is, therefore, ever contemporary and filled with guidance.

Over the years, I have found that retreats are prime opportunities to create the conditions of safety and trust that allow the inner life to emerge and insights to arise. To go on a retreat in the first place takes a willingness to let go of certain habits and routines.

This willingness to step into the unknown is part of any spiritual journey. It is modeled in Torah when God tells Abraham to "get going" in Genesis 12:1, to leave the family and the familiar for a deeper exploration of what is true.

I was personally inspired by participating, especially in silent retreats, and was blessed to have a chance to set up meditation retreats for Jewish leaders, which I taught with my own teacher, Sylvia Boorstein. On one of the first retreats, I learned a profound and enduring lesson from Sylvia. After four or five days of silence, we opened up on the last night to group sharing. One of the participants chose this time to put on a very critical spoof of the teachers and the teachings. I was in shock. I felt very hurt and misunderstood. I did not see the humor. I thought this person was confronting my beloved teacher and all our efforts to create an atmosphere of patience, kindness, and sincerity. I felt my face flush. My mind raced. I wanted to defend my teacher, the teachings, and myself.

When Sylvia spoke, she had a wide smile on her face. Her demeanor was calm and pleasant. She thanked the person for the presentation. That was it; no calling to task, no reprimand. I was stunned. As it turned out, this student became a great advocate of the work we were doing and a teacher in her own right. In *Pirkei Avot* 1:6 we are advised, "Judge all people meritoriously." It is good advice; it takes a willingness on the part of the teacher to avoid confrontation. If someone is having a hard time and this is expressed in anger, sarcasm, doubt, fear, harshness of one kind or another, it is only a demeanor of calm and acceptance that can free the heart from the grip of these aversive mind states. Such a simple prescription and it is so hard to follow. I need to practice resisting the tendency to blame the student that doesn't "get it" and instead hold that student in a calm and loving presence. I have had many experiences when my memory of Sylvia's gentle smile reminded me of the more generous and skillful approach.

The Value of Embodied Practice

Another story: I have always enjoyed physical activity. I was a swimmer in college, did karate and tai chi in my twenties and thirties, jogged till my mid fifties, and have embraced a pretty serious yoga practice for the last dozen years. Rabbi Myriam Klotz introduced me to an integration of Torah and yoga. What a thrill to discover that Torah texts could be illuminated through moving my own body. I began to teach yoga as part of the Institute retreats. I was assigned the beginner class. These are the folks that would skip yoga if it were optional. They might go for a walk, play basketball, or just read. Yoga had no appeal for them. Or there were folks with injuries, with negative body images, or just plain stiff joints. Stretching did not sound like fun. In our retreats we choose a common theme that threads through all the teaching and practice modalities such as payer, text study, meditation, and yoga. Let's say the theme is "descent for the sake of ascent." We can explore this idea with our bodies as well as with our minds, our voices, or simply sitting and noticing the rhythm of our breathing.

I find it is so important to remind people that they are always exploring their edges. In text, prayer, or conversation, they might have different places of comfort. In yoga, I ask them to meet their place of discomfort and hang out there. In fact, to bring an attitude of kindness, acceptance, and respect to their very own place of discomfort. The container of silence helps makes this possible. In the silence I see arising and passing. I see the life force itself as it moves and changes. I feel this movement in my own body. I feel how being grounded and rooted allows for rising up, freedom, and expansion. The poses are not important. Even flexibility is not important. It is access to another way of seeing and learning. It is an embodied modality. No one can argue about it. We are practicing a relationship to the truth of this moment of experience. It is not book learning. It is very important to continue to appreciate the effort my students are making and to continue to remind them of the purpose of this practice. It is practice. It is a mirror to the truth of our experience in this moment.

Many of the "beginner yoga" students experience significant changes in their lives. They understand what it means to practice something. They make a deep connection with their own bodies as sources of wisdom and love, deserving of respect and good care, whether or not they measure up to some imagined or superimposed cultural fantasy. They learn about compassion and the universality of change from their very own bodies. They experience the qualities of freedom from bondage, joy, deep rest, rededication of the sacred center, and the possibility of return and forgiveness, in their very own bodies. These are the themes we work with in the Jewish calendar and in all our lives.

Pirkei Avot 1:17 puts three thoughts together for us: "All my life, I was brought up among the sages and I have never found anything better for a person than silence. Study is not the most important thing but practice is, and too much talk brings sin."

This last statement cautions every teacher. Experience in silence allows teachers to cultivate wise speech, to discern when there is "too much talking." It prompts these questions: How much of what I say as a teacher is self-serving? How can I turn my tendency to preach into an occasion to ask a student to turn toward his or her experience and truth? How often do I ask myself before I speak: "Is this truthful? Is this necessary to say? Is this the right time to say it? Can I say what I need to say in a kind way? How attached am I to my own virtue and virtuosity?"

I have gone on to teach yoga to children. This is great fun and they get it so quickly. I especially love to do *Magid* yoga as part of the seder. I invite a room of folks from two to seventy-eight to join in the yoga of the story of Passover. Feel the curled up pose of the child, the dignified and proud princess standing at the river and reaching in to rescue the baby. Experience in your bodies a staff turning into a serpent; the raging might of Pharaoh, the quiet courage of Moses, the iridescence of the bush, and the proliferation of the frogs. On and on. They love it and it penetrates in ways that words and even pictures cannot. In fact, we go back to the seder table with more energy, more open to listen to the words and to each other. Every other holiday, indeed every Torah portion, has the potential to come alive in this way and to integrate with one's felt experience, touching into roots of deep wisdom, aliveness, and sharing.

What makes me effective as a teacher is doing what I love to do. It is giving up a whole lot of self- consciousness. It is not being afraid of looking silly. It is taking my own practice very seriously and always finding teachers that I can rely on and trust. It is never pushing too hard. It is always being curious. It is feeling deeply into what is my truth. Not easy! Of course, that requires knowing the texts, the poses, the tools—if not as an expert, at least as a responsible user.

When I Think I Am Right

I would like to share a story about telling a story. I was introducing mindfulness meditation to a group of rabbis shortly after the first

Obama election. I was telling a story I had told a few times before and I understood it as a good description of the nature of the mind, how the mind tells stories to understand reality that actually may have little relation to the truth. Sometimes, especially after being in silence without outside stimulation for a while, we come to realize that the mind has a mind of its own. "I," whoever that is, is certainly not controlling "my" thoughts.

The story was about an experience I had on an extended silent retreat shortly after 9/11. I was walking past the home of the lead meditation teacher who lived next door to the retreat center. I noticed an American flag waving on his property. I thought to myself, "How strange. I can't imagine this highly esteemed spiritual teacher is going to succumb to the knee-jerk patriotic display of the flag in the post 9/11 universe." I started trying to explain to myself what this might mean, including the desire to fit in with the rural population that surrounded the retreat center, to purchase some credibility in the eyes of the neighbors and so on. I had it fairly well rationalized when, on the way back from my walk, I noticed that the flag was not at my teacher's home at all but at someone else's.

This was one illustration among many and at the end of the talk to the rabbis, a young woman rabbi from the Midwest approached me looking extremely upset and angry. She said that she did not appreciate the trashing of the flag implied in my story, that she was a Republican and had voted for John McCain, which she considered perfectly responsible as a Jew, a rabbi, and an American. My story made her feel like she did not belong in this particular community if she were not an Obama voter. I was taken aback. It was the last thing I was thinking, but my own assumptions and politics had clearly sifted through what I thought was a "spiritual" teaching experience. I knew enough in that moment to tell her, I was really sorry to have upset her, and I would like to give her comments some more thought. I ended up admitting my bias and also apologizing for my own lack of awareness. I wanted her to feel comfortable in this group, doing the spiritual work, yet I was challenged to truly respect someone whose politics were that different than mine.

Pirkei Avot 4:1 asks us "Who is wise?" Then it answers: "The one who learns from everyone." It was not pleasant to have a mirror brought up to my face that revealed my own blind spots. I still think it is a good story, but I am challenged to tell it in a way that does not humiliate or belittle those whose views differ from my own. A teacher has to open wide embracing arms to every student that shows up and sincerely wants to learn. This particular student did want to learn. She stayed around for the rest of the retreat. I learned from her, I suspect, even more than she did from me.

A Moment of Spiritual Teaching as *Chesed*

Sometimes spiritual teaching emerges in the moment. It is an act of grace. There are so many opportunities in our interactions, especially with children, to open a perspective that heals and frees rather than deepens tension, hurt, or conflict. The core mandate of a Jewish spirituality is teaching our children *"V'shinantam l'vanecha"* (Deut. 6:7 and the daily prayer book). This is teaching centered in love and spirituality rather than mastery of content. It teaches trust in the knowledge that one is safe in this moment because this too is a holy moment. It teaches that the source of life's contentment is in a connection to the whole, the unity of life itself, in being with Being, rather than in having *more*, doing *more*, or even knowing *more*.

Having grandchildren has opened me to wonderful spiritual teaching and learning opportunities. I loved being a parent, but this is completely different. The grandchildren break my heart open. They are so innocent and so vulnerable. Children do have all kinds of wondrous ways to get power over adults who in size, authority, and resources appear so much more powerful. This is an interesting nexus for spiritual teaching.

My husband and I were taking care of our then five-year-old granddaughter who was free after a half day of kindergarten. We took her to lunch at Ikea where she really wanted to go and where they have videos and a game room for kids and yummy fish sticks, French fries, and chocolate milk. We wanted to buy a gift for her brother who was turning two. They didn't have anything at Ikea, so after lunch and some playing we went to Target. We found the basketball set very quickly, and our granddaughter asked me if I could get her something. I knew she needed a dark turtleneck for her school uniform so we found one in her size and then she said she needed new pj's. "Fine," I said, and we picked up a fuzzy one piece with princesses. Then she started asking for a toy or something else—an umbrella, a doll, a set of this or that. I did not want to get her anything else. I noticed that I was becoming less patient as she kept asking me. She said. "C'mon Grandma, just one thing and then I will stop asking." I didn't want to give in. I was annoyed at her. I was thinking I was not going to give in but I didn't want her to be upset either. Yikes.

That was when the moment of *chesed* descended. I paused. I took a few deep breaths. I bent down so we were eye to eye. This is very important. I said, "Honey, I know how it feels when you come to a place like this. Everything is calling to you. Everything looks so shiny and beautiful and makes you feel like you really want it. I know this feeling too. The people who own this store are counting on you feeling this way." She nodded. She knew what I was talking about. I said, "Let's just feel what this feels like." I paused. "It is desire, wanting, needing to have something. I feel it too. But, you and I both know that as soon as we buy whatever it is and we think it will make us feel great and happy, well almost right away, we want something else, or as soon as we get it home, or pretty soon, it ends up in some corner or pile somewhere." She was quiet. She looked at me with those enormous dark brown eyes and she was quiet. I paid for the toy, the pj's, and the shirt. We walked out of Target. Just as we got to the door, she said, "If it were my birthday, you would have gotten me something, right, Grandma?" "Yes, sweetheart."

In *Pirkei Avot* 4:28, Rabbi Elazar Ha-Kappar taught, "Envy, lust and honor will ruin a person's life." How do we cultivate skills to meet the envy, lust, and craving for honor that beset us our whole lives? How do we remember that there is a power in the world that is stronger than these forces? Our culture is filled with invitations to increase desire for the ephemeral and the insubstantial; for constant external validations of our worth. From an early age we are schooled in relentless comparing and competition. Spiritual training is countercultural. I asked my granddaughter at five years old to take a step outside the competitive consumer culture; to know that she was okay in this moment, to recognize the delusion that she would be satisfied by having the next thing.

Rabbi Akiva used to say "Beloved is the human being, for he/ she is created in the Divine image; it is indicative of a greater love that it was made known to them that they were created in God's image, as it is said: 'For in the image of God, God made the human' (Genesis 9:6)" (*Pirkei Avot* 3:18). The deepest spiritual teaching is to honor and love ourselves as the divine image. This does not depend upon any achievement or characteristic. It is our being human itself which is a divine gift. How do we learn this lesson? How do we as teachers stay connected to our *tzelem* so that this will link us in love and honor to our children, our students, and each other? How do we stay connected to our sacred root? This is the purpose of all spiritual practice. It is the source of freedom. It lies within each of us and cannot be denied to us. When I was still enough to bend down and look into my granddaughter's eyes, I spoke from one *tzelem* to another. This is how we transmit spirituality.

The Spirituality of Freedom

One last story. I am sitting in spiritual direction with my own director who is a Protestant pastor. I am very fortunate to be in this room and to have found her in my new home. She lives only a ten-minute walk away and I feel very safe with her. I was planning to leave in two days on a kayaking meditation retreat in Southeast Alaska. I have been on this trip three times before. It is amazing in every way. I teach meditation in a pristine wilderness to a group of Jewish activists and leaders. The guide and leader is a beloved and brilliant teacher—lover of this land and this sea and of spirit. I am explaining to my director how I have had a lot of pain for the last year or more and I have not been able to find a resolution for the degeneration in my cervical spine. I have to figure out a way to get my gear to Newark where I fly to Seattle and then Petersburg, Alaska. I am anxious. I have not even contemplated canceling this trip because of my neck. I have not really thought about possible consequences of kayaking for a week in the wilderness, camping out, schlepping gear and kayaks. It was something I promised I would do; something I had done; something I simply would rally my strength to do.

She listened. Then she asked me to consider how I would feel if I didn't go on this trip. I went inside. I asked my bones, my muscles, and my inner organs. I realized that I would be enormously relieved. I would be truly happy not to go. Then she asked me why I was going. It was clear. I couldn't break a commitment. How would people think of me? I couldn't abandon the trip. I was not that kind of person. I was responsible. I sat with one side and I sat with the other side. I sat with the truth of my body and heart and I sat with the patterns and habits of a lifetime. I left the session and knew that I did not know what I was going to do, but I did know that I had a choice. This was something I did not know when I walked into that room.

That is what we teach. We teach freedom. My spiritual director allowed me to see that I had a choice. So much of life is lived mechanically and habitually. A spiritual life is about waking up and seeing and becoming freer, more intentional in how we live our lives. This is how I try to help others. Again it is *Pirkei Avot* 4:1: "Who is a hero, a person of courage, a strong person? The one who subdues his/her personal inclination, as it is said, 'One who is slow to anger is better than the strong man, and a master of one's passions is better than a conqueror of a city' (Proverbs 16:22)." My inclination is what appears to keep me safe. It is what is known and easily available. It is what obscures my clear thinking. I don't wish to repudiate it but I want to transcend it. This gives me freedom. This cultivates wisdom as well as strength. I didn't go to Alaska. I took care of my own body. I didn't risk jeopardizing the trip for others if I had had a crisis. I faced my compulsive nature. I took a step into a kinder and more generous way of living with myself as I age.

The last *Pirkei Avot* to share comes from Yochanan ben Zakkai, who received the tradition from Hillel and Shamai. He used to say: "If you have learned a great deal of Torah, do not pride yourself in it, because you were created for that purpose" (*Pirkei Avot* 2:9). As a teacher I have experienced great terror and lack of confidence, which I think is very common among spiritual teachers. After all, I know how imperfectly I practice what I teach. I know my own cravings, flaws, and doubts. How can I get up before others and bring them closer to God? On the other hand, it is also easy to think that I have so much to offer that the nice things people say about me are really true and that altogether I am pretty great. Most of us wobble between those two edges of self-importance and self-denigration. It is good to see these mind states when they arise. They are equally misleading. As we inhabit the seat of the teacher we develop a balance between confidence and arrogance. The phrase "you were created for this purpose" holds the midline and sustains the balance. If you are doing this, you are meant to do it. You are meant to do the deep soul work that you offer to others, and you are meant to be aware of how limited you are. You are meant to love teaching while it frustrates and exhausts and uplifts you and makes you so happy and so sad.

A teacher of spirituality is a guide on a journey. You must be on the journey, learn the terrain. You must know how to keep your students as safe as you can. You must know where the rough spots are, where the road curves and the incline gets steep. But you are also on the journey. You are only in your own skin, not in theirs; as responsible as you are, you cannot make someone not turn back or get further than they are willing and able to go. You are only a steward of a mystery that is immense, vast, and ultimately unknowable. You are supported by the greatest power of all, the power of *t'shuvah*/return. You set your compass, your intention, and then, when you stray, as you inevitably will, you return, you forgive, you remember where you are—again and again.

Note

1. Mordecai Kaplan, *The Future of the American Jew* (New York: Reconstructionist Press, 1981), 210.

Section Four: The Arts and Jewish Spirituality

(Re)Learning *L'Hitpaleil*: The Performance of Prayer as Spiritual Education

Tamar Heather Havilio

Ever since rabbis and cantors turned to face their congregation, the practice and the pedagogy of Jewish prayer have undergone important changes. The result was not only a heightened self-consciousness on the part of the prayer leader, but also a counter-intuitive interplay between the prayer leader and her congregants now praying face-to-face. This shift may not seem so radical, but it has actually created consequential changes in prayer leaders, teachers, and congregants that directly address not only what Jewish tradition has to teach, but our method and manner of teaching prayer. This alteration of the direction of the prayer leader has turned the focus of praying from a more inner exploration and expression of text to the outer aesthetic of prayer production. As an example, the pray-er consequently focuses more on the "watching" of the prayer leader as a critic rather than his own internal self-investigation. This article addresses this change in prayer direction, the effects on the external and internal pray-er and prayer leader as seen through three Jewish texts, and then offers a new way of teaching or (re)learning *l'hitpaleil* through the creation of a pedagogy of exploring first, prayer initiated within the body.

Traditionally it matters more how we perform *t'filah* than what we feel when we perform it.[1] While the discipline of understanding

TAMAR HEATHER HAVILIO was invested as cantor at HUC-JIR/School of Sacred Music, New York, in 1996. Since 2002 she has been leading the Prayer Workshop and is currently Head of Cantorial Studies at HUC in Jerusalem in both the Year in Israel and Israeli Rabbinic programs.

the prayer text as words spoken is important, the development of one's individual subtext is also significant for any pray-er, leading or following. This tension between an external aesthetic of prayer and the inner world of prayer can be seen in many Jewish texts. This work focuses on two modern critical analyses of the effects of this "turnaround," followed by one ancient text that explores the idea of reaching prayer through a state of finding presence. First is an excerpt from Rabbi Abraham Joshua Heschel's observations of prayer leader as "proxy" or master of ceremony in his book *Man's Quest for God*, next is Cantor William Sharlin's short, unpublished essay on the performance of the cantor and his loss of his "aloneness in prayer" upon facing the congregation, and finally we discuss the Chasidic Master's search for presence in prayer in *Mishnah B'rachot* 5:1. These texts consider the teaching of textual embodiment and inner awareness in context with the theories and practices of groundbreaking Jewish theatre practitioner Richard Schechner.

Finding one's inner voice becomes the root of reaching and teaching others as a transformative prayer education. The theory here is that we find our voice by understanding the text in ways that demand first action from the body. Schechner, also the founder of the Performance Studies department of NYU's Tisch School of the Arts, demonstrates this in two workshops. The first is through a physical slowing down of the body within a set time and space and the second is an emotional exploration of the performance of textual embodiment through the development of emotional intelligence of the enteric nervous system, or the "brain in the belly."[2] This is a prayer education that begins from the discovery of a physical emotion or "gut feeling" that initiates one to pray, as in Hannah silently praying to become pregnant in the Book of Samuel. As the body literally slows down, inner emotions are able to be discovered. These emotions are then activated in a separate workshop in areas of the space on the floor that have designated feelings as Indian *rasas*. Indian *rasas* are not the external emotion that one sees and experiences from facial expressions, but rather the energy from within that one can almost "taste" as one experiences the other's inner emotion. Participants "jump" from emotion to emotion (from love to anger, jealously to joy, and back again) while reciting Jewish prayer texts. This range of emotions models a density of spiritual feeling and an exploration of the interpretation of Jewish texts *from what we discover we feel* in the body.

Prayer Responds to When the Prayer Leader "Turned Around"

In 1954, nearly one hundred years after the birth of Reform Judaism in Germany, in his book *Man's Quest for God*, Rabbi Abraham Joshua Heschel wrote about this conflict of the change in prayer in his essay, "Praying by Proxy."

> Services are conducted with dignity and precision. The rendition of the liturgy is smooth. Everything is present: decorum, voice, ceremony. But one thing is missing: Life. One knows in advance what will ensue. There will be no surprise, no adventure of the soul; there will be no sudden outburst of devotion. Nothing is going to happen to the soul . . . Our motto is monotony. The fire has gone out of our worship. It is cold, stiff, and dead . . . We have developed the habit of praying by proxy. Many congregants seemed to have adopted the principle of vicarious prayer. The rabbi or the cantor does the praying for the congregation. The men and women would not raise their voices, unless the rabbi issues the signal. Alas, they have come to regard the rabbi as a master of ceremonies.[3]

Heschel's frustration with the state of Jewish prayer services is exclaimed in his emotional language. The "seeing" or watching Jewish prayer as primarily an aesthetic-centered prayer, and the bimah "turned around," inevitably caused the pray-er to become the spectator or critic and the prayer leader to become the presenter or proxy of prayer.[4] This perhaps changed the direction of the original prayer gaze. This gaze looks simultaneously forward towards the back of another body and not the face, and then forces the eye inward to focus on the inner before one can approach the external other.[5] If one only focuses on what the eye "sees" or watches from the expressions on a face, this creates a different prayer experience. Heschel's reaction is evidence of a genuine frustration of the absence of a praying body that relies upon both pray-er and leader together.

Another example of this functional and aesthetic prayer change when the leader "turned around" was in an unpublished, undated article (1970s) entitled "When the Chazzan Turned Around" by Cantor William Sharlin:

There is no question that with the arrival of the emancipation and the Reform movement, a major change in the form and character of Jewish worship was inevitable . . . If, however, one were to ask which single event affected crucially the transformation of the inner character of worship, one would have to consider seriously the phenomenon of the turning about of the chazzan, for it was his facing away from congregation on the one hand, and his subsequent turnabout, which touched deeply upon the inner dynamics of the service and influenced even more directly the very nature of chazzanuth. Specifically, this influence manifested itself in the degree of spontaneity experienced by the chazzan's ability to express was crucial, for in both cases this ability or lack of it acted potently upon the worshippers. How did the chazzan function when he faced the Ark? His position was paradoxical. On the one hand he was surrounded by a community of worshippers whose presence he felt very deeply, and on the other hand, he isolated himself from them whenever he entered into prayer. This he achieved by establishing around himself a state of privacy which enabled him to release his innermost thoughts and feelings, for only with the power of solitude does one dare to reveal the deeper part of oneself.[6]

In this essay, Sharlin explains this dualistic premise unique to Jewish prayer when the leader and congregation are facing in the same direction as they stand to pray; alone and together at once. The musical improvisation on the prayer text requires one to feel intimately connected to the text, music, and the emotion of longing for God. Instead of this longing in prayer, the prayer leader faced a dilemma: to entertain or please an audience with his face or to plead for something beyond himself that does not have a face. Richard Schechner explains when ritual becomes entertainment with his efficacy/entertainment dyad:

Whether one calls a specific performance "ritual" or "theatre" depends mostly on context and function. A performance is called one or the other because of where it is performed, by whom, in what circumstances, and for what purpose. The purpose is the most important factor determining whether a performance is ritual or not. If the performance's purpose is to effect change, then the other qualities under the heading "efficacy" will also be present, and the performance is ritual. But if the performance's purpose is mostly to give pleasure, to show off, to be beautiful, or to pass the time, then the performance is an entertainment.[7]

When the *chazan* (prayer leader) turned around, the prayer was subject to the need to please a consumer through an "acted out" visual experience. This is in order to perform a prayer service not intentionally as an entertaining performance, but it communicates "not-not"[8] an entertaining performance.

Lawrence Hoffman addressed performance of prayer in an article entitled "Re-Imagining Jewish Worship," where he states:

> In a way we are returning to an age of orality, where performance of prayer matters more than the fixed words . . . The question of leadership has expanded now, to include the theology and artistry of being a sheliach tzibbur—how to orchestrate the seating, fill empty space, provide the right acoustics and honor individualism within the same experience.[9]

Here Hoffman eloquently states the facts of Jewish prayer as performance. However, the pray-er and prayer leader are often caught up in the details of the production values of the performance and not the actual prayer as personal subtext of the text; a ritual guided by transformation. The emphasis on the actual performance of the prayer service as a production has just increased because of this cycle of "watching" the prayer as an entertaining performance driven by spiritual marketing.[10] Cantor Sharlin goes on to state:

> When the cantor eventually made his turnabout it was inevitable that he should lose his privacy—his self-entity. Unfortunately this loss led to a new experience in Jewish worship—that of self-consciousness . . . Just as spontaneity travels quickly from pulpit to congregation, so does self-consciousness. So we now find worshippers, disabled by their dependency on the pulpit, exercising caution and restraint that prevent a more meaningful experience. It is interesting to note that during those rare moments when the rabbi and cantor face the ark, one immediately senses a change of mood as the atmosphere of privacy reappears for a moment.

Sharlin is a cantor concerned with this turnaround, not only as detrimental to the cantorial art of *chazanut*, but threatening the function of Jewish prayer as a theological quest of the individual and the community in prayer. The self-conscious prayer leader can then be treated as any performer that deals with his own "self" in performance. The anxious emotions of the self-conscious prayer leader travel to the emotional experience of their congregation. The congregant then is preoccupied with the energy of the nervous prayer leader pressured to "do something" to his congregation.

All performing work begins and ends in the body.
—**Richard Schechner**

The presence of the physical body is central to the historical development of Jewish liturgy, which in the beginning thanks God for the return of our breath upon waking and concludes with the praising of the gift of life in the absence of the body in the Mourner's *Kaddish*. The performance of the body in prayer is then literally brought back to awareness by the physical embodiment of not just the actions implied in the text, but rather being the text from within. In Performance Studies, one investigates the performance of the leader and her audience upon various stages: religious, political, and commercial. The performance theorist then learns how the field of one affects the performance and aesthetic of the other. In performance and social performance theory, the personal body is the first place of investigation as it affects the political and therefore the corporate performance as a whole entity.[11]

Performance Studies theories can only help and enable the prayer leader and the pray-er (re)learn how to pray with a Jewish gaze—inwards and then outwards and back again, without necessarily turning around. It also inspires the prayer leader and pray-er to be as believable as the actor on the stage or political arena. The performance, whether on the bimah of a synagogue or other arena, must be authentic to the person embodying the role. Otherwise audiences will not trust or believe the person leading them in prayer, as in other forms of social performance. These theories and practices help to explain and treat the self-consciousness that evolved from praying face-to-face. In *Environmental Theatre*, Richard Schechner explains the role of the performer like that of a shaman:

> A performance is always about two things: the performer's body and the story. The performance stimulates the audience to react *in their bodies* to what's happening to the performer. The stories are variations on a few basic themes, all of them involving dismemberment and reparation. The performer says to the audience: "Watch my insides being removed, watch as I spill my guts

in front of you, to you, for you; watch how I am healed. In watching the audience participate in a cycle of conflict, agony, death, dismemberment, and repair . . . During each performance the performer tries to find for himself—and undergo in front of the audience—the process of birthing, growing, opening up, spilling out, dying, and re-birthing . . . This is the kernel of theater's most personal experience, located at that place where art, medicine and religion intersect.[12]

Here Schechner reveals the purpose of the shaman, which indeed could be translated to the goal of the Jewish pray-er or prayer leader in its intention to self-reflect. The Jewish prayer gaze from the point of view of the prayer leader looking up and away from the congregation creates a place where the prayer leader has the possibility of shedding his masks and inspiring through his own vulnerability as Cantor Sharlin claims. Both the dichotomy and irony here found in the prayer leaders and their creation of prayer services that mostly function as entertainment is not coming from an intentional goal of the prayer leader. He wants to be praying rather than entertaining, but the latter has gained him more self-confidence and the former often causes one too much public, emotional pain and vulnerability. Because of this turnaround, the audience also became the critic not of oneself in prayer, but rather what is before him that he watches. According to social and performance theories, the leader has to begin the process of (re)connecting themselves emotionally, and then the audience will follow by way of a corporeal and emotional exchange.

Most pedagogies of Jewish prayer focus on the doing or performing of the commandment to pray three times a day, as in Western theatre training of presenting a set text in a specific genre, "as if." In liberal movements of Judaism often a student will enter a seminary to become a rabbi or cantor without ever leading or praying Jewish prayer. The prayer language is often foreign (Hebrew), and the student of prayer tries to find his authentic text within the prayer or she becomes so enamored of the "role" she plays being a pray-er and leader "as if." In this pedagogy they learn to play rabbi, cantor, teacher "as if," and they often become enamored with the role as a character and consequently they do not find their own authentic voice as "being a cantor, rabbi, or educator."[13] This (re)learning pedagogy of the performance of prayer focuses on the body in prayer and then the body's text as revealed through the performance of the body as *being* prayer text. The leading performer then enables the experience first himself to be emotionally authentic in order for the others to be drawn into participation. Schechner states in *Environmental Theatre*:

> These are the four steps to the performer's process. One doesn't go up these the way one goes up and down a staircase. They happen simultaneously, each feeding off of the others. The four steps are life rhythms—like breathing, eating, sleeping; they sustain a performer without exhausting him. The four steps are:
> 1. Getting in touch with yourself.
> 2. Getting in touch with yourself face to face with others.
> 3. Relating to others without narrative or other highly formalized structures.
> 4. Relating to others within narrative or other highly formalized structures.[14]

The steps here inspire an authentic performance on any performance stage. Schechner states that a performer must be able to be in touch with herself and then acknowledge that consequently she can be in touch with herself in performance "face to face with others." Once the performer of prayer understands and copes with his/her own self-consciousness, another form of presence occurs that is beyond the self and into the other. The text then is understood by how the body in prayer is breathing, singing, dancing, or swaying not only through what the eye sees; but what the congregant feels emotionally in their own body.

Performance Studies Meets *Mishnah B'rachot* 5:1

In the summer of 2002 at the conclusion of my M.A. in Performance Studies at NYU, I took Richard Schechner's East Coast Artist's Performance Workshop with Richard and two theatre artists, Michelle Minnick and Paula Cole. Once we began the slow-motion body work in total silence in the "crossings" exercise, I found something from within the space that was both internal and communal, like Jewish prayer.[15] I felt a heightened awareness of my body within the context of the others next to me within the silence and the slow motion. We added elements to the exercise each day and the final ritual, after three intense weeks, was an elaborate slow-motion dinner party. Revelation, for me, occurred in this moment. I wrote in my journal, "Crossings slow-motion exercise is the Sabbath IN the body—an internal present progressive now." Perhaps this is a way to teach presence in prayer, how to enter the Sabbath as not a place or destination, or one-to-two-hour ritual, but as a holy other, a presence of *being* the Sabbath. Once the pray-er or leader are able to be less self-conscious in front of one another, there is a moment when the ritual performers find presence in the understanding of their mutual longing for the presence of something holy. Simply stated, they find this mutual longing something other than their daily norm of constantly dwelling in the past ("What *did* I do?") or thinking into the next future moment ("What *will* I do?"). The Chasidim in the Mishnah were seeking this specific presence in *Mishnah B'rachot* 5:1:

> One does not stand up without *"Koved Rosh"* (honorable head, heavy head, right mind, reverent mood). The Chasidim of old would first *"shoheh"* or wait in slow-motion an hour and then re-cite the Tefillah (the standing prayer), so as to direct their minds to the place (the holy place/One). Even if a King were to greet him, he may not return the greeting. Even if a snake were to be curled at his heel, he may not break off.

There are two important concepts here that could become lost in translation: *koved rosh* and *shoheh*. *Koved rosh* is often translated here as "reverent mood," which could be a sign of the emotional connection to the state of which one must enter a prayer place (the word for God here is *Makom* [place]). Literally *koved rosh* is either honorable or heavy head. They had to direct their mind to the prayer within an hour as they *"shoheh,"* which is often translated as "wait." However this is not used in modern Hebrew as wait in the sense of waiting for something to happen to you or around you (a bus to arrive, an event to begin), but rather it is a waiting that is from within as preparation for something to happen, as *presence*. This actually could be waiting in the sense of slow-motion from within the body by connecting the brain in the head, with the belly and the groin, as the development of emotional intelligence.

Here is where *Mishnah B'rachot* meets Performance Studies. In 2004, at Hebrew Union College in Jerusalem, I conducted my first "Praying Body Workshop" with eight cantorial and one rabbinic student. For lack of a black box theatre, the workshop took place in the college bomb shelter. The students were instructed to wear loose fitting clothing and come prepared to move. The workshop began by creating a "sacred space." Before entering the bomb shelter, the group stood at the entrance. I gave them a detailed set of rules for the exercise and told them to enter the space in silence. They entered the space and saw a rectangular shape outlined on the floor with stage tape with two boxes outlined on the floor on opposite sides of the rectangle.

The detailed instructions were:

1. Place yourselves four on each side of the "crossings" space.
2. Take off watches, anything that will inhibit movement.
3. There are thirty minutes to cross the space once in slow-motion (Later workshops became forty-five minutes to one hour). The original exercise takes place in three hours.
4. Enter the space once you have decided in which direction that you will cross over.
5. You can nonverbally communicate within the space.
6. You have two "time-out" spaces, one is to observe the crossings, and the other is where you can sing a prayer or musical text that is prayer to you. You cannot stay in the time-out places for long.
7. I will let you know when there is two minutes left to the exercise.

Figure 1 shows a diagram of the tape on the floor that creates the workshop space. Before I say "time" to begin, I demonstrate the body moving in slow motion. In order to understand this concept, one has to first try moving their hand in slow-motion. One's breathing slows and the body becomes ultra-aware of each little movement of the body.

The group revealed both struggle and revelation in the space and time literally set before them. At the conclusion of the hour, I gathered them in the middle of the space and asked one of the students to lead us in blessing the Sabbath candles. We all took our

Figure 1. Diagram for "Crossings" Exercise as the "Praying Body"

hands and waved them in three swirling circles before our closed eyes and chanted the blessing. I asked them to open their eyes and the group debriefed the experience. Suddenly the students began to talk: "It was difficult at first. I tried to move slowly but sometimes it was too challenging. I could not do it. I felt so free. It was holy to me."

The exercise was both individual and communal, as in Jewish prayer. One of the students, Sara, wrote as a response:

Yesterday, our class performed the "crossings" exercise in the HUC-Jerusalem shelter. Nine of us made our way downstairs to the unfamiliar, unexpected space, where we were told to take off our shoes and stand at the edge of a carpeted area. Four of us stood on one side, five on the other. The object of the exercise: to cross the carpet, in silence, in thirty minutes. At any given moment, two of us could remove ourselves from the action and observe. What was this exercise for me? For me, it was revelatory. After the first initial moments of akwardness and levity, I found myself sinking into the silence and enjoying the stillness. There was something about the limitations of the exercise—no talking, no looking at watches, no rushing to the other side—which made me look deep within myself. Instead of hurrying across or chattering to fill the space, I found myself seeking alternative ways of moving, communicating, of BEING. What I found inside of myself was a sense of unadulterated freedom and joy and CLARITY . . . I was FREE in the cordoned-off section of time . . . I found myself seeking closeness to others. Without the presence of speech, I felt empowered to be near others, to use their presence to strengthen my own. I found that I could be more honest than I almost ever am in reality. By drawing near to my classmates, I was telling them, "I need you right now," without ever having to say a word. My journey was shaped very much by them, and I was helping to shape their journeys as well. As I connected to my classmates, I also found myself drifting, drifting in a fog. The music and the voices would enter this fog and then be, somehow engorged by it. I was so open to the world around me, so tuned into the sounds, sights, but also so very tuned with myself . . . Without speaking, I revealed more of myself to this group that I ever have through words. Contrariwise, I think I learned more about my colleagues than I have in four years. We allowed one another a view inside, deep inside. Whether we knew it or not, we each were saying, "Look at me for who I am, who I REALLY am," and that was so very powerful. When we finished, we all felt very close and very vulnerable. There were tears, and there

were honest, candid statements. We spoke to each other without valence or walls. We were able to bring the exercise into our
conversation. We were able to know one another. We were able
to trust each other with our feelings. I revealed myself yesterday.
I revealed a part of me that is young, that wants to break free of
rules (all rules and restrictions I place upon myself and my life),
that wants to scream and shout and love and embrace and cry
and laugh. I revealed the woman who wants to leave the little girl
behind, and the little girl who refuses to be abandoned. I revealed
my fears of being alone, of being unliked and unloved. And in
my colleagues, I found receptivity. I found acceptance. I found
love.[16]

It is in this space that is "pre-prayer," that allows the pray-er or
prayer leader to reach a sense of self-awareness, within a communal place and the state of the present progressive now. Some students have commented on learning humility, how to take time, and
they learned an inner time and space. The intention to expand the
workshop from "crossings" to the *rasa* boxes with Jewish prayer
enable the pray-er and leader of prayer to emotionally connect to
the prayer texts while simultaneously connecting to others.

The *Rasa* Boxes Meet the Prayer Leader

Once the body has opened up to the awareness of their body in
relation to others within a set and silent space, one is more open
and clear to the emotional interpretation of prayer texts, ancient
or modern. The individual *rasas* (anger, love, disgust, fear, humor-
laughter, grief, strength, awestuck, and completeness), as emotions that are felt, are drawn out on the floor in chalk before the
participants. The participants first individually experience the *rasa*
in each box and the emotions are defined by the body's reaction
actually inside of the feeling:

> The performer becomes a partaker herself. When she is moved by
> her own performance, she is affected not as the character, but as a
> partaker . . . Where does she experience these feelings? In the ENS,
> in the gut—inside the body that is dancing, that is hearing the
> music, that is enacting a dramatic situation. The other partakers—
> the audience—are doubly affected: by the performance and by
> the performer's reaction to her own performance. An empathetic
> feedback takes place. The experience can be remarkable.[17]

This in essence can be the same as the praying body; the prayer leader and pray-er partake in the experience of praying with empathy as a shared experience into the emotional want of something better than where they are when they begin. The direction of the prayer gaze, whether facing the congregation or the holy ark, can become like the *rasa* as expression of the internal emotion, creation and experience of feelings, and revelation of the "soul." This is not made manifest as poetry beautifully read, but rather a "throwing up" or a "birthing" of the belly's song through the emotion of the individual's encounter with the text.

This liturgical purgation can begin with the transformation of the Indian *rasa* boxes into Jewish *t'filah* (prayer) boxes marked on the floor (see Figure 2). These boxes become an outlet for the body's initial prayer response even before they add the layer of a prayer as text, spoken, or sung.

According to the *rasa* boxes, each performer begins alone in a box on the floor, and then others may join. In this prayer box, the students first become in touch with these feelings through the body. One will stand on the periphery of the box and then enter into the *rasa* and change emotions from jumping between each one. Following, another performer enters the boxes as the two encounter a different awareness through the other. For example, one expresses anger and the other love in order to experience the different levels of emotional connection to the other. Here the body emotes through an external physical manifestation of the internal emotion without a set text. The next step of the exercise is when each student adds another layer and memorizes a prayer text. Then they enter the boxes with the prayer and the expression as embodiment of that *rasa* emotion. In this part of the workshop, the body speaks

Strength/ כח אנרגיה	Fear/פחד (evil)	Anger/כעס
Humor-Laughter/ חוש הומור	Completeness/שלום	Disgust/מגעיל
Love/אהבה	Grief/יגון	Awestruck/ מלא יראת כבוד

Figure 2. The *Rasa* Boxes Made into Jewish Prayer Boxes

and chooses its own emotional destination through their personal reaction to a text. This creates within the praying body an emotional knowledge as recall, or a sixth sense of the performing of the text. Consequently because of this training, the prayer text has the possibility of emotionally communicating something that was written in the past, in the here and now, again as the present progressive now. The subtext is then delivered from emotions within the body and therfore felt in the others in the same prayer experience. The student will not just be reading the prayers "as if" the rabbi or singing the sacred texts "as if" a cantor, but rather he will be himself performing the text as *being* the prayer by emulating the inner emotion of the prayer. The *rasa* boxes are yet another key element in (re)creating the pedagogy of prayer leaders and pray-ers. Within the slow-motion body work in the "crossings" exercise the pray-er learns to "*shoheh*," as presently waiting, and embodies the Chasidic Master's of prayer quest for *koved rosh*. This teaching of the outer to the inner and then back again is reinitiating the Jewish prayer gaze, void of the pressures of just a seeing and hearing visual exchange.

Within the prayer service the main themes of the service are: creation, revelation, and redemption. In theses narratives lie the emotional and intellectual development of the Jewish people. As a teacher and guide of the *rasa* boxes, Michelle Minnick writes:

> "Emotion," like space, time, and other elements of staging, becomes simply another tool to be used in the process of exploring and developing performance work. The Rasaboxes can free performers from questions about "motivation," allowing them to think of and use emotion in a more playful and adventurous way. Finally, emotion—which is so often blocked, or internalized in Western acting—moves into the body, where it can energize the space *between* one performer and another, and between performer and spectator.[18]

This is the essence of Jewish prayer and prayer leading. This pedagogy of (re)learning Jewish prayer in the body reveals the praying body and brings him *back to life as presence in the present progressive now* by releasing emotions of his "aloneness." Heschel and Sharlin both called out for a new kind of prayer leading where the praying body becomes her text and transmits text by way of emotional intelligence of an energizing kind. This prayer is not for the spectator but for the investigative pray-er of prayer; the one who transcends the ritual into being and therefore feels the prayer not only in himself, but also for the other. Like the Chasidim who stood and waited for an hour before entering prayer, this work encounters a holy presence as the physicalization of a present body and a *koved rosh*. In a deep sense of awareness of the between-ness of pray-er and the prayer leader, prayer as merely observation becomes irrelevant as one's inner prayer, simultaneously alone and together, is *(re)discovered*.

Notes

This article's title is inspired by the book *Acting (Re)Considered: Theories and Practices* edited by Phillip Zarilli (New York and London: Routledge, 1995). It was one of the first collections of essays on theory and practices of acting when acting pedagogies made a switch from the "West" to the "East." This book demonstrates this evolution from the old school of Uta Hagen and Stanislavski, where the actor trains " as if" the character into the new schools focused on the physical/intellectual/emotional techniques of Meyerhold, Chaiken, and Grotowski.

1. A perfect example of this is the focus on how a bar/bat mitzvah "performs" his/her *parashah*. What we see is the focus of the ritual, not on the inner prayer or transformation of the child. (Re)learning prayer does not go into the details of the prayer pedagogy of children, but on a simpler level could become the basis for prayer education in elementary and secondary Jewish education. I have worked with prayer and the development of subtext of prayer with many youth ages including *b'nei mitzvah*.

2. Richard Schechner, "Rasaesthetics," *The Drama Review* 45, no. 3 (Fall 2001): 35, http://rasaboxes.org/wp-content/uploads/2009/01/rasaesthetics-copy.pdf.

3. Abraham Joshua Heschel, *Man's Quest for God* (New York: Scribner, 1954), 49–50.

4. This concept of a presentational Jewish prayer was seriously debated and compared with Greek Theatre in Michal Govrin, "Jewish Ritual as a Genre of Sacred Theater," *Conservative Judaism* 36, no. 3 (Spring 1983): 15–34. Her main argument was that Jewish sacred theatre was never intended to be Greek Theatre, whose main goal is to imitate and portray the gods in a story. Jewish sacred theatre, she claims, is not about seeing, but between the Jew and her longing for God. It is something way beyond seeing. "Translating Jewish traditions into formal tools taken from other ritual-theatrical traditions might make the tradition devoid of its very essence."

5. In *Parashat Ki Tisa*, Exod. 33:17–23, Moses asks to see God's face and God's *k'vodi* (presence), and God says: "But you cannot see My face, for a human being may not see Me and live." God asks Moses to basically look away while his "presence passes by and then I will take My hand away and you will see My back, but My face must not be seen." This concept of presence without the face, but the back, is also in Japanese theatre where the back actually "sees." I am very interested when the face is face-to-face that a very different presence occurs, which is embedded in self-consciousness. When Moses feels the presence of God from his back, this is a very different exchange of the physical presence of a body in prayer. The eyes focus on something not there and yearn to capture a presence beyond what they see.

6. William Sharlin, "When the Chazzan Turned Around" (unpublished essay, 1970).

7. Richard Schechner, *Performance Studies: An Introduction* (New York and London: Routledge, 2002), 71.

8. The term "not-not" is how Richard Schechner explains when any given performance may be not intended as a specific performance yet still has the qualities of that given performance: the prayer service was not a ritual performance and not-not a ritual performance.

9. Lawrence Hoffman, "Re-Imagining Jewish Worship," *CCAR Journal* (Winter 2002): 79.

10. I do not claim that when we were all facing one direction, only forward, that the audience did not become the critic. However the "turnaround" discouraged a directional Jewish prayer gaze that may be the first Jewish gaze of the internal investigation first before the eye can take in the external. The (re)learning of *l'hitpaleil* faces this challenge in order to (re)learn or initiate this gaze.

11. Jeffrey Alexander, the codirector of the Center for Cultural Sociology at Yale University, developed a technique of studying social performances through cultural pragmatics. His main paper on this is "Cultural Pragmatics: Social Performance between Ritual and Strategy," which is published in his book entitled *Social Performance: Symbolic Action, Cultural Pragmatics, and Ritual* (Cambridge University Press, 1998). Alexander works closely with Joseph Roach, the director of Yale School of Drama, on investigating how sociology can learn from how the actor learns how to create believability on stage. If the prayer leader does not believe in the text that she prays, then the pray-er is "defused" from the prayer experience. (Re)learning *l'hitpaleil* focuses on Alexander's idea that the performance of prayer as efficacious ritual has to be (re)fused in order to be successful ritual as transformation.

12. Richard Schechner, *Environmental Theatre*, new and expanded (New York: Applause Books, 1994), 172–73.

13. This "as if" term comes from Constantin Stanislavski in the late 1800s Moscow Theatre training, which later was developed by Lee Strasberg, Stella Adler, and Uta Hagen into Method Acting. The main question for the student of Method Acting is "How can I, myself, perform this scene as if my character would do so." If one only learns to become a pray-er or prayer leader then perhaps they do not fully embody who they are as a praying body, but rather play the prayer leader or pray-er "as if" a picture in their memory of what this should look and sound like.

14. Schechner, *Environmental Theatre*, 129.

15. Schechner took this slow-motion in the body work from Robert Wilson's staging of certain operas. At a moment of high drama (someone falling in love or a murder), he would place the performer in slow-motion. Wilson combined elements of slow motion also to create a cinematic feeling.

16. Rabbi Sara Sapadin (NY07); she spent her Year in Israel in 2004.

17. Schechner, "Rasaesthetics," 46.

18. Michelle Minnick, "Rasaboxes Performer Training," in ibid., 41.

Jewish Early Adolescent Spirituality

Micah Lapidus

Introduction

It's a typical Monday morning at The Alfred and Adele Davis Academy, Atlanta's *m'chinah*—eighth grade Reform Jewish day school. Second period ends, and two hundred middle school students spill into the hallways and head down to the gym for *t'filah.* For the next forty-five minutes the gym will become a "gym-agogue" as students and teachers come together in prayer.

As the director of Jewish and Hebrew Studies at The Davis Academy, *t'filah* is an important part of my weekly routine. I either directly participate in or oversee approximately twenty-five *t'filot* on a weekly basis as our students gather in various groupings on Monday, Thursday, and Friday mornings.

Over the last number of years I have become increasingly fascinated by middle school *t'filah.* My colleagues and I strive to make middle school *t'filah* into something that resonates with our students. Even more than resonating with our students, it's my hope that these thrice-weekly gatherings will be inspirational, relevant, and transformational in their lives. I hope that they will leave The Davis Academy with something greater than siddur fluency. I hope that they leave Davis with the foundations of an authentic spiritual practice that will grow with them as they continue their journeys as Jews and human beings.

In order to realize the vision of providing middle school students with the tools necessary for spiritual growth, I quickly discovered that I needed some tools of my own. Specifically I needed a much

MICAH LAPIDUS (C08) is the director of Jewish and Hebrew Studies at The Alfred and Adele Davis Academy. He also serves as the president of PARDES: Day Schools of Reform Judaism and is a Jewish songwriter and composer whose music appears on his first album, *Be a Blessing*, as well as in *URJ Books and Music Shabbat Anthology, Volume VII.*

richer understanding of the phenomenon of early adolescent spirituality. What does spirituality look like during early adolescence? How does Judaism or religion generally facilitate or complicate spirituality? How is spirituality nurtured during adolescence? How is it threatened? As a Jewish educator, I had to figure out how to most authentically and meaningfully promote a spiritually robust environment for my students.

Rather than continuing down the same path of having hopes and visions but lacking data, I employed a twofold approach to answering these questions. First, I began reading. Second, I began paying attention to my students in new and different ways. In addition to viewing myself as their rabbi and teacher, I also started to view myself as a researcher, deeply dedicated to illuminating a particular research topic: early adolescent spirituality. Unlike some researchers that try to approach their topic objectively and quantitatively, I decided that I could only approach my topic qualitatively, with all my biases, assumptions, concerns, and hopes. Rather than conducting research "on" my students, I see myself as trying to understand my students so that, together, we can deepen our mutual understanding.

While my reading and my research are ongoing, my initial work in this area has enriched my understanding of the phenomenon of early adolescent spirituality. Now more than ever, I believe that early adolescent spirituality must be appreciated, protected, and nurtured. Now more than ever I believe it is the role of Jewish education to champion this important cause.

Reading

One of the major difficulties in researching spirituality is the amount of white noise that there is on the topic. It's my opinion that we suffer currently from an overabundance of language for describing spirituality that is impoverished in its ability to adequately describe it. Overabundance because everything and anything can be spiritual; impoverishment because we have not truly given this topic its due, at least in liberal Judaism.

The single most influential book I have read on the topic of childhood spirituality is *The Spirit of the Child* by David Hay with Rebecca Nye.[1] Hay and Nye's work has been helpful for me because it provides both a context and a framework for thinking about childhood spirituality. While their research was conducted with children between the ages of six and seven as well as between the ages of ten and eleven, their work may also be applied (with some adaptation) to early adolescents between the ages of twelve and fourteen. While they do not write in a Jewish context whatsoever, I agree with others who note that their work has implications for Jewish education and warrants greater attention from the Jewish community.[2]

The preliminary chapters of *The Spirit of the Child* suggest that spirituality has become an increasingly vague concept in modern Western society. They argue that societal disagreement about the value and character of spirituality weakens our collective ability to instill spirituality in children. Here I would simply note that my experience attests to this reality. While a Jewish day school seems like the ideal venue for nurturing spiritual growth in early adolescents, I have experienced a good deal of ambivalence. My suspicion is that there is both discomfort on behalf of some adults as well as a lack of collective agreement on behalf of the faculty as to what spirituality is and what mandate, if any, teachers have to promote it. Interestingly, Hay and Nye argue that rather than being a vague or culturally constructed concept, spirituality may have biological foundations that make it a natural part of human experience. Regarding the relationship between religion and spirituality they note that, "All of our human experience, without exception, is mediated to us and at least partially created by the social institutions of the culture to which we belong."[3] It cannot be denied that religion is one of the dominant cultural institutions that mediates the individual's experience and understanding of spirituality. Yet they insist that while religion is a major consideration it is not synonymous with spirituality nor can it account for the full range of spiritual expression. They claim that in order to protect childhood spirituality as well as promote spiritual growth in children we need a better understanding of the phenomenon of childhood spirituality. In addition to being a difficult topic to research they also identify what they call "the shortage of competent research."[4] They suggest that competent research must, at its core, be about listening to children.

Rebecca Nye carried out the task of listening to children. She conducted a number of semi-structured interviews and then analyzed the transcripts to see if there were any common themes using a grounded theory approach. She came to two conclusions relevant to our work as Jewish educators. First, she determined that each child had his/her own distinctive way of making meaning of his/her spiritual life. Whatever common themes might emerge, there remains a deeply personal "signature" for each child.[5] In our work as Jewish educators we must continually strive to recognize and celebrate each unique signature that we encounter. We must also strive to recognize and celebrate our own signature so that we might become more aware of the meanings and interpretations we bring to our work. In addition to the personal signature, Nye also discovered some important common themes. When taken together these common themes became the framework that Nye developed for identifying and understanding childhood spirituality as "relational consciousness."[6]

Hay and Nye's data analysis led them to conclude that the core of childhood spirituality is "relational consciousness." They found that there were parts of their interviews when children demonstrated a heightened consciousness. At such times the children spoke with excitement, energy, and self-awareness. Hay and Nye describe this consciousness as "meta-cognition."[7] They realized that all of these instances of heightened consciousness occurred when the children were speaking about various types of relationships such as their relationship to self, family and friends, nature, and God. They came to refer to these relationships as child-self, child-people, child-God, and child-world. Hay and Nye do not intend for "relationship" to be understood in the mundane sense, but rather as a kind of intersubjectivity, a deep engagement.

Hay and Nye also realized that children expressed relational consciousness in different ways: through art, fiction, philosophical monologues, fantasy, self-questioning, and others. They also found that some children embraced this part of their life experience while others were embarrassed by it. They found that children's attitudes towards their own relational consciousness could change over time and that some children experienced it as calming, while others experienced it as perplexing or foreign. On the basis of her interviews, Nye proposed that "relational consciousness" was the most authentic way of thinking about childhood spirituality.

One of the most important aspects of the "relational consciousness" framework is that it fully liberates spirituality from religion. Moreover it makes spirituality something that is available to the majority of children. Spirituality becomes more about the individual quest for connection and meaning then it does about the socially mediated experience of formal religion.

Analyzing Data

As a Jewish educator, I believe that all people are capable of living meaningful and spiritually vibrant lives. One of the things I most appreciate about Hay and Nye's relational consciousness framework is that it knocks spirituality off of its metaphysical pedestal. It makes spirituality something that every child, every adolescent, and every adult can access. I find this to be empowering and exciting.

I agree with Hay and Nye that the only way to deepen our appreciation for early spirituality is by listening. At the same time I believe there are many different ways of listening. There is the listening that comes from intentional conversations such as interviews, and there is the listening that comes from interacting with early adolescents in a variety of contexts, observing them, and also paying attention to the meanings and messages they consciously and unconsciously broadcast to the world. I believe that all of us who work with Jewish children and adolescents are blessed to have many opportunities to listen. One way of listening to early adolescents speak about their spiritual lives is by analyzing their artwork. It may be that a better phrase than "listening to" would be "listening for" insofar as it captures an intentional sensitivity to relational consciousness without prompting the students in advance.

In this section I will present and analyze several samples of student work. I will apply Hay and Nye's relational consciousness framework to each piece of art and comment about what I "hear" going on in each piece. I hope that engaging in this type of analysis will illustrate the idea of relational consciousness as well as inspire colleagues to engage in this type of listening and/or report on the different forms of listening that we are doing.

Before presenting student work I would offer a few qualifications. First, the student work that is presented here is presented anonymously and with the permission of the students and their parents. Second, the work that is presented here is exceptional but not unique. While each sample bears the personal signature of the artist or author, the truth is that The Davis Academy Middle School alone is home to thousands of samples of student artwork and coursework that illustrate the relational consciousness framework. I collected these samples during the 2011–2012 academic school year as part of my research into the topic of early adolescent spirituality.

Image 1 is an excerpt from a "spiritual portfolio" assignment that is part of The Davis Academy's Eighth Grade Jewish Studies curriculum. In this case the student was asked to write a one-hundred-word response to any of the themes that were introduced in the class's study of *Kohelet* (Book of Ecclesiastes).

The "Double Mini Saga—*Kohelet*" illustrates several important components of the relational consciousness framework. Most prominently we see the author in the context of the child-self as

double mini saga- kohelet

do you ever grow too old to celebrate like youth?

eat, drink, and be merry

what is considered a child? an adult?

me, adult in the jewish community and to god

does that mean i cannot celebrate like a child?

summer camp, birthday parties, and sleepovers

am i too old?

joy, heart, and playfulness of a kid

responsibilities and maturities of an adult

which group do i belong in?

god doesn't give a certain path for me

but his guidance is there

all people of morning and night

it is always the time to enjoy the good things in life

Image 1. "Double Mini Saga—*Kohelet*"

she is relating to her own self.[8] We see her reflecting on her transition from child to adult. We see her questioning societal definitions and trying to figure out what category she fits into as well as which category she wants to fit into. Additionally we see her asking questions about her relationship with God. She asks herself what God requires of her as a Jewish adult and also expresses her feeling that God is with her without providing her with a "certain path." Hay and Nye suggest that relational consciousness can involve a "quest for understanding" and "inner conflict."[9] I feel that this piece illustrates these aspects in a way that bears the personal signature of the author but that also speaks to a broader Jewish typology. The author of this piece strikes me as refreshingly honest, aware of her liminality, and searching for understanding. I think it is particularly wonderful that the entire piece is in response to *Kohelet*. While Hay and Nye do not consider the individual's relationship with their faith tradition to be one of the contexts for childhood spirituality, I would suggest that it is a logical and even necessary extension of the framework into early adolescence to view the relationship between self and religion as a context for relational consciousness.

Image 2 is also an excerpt from an eighth grade spiritual portfolio. In this portfolio assignment, students were asked to present their favorite piece of artwork and offer an explanation for their choice. This student selected a painting by Georges Seurat.

One of the processes that Hay and Nye include in their relational consciousness framework is "self-identification."[10] In this example I see an early adolescent identifying with a character from a painting. The identification between the student and the character is worth considering more closely. Based on the student's reading of the artwork she identifies with this character because the character is in the dark but looking towards the light. According to this student, the light represents happiness and the dark represents sadness. Interestingly the student says that the picture makes her feel calm even though she identifies with the character that is standing in the dark (i.e., in a place of sadness). It seems that the student is acknowledging her own feelings of sadness in a way that allows her to feel these emotions without being stirred from a deeper sense of calm that comes with knowing that the light awaits her. Identifying with the character in the painting seems to give this student a measure of comfort, helping her to understand that her

When I look at this picture, I see many things. First, I see people in the light and
the dark, which symbolizes happiness and sadness. This picture makes me feel
calm due to the soft sailing boats in the background. The woman with the two
dogs speaks to me the most. She is standing in the dark, but looking towards
the light.

Image 2. "Towards the Light"

emotions have been experienced by others before her and are a part of life. It is also worth noting that this student expresses her spiritual worldview through the language of nature: light and dark, blue waters, and so on.

Image 3 represents a student submission to a Holocaust art competition. It depicts an image of Adolph Eichmann as a devil with the following text written by Leonard Cohen wrapped around the image:

> All there is to know about Adolph Eichmann. Eyes: Medium; Hair: Medium; Weight: Medium; Height: Medium; Distinguishing Features: None; Number of Fingers: 10; Number of Toes: 10; Intelligence: Medium. What did you expect? Talons? Oversize Incisors? Green Saliva? Madness?

Image 3 shows a student grappling with questions of what it means to be human as well as why there is evil in the world. The relational framework context most relevant here would be that of

Image 3. "All There Is to Know about Adolph Eichmann"

child-people.[11] Additionally, Hay and Nye suggest that relational consciousness can sometimes involve "moralizing." In reflecting on Adolph Eichmann and the mundane nature of evil, I "hear" an early adolescent trying to make sense of one of the most troubling questions of all: How ordinary people can be capable of such extraordinary evil. In trying to relate to the figure of Adolph Eichmann, the artist is teaching an important moral: that the propensity for evil is something that resides within ordinary people. A piece of art such as this presents all sorts of opportunities for a Jewish educator to engage the student in spiritual reflection and spiritual growth. Acknowledging works such as these and using them as departure points for additional conversations and explorations should be commonplace in Jewish education.

Image 4 was submitted jointly by two students in response to a seventh grade Jewish studies assignment entitled, "Where Do You Find God?" The image reproduced here is a small part of a much larger piece that illustrated a biblical passage from I Kings 19:11–13, where Elijah encounters God as a "soft murmuring sound." Interestingly, while the biblical passage makes it clear that God is *not* in the wind, *not* in the earthquake, and *not* in the fire, the students constructed their artwork (which includes wind, earthquake, and fire) by writing the word "god" repeatedly. Reading their image suggests that God *was* in these natural occurrences. This reading appears to be in tension with the biblical text. At the same time the students offered the following statement with their artwork:

> God is everywhere. In a rambunctious crowd God is that small, still, and silent voice. God is the spark or ember that causes the wildfire. God is the cause of the tornado and the earthquake. God caused these things but wasn't in them. It's not the big things but the little things that count. God just is.

The relational consciousness context of this work is clearly that of child-god.[12] When I read this piece I can hear the student artists philosophizing about the nature of God. It's hard to determine how much conviction or certainty they bring to their conclusion that "God just is." One of the processes associated with relational consciousness is "forcing a conclusion."[13] It seems like the tension between the image, where God is literally in the fire and the earthquake, and the artist statement, where God is the cause without

Image 4. "The Still Small Voice"

being "in" them, is prematurely resolved. The statement, "It's not the big things but the little things that count" seems like a falling back on a truism from a parent or teacher rather than a deep synthesis of the theological point. All of this sits comfortably within the relational consciousness framework of child-god. How grateful would any Jewish educator be to encounter two students who were engaged in such meaty theological reflection?

Implications for Jewish Spiritual Education

One of the key insights of the relational consciousness framework is that it makes spirituality a universal feature of the human experience. Many adults cling to the notion that true spirituality resides only in those children and early adolescents who demonstrate a certain measure of genius or precociousness in their spiritual acumen. Rather than preserving spirituality as the special domain of a few highly sensitive individuals relational consciousness is accessible to all children and adolescents. This allows for growth and development so that spirituality can be found in even the most inchoate relationships and awareness as they become patterns of meaning making.

Another benefit of the relational consciousness framework is that it offers a shared language for Jewish educators to adopt in regards to spirituality. Jewish schools, camps, and synagogues are uniquely positioned to promote spiritual growth and spiritual education. However obvious and assumed this may be, the fact of the matter is that spirituality is not being consistently taught or promoted. This is likely due, in part, to the fact that there is not agreement about what spirituality is. It is also likely due to the fact that many educators do not feel the need or the responsibility to educate children spiritually. By placing an emphasis on relationships it should be possible for all educators in Jewish institutions to rally around the idea of recognizing and promoting spiritual growth. Some educators may be more comfortable and more equipped to help students grow in relationship to "self"; others may be better at helping students explore their relationship with other people or with God; but all educators should become accustomed to listening for spirituality in their students.

Listening to our students, particularly during early adolescence, can be transformative for religious educators. Our task is to ensure that formal religion can be a vehicle for individual spiritual growth. To use Hay and Nye's vocabulary, we must figure out how a socially mediated religious experience like *t'filah* can be meaningful to the individual child with his/her individual personal signature. We must also figure out how to infuse our houses of learning with a deep appreciation for relational consciousness. When we see examples of student artwork and coursework, we can use them as a platform for engaging in discussion with students, parents, and colleagues. We can shine a light on spirituality and ensure that it flourishes in our midst.

Notes

1. David Hay and Rebecca Nye, *The Spirit of the Child*, rev. ed. (London and Philadelphia: Jessica Kingsley Publishers, 2006).
2. Most notably: Michael Shire, "Spirituality: The Spiritual Child and Jewish Childhood," in *International Handbook of Jewish Education: International Handbooks of Religion and Education*, vol. 5, ed. Helen A. Miller, Lisa D. Grant, and Alex Pomson (New York: Springer, 2011), 301–18.
3. Hay and Nye, *Spirit of the Child*, 25.
4. Ibid., 49.
5. Ibid., 94
6. Ibid., 109.
7. Ibid.
8. Ibid., 114.
9. Ibid.
10. Ibid.
11. Ibid.
12. Ibid.
13. Ibid.

Storytelling and Spirituality: Sacred and Shared between Generations

Peninnah Schram

According to legend, just before a child's birth, an angel gently strikes the place just above the middle of the child's upper lip in order to erase all of the Torah learning its soul had learned in the womb. It is said that is why humans have a slight indentation above the upper lip and must spend the rest of their life relearning Torah. Doing so nourishes the *n'shamah* (soul/spirit), as food nourishes the body. Judaism relates the quality of one's soul to one's performance of mitzvot, to reaching higher levels of understanding, and to feeling a closeness to God. It is our *n'shamah* that makes us human (*Midrash Tanchuma, P'kudei* 3).

This search for learning Torah is the search for spiritual learning through the sacred stories we have in our Jewish oral and written traditions. It is a search to know "our" family stories, both our personal family and our greater Jewish family, so that we feel connected to a group. However, there is an additional dimension to this search, namely, to connect to some force beyond ourselves and, yet, within ourselves. As it says in Torah: "And let them make Me a sanctuary that I may dwell among them" (Exod. 25:8). Avivah Gottlieb Zornberg comments, "The essential space is the space within the human heart."[1]

If we open ourselves to spirituality, God dwells within each of us and among all of us. By bringing these dimensions into our

PENINNAH SCHRAM, storyteller, is professor of Speech and Drama at Yeshiva University. She is the author of twelve books of Jewish folktales. The anthology *Mitzvah Stories* was published in her honor. She is a recipient of the prestigious Covenant Award for Outstanding Jewish Educator awarded by the Covenant Foundation and the National Storytelling Network's Lifetime Achievement Award. For an annotated bibliography of collections of Jewish stories and recordings, e-mail Peninnah1@aol.com.

lives, we can become more compassionate people who perform mitzvot (acts of loving-kindness and righteous deeds). It is in hearing shared stories, sacred and secular, that we learn to empathize with others and reach out to them.

In other words, we learn in Leviticus 11:13, 19, that the *chasidah* (a bird that Rashi identifies as the stork) is an "abomination" because the *chasidah* is kind only to its own species and not to any others. This bird is to be "detestable unto you" since selfishness is not an admirable Jewish trait.

Where and what are these stories? To begin, Jews have a great treasure of sacred literature that encompasses both Written Law (*Torah Shebichtav*) and the Oral Law (*Torah Shebal Peh*). In addition to Torah, Talmud, and midrashim, we have a rich secular oral tradition including folktales, fairytales, fables, parables, tall tales, mystical and supernatural tales, as well as other genres. All of these Jewish stories—or Jewish variants of world folktales—contain what Jews have always considered significant, specifically, the faith, values, traditions, history, geography, and customs of the Jewish people. As folklorist Richard Dorson has stated in his Foreword to Dov Noy's *Folktales of Israel*, "Among the Jewish people the telling of stories and the learning of the faith are interwoven in a manner unparalleled in other countries of Western civilization."[2]

Through all of these stories, sacred and secular, we transmit the spirituality of the Jewish people, namely, the relationship of a person to God and one person to another. As folklorist Angelo S. Rappoport wrote in *The Folklore of the Jews*, "The Folklore of the Jews is distinguished from that of other nations, primitive and even civilized, by its *monotheistic* and *ethical* background."[3] All of the stories, songs, and proverbs mirror the soul of our people painting a composite portrait of who we are as a Jewish people.

In this essay, I will explore the power, importance, and spirituality of storytelling. I will also focus on the relationship between the storyteller and the story listener. There is no substitute for the voice of a parent, rabbi/educator, or young people telling one another stories. After all, the voice is produced by breath (*n'shamah*). In Latin, breath is *spiritus*, which can also mean inspiration, from *spirare*, to breathe. We can then see how breath/inspiration and voice are tied together in order to bring forth feeling and bring to life an idea or action. In this way, by telling and listening to stories the storytelling educators and listeners breathe together with their hearts beating in synchronicity. By telling stories "by heart," the teacher does not present the lesson as a linear straightforward speech, but rather in an inspired, fluctuating, undulating, interactive, fluid manner reaching into the heart (the "seat of memory").

According to the Torah, the Talmud, and folklore, the heart is considered to be the seat of wisdom combining both the cognitive and affective realms. "A man's whole wisdom is in the heart" (*Kohelet Rabbah* 1:7). In addition, the heart is also considered the seat of memory and recollection (Deut. 4:9). When I use the term "by heart," what I mean is that the story comes from a deep place within us with bridges to sensual associations, feelings, connections, and secrets that we make and keep in our memory. Stories transmit the experiences, history, and lessons of past generations. This is part of the teaching that Moses passes on to the Israelites in Deuteronomy 31:13, "Their children, too, who have not had the experience, shall hear and learn to revere the Lord your God as long as they live in the land that you are about to cross the Jordan to possess." So we are all called to be "holders of the story" in order to keep alive the wisdom of the past.

Storytelling is the most human activity. People have an urge to tell someone about an adventure, where they were when there was a crisis, when they experience a life-cycle moment, and on and on. What happens after the shared telling? Most often, the storytellers experience a catharsis. Tears of joy or sadness shared in community offer healing and hope with a perspective that restores the energy for life. Telling the story can possibly illumine options and alternative approaches to resolve negative emotions. Above all, the story becomes part of that person's history and a shared experience with the listeners.

As Roger Schank writes, "We need to tell someone else a story that describes our experiences because the process of creating the story also creates the memory structure that will contain the gist of the story for the rest of our lives. Talking is remembering."[4] Talking sets the story in the heart. The word "ear" is embedded in both words: hear and heart. Thus, we tell stories with the voice from the heart to reach the ears and hearts of others. Telling stories is sharing.

The philosopher Walter Benjamin, in his essay "The Storyteller," wrote: "The storyteller takes what he tells from experience—his own or that reported by others, and he in turn makes it the experience of those who are listening to his tale."[5] In effect, storytelling promotes a dialogue among the storyteller, story, and listener.

Scholars in the field of communication are discovering that the oral transmission of tales is literally mind-expanding. In his *Scientific American* article entitled "Paleoneurology and the Evolution of Mind," Harry Jerison states, "We need language more to tell stories than to direct actions." He continues:

> In the telling we create mental images in our listeners that might normally be produced only by the memory of the events as recorded and integrated by the sensory and perceptual systems of the brain.
> . . . The role of language in human communication is special because we have the vocal and manual apparatus to create spoken and written language. In hearing or reading another's words we literally share another's consciousness, and it is that familiar use of language that is unique to man. The point, however, is that it was necessary to have a brain that created the kind of consciousness communicated by the motor mechanisms of language. That new capacity required an enormous amount of neural tissue, and much of the expansion of the human brain resulted from the development of language and related capacities for mental images.[6]

More recent research by interpersonal neurobiologists has found and confirmed that there are dynamic changes to the structure and functioning of the brain as a result of relationships and shared narratives. In her article "Neuroscience and Spirituality: Implications of Interpersonal Neurobiology for a Spirituality of Compassion," Andrea Hollingsworth develops four criteria as components of a "spirituality of compassion." Hollingsworth's fourth criterion focuses on the importance and power of shared narrative, reinforcing the findings of Walter Benjamin and Harry Jerison, quoted above:

> Telling our own story to someone else, or listening to someone narrate his or her story, asks us to be affected by and share in the state of the hearer or speaker in such a way that we hold on to our own perspective even as we attempt to indwell the experience of the other person. Shared narratives, therefore, are the fourth condition for the emergence of empathy in humans and constitute the fourth component of a spirituality of compassion.
> Stories are naturally bound up within human spirituality; speaking, reading, and/or hearing sacred narratives from our

traditions are at the heart of many of our experiences of the divine . . .The combination, therefore, of neural integration and empathic connection with others and self, and deep personal meaning and transcendent participation, means that storytelling holds potential to raise us to greater levels of concern for the pain of others and motivate us to stand in solidarity with those who are suffering by weaving their stories into the fabric of our own.[7]

In Bruce Feller's article "The Stories That Bind Us," he reports on research by psychologists Drs. Marshall and Sara Duke. They found that children with learning disabilities who knew about their family's history were more resilient when they encountered challenges and dealt with stress. According to Dr. M. Duke, "The answers have to do with a child's sense of being part of a larger family." In other words, children who knew their family narrative "know they belong to something bigger than themselves...Talking also means telling a positive story about yourselves...The bottom line: If you want a happier family, create, refine and retell the story of your family's positive moments and your ability to bounce back from the difficult ones. That act alone may increase the odds that your family will thrive for many generations to come."[8]

We may apply this paradigm to the Jewish people and the telling of our stories. Our Torah and our entire history contain stories about how we did well and succeeded and also how we wrestled with problems and defeats. Yet, we bounced back—we survived—and continued on as a united community of Jews all around the world. When we know our history, when we understand that we belong to the Jewish People, that there is a force beyond ourselves, and yet within each of us, that we are not alone in the world, we create group immortality by living and telling our stories. We tell our stories in order to live a life filled with compassion leading to ethical behavior.

In order to make these connections, I will summarize three inspiring stories in the oral and written traditions. They illustrate how nonlinear and nonthreatening teaching can integrate shared experiences and introduce children and adults to the deeper meaning of rituals and performance of mitzvot.

As Elie Wiesel has said, "I'd rather share than teach." While teaching means reaching out, the sharing of stories becomes an interactive connection that goes beyond teaching. These folk and personal narratives are retained in the imagination, connect to what we learn in Torah, and expand empathetic feelings and lessons into our new consciousness.

I.

In Genesis 18:2–8, Abraham welcomes his three guests and offers them hospitality. In verse 16, Abraham sees that they are ready to depart: "The men set out from there and looked down toward Sodom, Abraham walking with them to see them off." From this verse, we understand the mitzvah of accompanying our guests a certain distance when they are leaving our home.

How does one begin practicing such a mitzvah? Rabbi Benji Levene has written a deeply moving story about his grandfather, Reb Aryeh Levin, the Tzaddik of Y'rushalayim, who always escorted his guests from his home to the main road. He would also accompany someone to help a person find the right destination.

His story is entitled "The Escort." As a young rabbinical student in Jerusalem, Benji read an article in an Israeli newspaper and learned of his grandfather's practice of accompanying guests to the main road. His father tells Benji how his own father, Reb Aryeh, many years before, had promised to deliver a message to the wife of a Jewish man who had been taken prisoner by the British. This Jew had been fighting in the underground to help establish a Jewish state in the Land of Israel. However, when Reb Aryeh could not find the right street, he knocked on the door of a house hoping to get directions. Upon hearing his request, the young woman brought Reb Aryeh directly to the right address.

Reb Aryeh asked her why she had taken him instead of just giving him directions, especially when it was close to Shabbat. She told him the story how, when her father was near death, he had told his children, gathered around his bed, that a person doesn't take honors or wealth when s/he leaves the world—a person only takes the mitzvot s/he performed in life. He tells his children to continue doing mitzvot but to also choose one special mitzvah that they would do whenever possible, even when difficult. This young woman selected the mitzvah of escorting people to where they needed to go. Reb Aryeh's request gave her the opportunity to fulfill this mitzvah.

When Reb Aryeh heard this, he wrote in his notebook how he had learned from a young woman an important lesson of fulfilling this commandment of accompanying people to where they needed to be. When Benji heard this about his grandfather, he decided to also choose this same special mitzvah for himself.

A few evenings later, Benji noticed an old man looking lost on a street in Jerusalem. He found out that the man was looking for a specific street and Benji wondered whether God was testing him so soon. He immediately took the man directly to the place he had been searching for. The man asked him why Benji had taken time to do this, especially since young people are always in such a hurry. Benji replied that it was because his grandfather always performed this mitzvah. The old man was curious to know who his grandfather was and when he found out, he was amazed because he was the reporter who had written the just-published article about Reb Aryeh. Now Reb Aryeh's grandson was escorting him through the streets of Jerusalem. Benji told him, "And do you know why? Because Reb Aryeh's grandson read your stories and learned how important and beautiful it is to escort another person on his or her way."[9]

This story, "The Escort," teaches us several lessons we can transfer to our own lives. First of all there is the theme of hospitality that should not end by closing the door just as the guest steps out of the house. Secondly, it is wonderful to help others who have lost their way. We can also see how important it is to choose a special mitzvah to perform whenever possible.

I would like to suggest the "special" mitzvot of:

1. listening and reading stories of family elders, including survivors of the Shoah (Holocaust)
2. asking questions, as Benji did in the story
3. retelling stories

Here are some kinds of follow-up questions you might ask of the elders:

1. What wisdom would you want to transmit to the next generation?
2. What mitzvot have you done or had performed for you during your life?
3. What mitzvot did you see fulfilled by someone else?
4. What stories did you hear in your family or school that influenced how you act in the world?

Let me illustrate this last question. While stories teach us, it is also the voice of the storyteller that creates the bond between the story and the listener. In the book *Mothers, Sisters, Resisters: Oral Histories of Women Who Survived the Holocaust*, one account moved me very deeply because of the role of story within the story. Rose Muth, while in Auschwitz, tells of relating parables to her sister that their father had told her. The remembered parable served as a blessing and a focus that helped Rose Muth and her sister survive:

> I had told her things that my father said. He prepared us for the hardship . . . through *meshalim* he gave us courage and taught us how to live in spite of difficulties.
>
> Just before we were separated, before we went to Wadowice, my father took us four girls aside. He told us a parable of two men. They were tired of life. They had difficulties and problems. They went to a river, stood on the bridge, and contemplated suicide. One of the men courageously jumped into the water and was gone. The other one shivered and went away. Which was the coward and which was the brave man? Of course, as children, we said it was the one who had the courage to jump into the river.
>
> My father said, "No, you're wrong. The one who took up the fight and continued to live and fight for what he wanted, this one was the brave man." I had told this to Estusia before, and she kept on repeating it to me. Other things that he told us made us have faith, to believe that some good would come of it. I feel that it was my father's blessing that helped me survive.[10]

Walter Benjamin said, "All this points to the nature of every real story. It contains, openly or covertly, something useful. The usefulness may, in one case, consist in a moral; in another, in some practical advice; in a third, in a proverb or maxim . . . To seek this counsel one would first have to be able to tell the story . . . Counsel woven into the fabric of real life is wisdom."[11]

We never know when we will need the wisdom given to us in the most beautiful way through a story. Therefore, stories must fill the storehouse of memory from early childhood on to help us live, feel connected to, and transmit our Jewish faith and values.

II.

Tears! A string of tears threads itself through the last four *parashiyot* of Genesis, which tell the story of Jacob and Joseph and his brothers.

Heartbreaking tears become transformed into hopeful, joyous tears. I recall that I had been told, a long time ago, that tears produced by sorrow and those produced by joy have different chemical compositions. Nevertheless, interwoven throughout—and in folklore too—is a mystical connection between tears and rain.

I remember that when I was a child my father used to tell me the story of Jacob and Joseph and the coat of many colors, or he would ask me to read the story to him. Every time the brothers showed the coat drenched in goat-blood and told their father of not finding Joseph, my own father would weep. I didn't understand what those tears meant. How could a child understand this emotion. But I now know that those tears were a gift and a deep memory.

This *parashah*, *Mikeitz*, opens "at the end of" two full years of Joseph's imprisonment. So we see that with endings there are new beginnings. Pharaoh has his now-famous dreams, which Joseph interprets with precision. As a result, Pharaoh appoints him his overseer. After seven years of plenty, the predicted famine arrives. No rains fall. Food is only available in the storehouses of Egypt, thanks to Joseph.

In this *parashah*, there are two deeply moving passages that connect to tears. The first is in Genesis 42:1: "Now Jacob saw that there was corn in Egypt, and Jacob said unto his sons: 'Why do you look one upon another?'"

At a time when food is scarce and people famished, how hard is it for a parent to see the children hungry? *Midrash HaGadol* (compiled by Rabbi Dovid al-Aldeni in the thirteenth century) notes that what we can learn from Jacob's story is that it is a parent's worst trial to have their children ask for food when there is nothing to give. No doubt Jacob shed tears at those moments.

This reminds me of a story, "The Gates of Tears," a folktale from Syria collected in the Israel Folktale Archives, that connects tears and rain in a compelling way. Versions of this story—with the theme of *"Rachmana liba ba-ei"* (God wishes the heart)—can be found in Ashkenazi and Sephardic folklore traditions and it is found only in Jewish literary and oral traditions.

There was a drought, but prayers and fasting by the rabbis and community did not bring rain to the land. One night the rabbi dreamed that he should ask Rachamim to pray for rain. Rachamim was a poor illiterate man and the rabbi could not believe the dream. However, he finally asks Rachamim to lead the prayers.

Immediately Rachamim leaves the synagogue and soon returns carrying a small clay pitcher with two spouts. On the bimah, as the ark is opened, Rachamim whispers something into one of the spouts. Then he holds the other spout up to his ear. Instantly dark clouds cover the sky and a heavy rain begins to fall.

When the rabbi asks Rachamim what he had done to bring the rain, he tells the rabbi how he sees his children going to bed hungry at night and he sheds tears that he collects in this special clay pitcher. He had also asked his wife to bury this tear-filled pitcher with him when he died. So he spoke to God in the first spout threatening to shatter the pitcher that was filled with his bitter tears, the outpouring of his soul, if God would not bring rain. He then turned the pitcher to listen and heard God say, "Do not shatter the pitcher."

The rabbi wept and concluded, "It is because of your tears that the rains came. How true are the words of our Sages: 'The Gates of Tears are never locked.'"[12]

Returning to the *parashah*, perhaps it was Joseph's tears that were needed to release the rains. Perhaps during the years of famine Joseph's heart hardened without nourishment since it was a time without rain, a time without tears. It was a time when he was alone without family and love, experiencing a sense of betrayal by those whom he trusted and loved. Nevertheless, when Joseph sees his half-brothers, and hears them express regret amongst themselves for what they had done to Joseph, "he turned away from them and wept" (Gen. 42:24). Sforno posits that these tears were because of his compassion for their distress. Joseph discovered empathy for his brothers. As it says in midrash, "only tears extinguish the burning coals of the heart."[13]

When Joseph could not weep, his heart, like the earth, remained dry and could not produce the human contact to bring about a family reunion, even with his beloved father. Only when Joseph could release his tears, then the reunion of the family, and between heaven and earth, were complete. I like to imagine that a good rain fell that night.

In a *New York Times* article, "I Cry, Therefore I Am," by Michael Trimble, he writes, "More recently, we've learned from neuroscience that certain brain circuits are activated rapidly and unconsciously, when we see another in emotional distress. In short, our brain evolved circuits to allow us to experience empathy and compassion, which in turn made civilization, and an ethics based on compassion, possible."[14]

III.

Tears as a result of seeing someone emotionally distressed is beautifully expressed in "The Princess Who Wanted to See God.": Molly Cone wrote this story to illustrate the Second Commandment: "You Shall Have No Other Gods—Only Me" found in Exodus 20:3. Let me summarize her story up to the closing climactic interaction between the princess and the wise old man:

> There once was a princess who had never cried because she always got what she wanted so there never was a reason to cry. One day she told her father, the king, that she demanded to see God. The king called the Chief of Law and Order but he could only show her a book of laws and punishments. Then her father called the Treasurer but he could only show her a room full of gold. Finally the king tried to find God himself, but never having searched for God he didn't know how to find God. He began to walk on a path away from the palace when he met an old man planting a fruit rree. When the king asked if the old man would live long enough to eat the fruit of the tree, the old man responded, and added "God willing, that is." The king asks the old man if he could show God to the princess. The old man agrees and asks the princess to visit someone. The princess goes reluctantly with the old man to a small shabby cottage. When she steps inside, she sees a young girl who is very poor but smiling as she remains seated. When the princess discovers that the girl cannot walk, the princess quickly leaves the cottage and follows the old man silently back to the palace.

This ending is taken directly from Molly Cone's story:

> When they reached the palace hall, the old many turned to her.
> "Are you ready?" he said.
> "Ready? For what?" asked the princess. She had been so busy thinking of the other girl that she had forgotten all about herself.
> The old man smiled. "You are ready," he said. To the princess' surprise, he put a mirror in her hand.
> "Now close your eyes, hold up the mirror, and look deep into your heart."
> The princess closed her eyes and held up the mirror. Suddenly tears began to roll down the cheeks of the princess who had never cried. Big, solf, wet tears.

STORYTELLING AND SPIRITUALITY

Why are you crying? asked the old man.

"I have been selfish all my life," she cried, "and I did not know it until I saw that poor girl." She put the mirror down and opened her eyes. "Oh, sir, do you think it would help if I brought her some good soup, and maybe a pretty dress to wear? Do you think that would help?"

The old man smiled. He took the mirror from her hand and put it carefully away.

"You have seen God," he said.[15]

In this story, the tear is an important symbol of understanding and repentance. Instead of talking about forgiveness, about what God looks like, the story shows it in ways that a child can visualize. The story has the power to change the way we talk about God.

These are some questions that the storyteller might ask after the telling: Have you ever searched for God? What does God look like? Have you ever cried over something serious or sad? Who helped comfort you? Was the dilemma resolved? What effect did the tears have on you and on others around you?

Whenever I come to the end of the Molly Cone story, I lower my eyes and keep silent for a few moments. I need time to make the transition to where I am physically. I know the listeners need the time, too. They have been on a journey with me. They have followed the search for God along with the princess, a young, selfish, and demanding spoiled child. The people in the audience need time to let the story settle into their minds and form the images in their mental storehouses.

The solution to the search is simply but effectively presented by the old man. He is an example, much needed in our society, of the older generation who has been there and who has so much to teach us and to hand down to us about the way we need to conduct our lives. A child listening to this story is able to react with empathy. If followed by a discussion, children can perhaps identify an elder to whom they go for comfort and/or advice when their heart is breaking.

Storytelling is a sacred responsibility that affects another's consciousness, emotions, and knowledge. Through hearing shared narratives we activate empathy and compassion. These emotions fill the *n'shamah* with wisdom, experience, memory, and meaning. We do this most effectively by telling stories face to face. We take this teaching from Exodus 33:11, "And *YHVH* would speak to Moses face to face, as a man speaks to his neighbor."

In this age of digital technology, young people's attention spans are changing and shortening. There is an ever-greater demand for instantaneous responses/answers. Their listening skills are being short-changed as well as the pleasure of interpersonal conversations. Yet, I maintain that, in spite of or because of these electronic devices, we need, more than ever, human interaction and sense experiences that come through the imagination and are evoked within the stories. It is through the senses that one recalls emotions. It is the emotions that cause one to act in concert with one's own group and to integrate the aspirations of the individuals with the ideals of their community.

The relationship between the storyteller and the story listener is dynamic, reciprocal, alive, spontaneous, and "in the moment." The response of the listener creates an energy that makes the story potent. The teller can adjust his/her voice, eye contact, and body language to make the experience personal and positive, and, thus, affect the listener forever. This transmission is not of facts but of an ability to make connections. It's a reciprocal process between two or more people in which there is mutual contact and trust. It's a shared story experience.

Everyone loves stories. Everyone has stories to tell. We can start by asking the young people about the stories of their names. In Judaism, we each have three names: the name given to us, the name others give us, and the name we give ourselves. Ask what is your name, your nickname, your Hebrew name, etc. Do you have a secret pet name used only by your parents or special friends? (No one need disclose that private name.) Why were you given those names? How did the parents choose that specific spelling of your name? Who were you named after? Tell us (or find out) who that person was and what characteristics that person had. If the name is a form of a biblical name, who was the biblical character and what were his/her characteristics and qualities? What kind of role models would they be for you?

Ask the students to remember what stories were their favorite as younger children. What story did they ask their parents to tell or read again and again? Write out the story as they recall it—before going back to the written or oral source of that story.

For those young people who are more visual learners, they might draw the story they love or of an experience in picture form as though it were a comic strip or drawing board. Then they can retell the story based on the drawings.

In our Jewish oral and written traditions comprising our *morashah* (heritage), we have a great treasure of stories of every genre. These stories, sacred and secular, transmit the faith, the values, traditions, and history of the Jewish people. They inspire and deepen the spirituality of the Jewish people, namely the relationship of a person to God and one person to another. Stories have the power to call forth deep emotions and move us to act, to engage in *tikkun olam*. Stories influence children and adults to live a life of *menschlichkeit*. I define a "mensch" as a compassionate resourceful hope-filled reaching-out-to-others *human* being.

I firmly believe that each one of us should and must wear that mantle of responsibility to transmit the stories of our own families and our Jewish people to the next generation in a most beautiful interactive way of teaching. We must tell stories—face to face—with our God-given gift of our human voices and listen to each other's stories. The voice is the messenger of the heart.

Notes

1. Avivah Gottlieb Zornberg, *The Particulars of Rapture: Reflections on Exodus* (New York: Doubleday, 2001), 332.
2. Richard Dorson, "Foreword," in *Folktales of Israel*, ed. Dov Noy (Chicago: The University of Chicago Press, 1963), v.
3. Angelo S. Rappoport. *The Folklore of the Jews* (London: The Soncino Press, 1937), 5.
4. Roger Schank, *Tell Me a Story: A New Look at Real and Artificial Memory* (New York: Charles Scribner's Sons, 1990), 115.
5. Walter Benjamin, "The Storyteller," in *Illuminations: Essays and Reflections*, ed. with intro. by Hannah Arendt (New York: Schocken Books, 1969), 87.
6. Harry Jerison, "Paleoneurology and the Evolution of Mind," *Scientific American* 234 (January 1976): 101.
7. Andrea Hollingsworth, "Neuroscience and Spirituality: Implications of Interpersonal Neurobiology for a Spirituality of Compassion," *Zygon* 43, no.4 (December 2008): 837–60. I would like to thank Dr. Gerald Katzman for bringing this article to my attention.
8. Bruce Feller, "The Stories That Bind Us," *New York Times*, Sunday Styles, March 17, 2013. This article was adapted from his book *The Secrets of Happy Families: How to Improve Your Morning, Rethink Family Dinner, Fight Smart, Go Out and Play, and Much More.*

9. Benji Levene, "The Escort," in *Mitzvah Stories: Seeds for Inspiration and Learning*, ed. Goldie Milgram and Ellen Frankel, with Peninnah Schram, Cherie Karo Schwartz, and Arthur Strimling (Philadelphia: Reclaiming Judaism, 2011), 265–68. Rabbi Levene has given me permission to tell this story.

10. Brana Gurewitsch, ed., *Mothers, Sisters, Resisters: Oral Histories of Women Who Survived the Holocaust* (Tuscaloosa, AL: The University of Alabama Press, 1998), 304.

11. Benjamin, "The Storyteller," 86–87.

12. Peninnah Schram, "The Gates of Tears," in *Stories Within Stories: From the Jewish Oral Tradition* (Northvale, NJ: Jason Aronson, an imprint of Rowman and Littlefield, 2000), 49–53.

13. Louis Ginzberg, *The Legends of the Jews*, vol. 5 (Philadelphia: The Jewish Publication Society of America, 1909–38), 351 n. 244.

14. Michael Trimble, "I Cry, Therefore I Am," *New York Times*, Sunday Review, November 19, 2012.

15. Molly Cone, "The Princess Who Wanted to See God," in *Who Knows Ten?* (New York: Union of American Hebrew Congregations, 1965), 14–20. This book has been reissued by URJ. Molly Cone has given me permission to tell this story.

Poetry on the Theme of the Symposium

She Said Yes

Barbara AB Symons

She said yes
and engaged with words of Torah.
Amen.

And then it happened.
Her eyes were opened
and her heart closed a little.
The story isn't True?
Capital T.

A deep sadness crept out of her eyes
and her mouth formed words of mourning.
She missed the tales of childhood,
the hard facts of how Noah loaded the animals
and the sea parted.

Yet she stayed engaged with those words.
She wrestled harder.
She sought truths
with a small t.
Amen.

BARBARA AB SYMONS (NY94) has served congregations in New York, Connecticut, and Massachusetts and is currently serving as rabbi and director of Education at Temple David in Monroeville, Pennsylvania. She lives there with her husband, Rabbi Ron Symons, and three children.

Akiva

Joseph Black

Perched atop a darkened snowy roof
Night after night
He maintains his tenuous grip.
Shivering, steadying himself with thoughts of Eternity
He listens intently, envying the discourse
Unfolding beneath his whitened knuckles.

Below,
Warmed by the hearth-light,
The bearded ones busy themselves
In endless argument.
Encircled by rhetorical flourish,
Oblivious to the desperate balancing act
Occurring above their heads.

Truth-seeking all too often requires climbing.

Teachers must be ladders—
Bridging the gap between
The seekers and the sought
The tangled and the knot
Things remembered and forgot.

With word, laughter, praise, and rebuke,
We are raised
Rung by rung
to loftier realms.

JOSEPH BLACK (C87) is senior rabbi of Temple Emanuel in Denver, Colorado. He has published several poems as well as five CDs of original Jewish music, two children's books, a songbook, and two videos. He and his wife, Susan Black, have two children—Elana and Ethan.

Akiva, as the story goes, was discovered and embraced.
He descended from his precarious post
Joining the ranks of the initiated.
Yet every night he still dreamed of stars.

We, who follow in his footsteps
Must first overcome
Our fear of heights.

Hide and Seek

Brad L. Bloom

I happened upon a synagogue
Only to hide behind a nearby tree
Delighting in the joyous pandemonium of children
Playing hide-and-seek
Like wind-scattered leaves.

I am more than a witness to this game
For once I too hid as a child
And played these games
When hiding behind a tree
Or brushing off a half-buried
Stone meant the world to me.

I like to hide and seek
And experience the adrenaline
Pulsing through me as I was about
To seize upon my friend who
Thought I had lost his trail.
Then we would return to the shade
Of nearby trees soothing the strain
Of afternoon heat.

Soon it would be time
For the children in the playground
To leap body and soul
Into the words of the Torah
Where God hides and we seek,
Uncovering the hidden, sacred presence
Which lies between every corner and crack
Where children love to crawl.

BRAD L. BLOOM (C84) is the rabbi of Congregation Beth Yam in Hilton Head, South Carolina, and is currently pursuing a D.H.L. at HUC-JIR in Jewish history.

Morning Prayer

Tamara Cohen

I want to understand boys.
Really, I just want to love my son,
teach him, learn from him,
walk humbly together each day,
doing good.

"Mommy, Mommy, come quick!" he calls,
pajama clad and early morning delicious I find him,
whole body curled around a vase of wilting tulips
on last night's uncleared table,
his curious hands cradle three gossamer fallen petals on the
    sweet edge of rot.
"They are going to die," he says, "and go up to God."

And then it's back to bad guys and good guys
and "Mommy, Mommy, let's play push down."

And it seems I have spawned an alien creature of a culture not
    entirely my own,
his muted explosions and rocket fire another mother tongue.

And I don't know if the mother on the playground
who says she doesn't want to encourage the love of Power
    Rangers
has some grip on control that I don't,
but here we are in a city filled with small children playing
    superheroes and villains
and some of us have televisions and some of us don't,
and some of us own guns and some of us hold signs against
    them.

TAMARA COHEN is a writer, activist, and educator currently completing her rabbinical studies at the Reconstructionist Rabbinical College.

And each of us here before You,
no capes on our backs,
no golden lassos with promising gleam,
only our daily mistakes,
our hopes and fears.

Astronauts

Judy Katz

Night is when the big questions come.
Tucked into the top bunk
you call Heaven,
your sister fast asleep on Earth,
you wait for those final moments
before the day's gates close
to hurl your most pressing questions
into the dark...*When did time start?*
Where is everything that died?
One night you said if Dad and I had just been astronauts
we would have understood everything—
as if all the mysteries of living
would be perfectly clear
if only we could get enough distance.

Lying beside you, eyes closed, the night sky
opening within me, I felt myself floating
weightless, and I pictured the earth.
There were no trees or people or bread or cars.
It looked like that photo we've all seen
taken from space—the blue and green sphere
with veils of white around it. I found it wholly
unfamiliar, almost unlovable. In the dark
I felt your skinny arm next to mine.
We didn't say another word that night,
just lay there, drifting, with our questions.

JUDY KATZ's work has appeared in the *New York Times Book Review*, the *Women's Review of Books*, *Lilith Magazine*, *upstreet*, and other publications, and has twice been nominated for a Pushcart Prize. She currently teaches creative writing at the Heschel School in New York City.

Call for Papers: *Maayanot*

The CCAR Journal: The Reform Jewish Quarterly is committed to serving its readers' professional, intellectual, and spiritual needs. In pursuit of that objective, the *Journal* created a new section known as *Maayanot* (Primary Sources), which made its debut in the Spring 2012 issue.

We continue to welcome proposals for *Maayanot* —translations of significant Jewish texts, accompanied by an introduction as well as annotations and/or commentary. *Maayanot* aims to present fresh approaches to materials from any period of Jewish life, including but not confined to the biblical or Rabbinic periods. When appropriate, it is possible to include the original document in the published presentation.

Please submit proposals, inquiries, and questions to *Maayanot* editor, Daniel Polish, dpolish@optonline.net.

Along with submissions for *Maayanot*, the *Journal* encourages the submission of scholarly articles in fields of Jewish Studies, as well as other articles that fit within our Statement of Purpose.

The *CCAR Journal: The Reform Jewish Quarterly*
Published quarterly by the Central Conference of American Rabbis.

Volume LXI, No. 1. Issue Number: Two hundred thirty-nine.
Winter 2014

STATEMENT OF PURPOSE

The *CCAR Journal: The Reform Jewish Quarterly* seeks to explore ideas and issues of Judaism and Jewish life, primarily—but not exclusively—from a Reform Jewish perspective. To fulfill this objective, the Journal is designed to:

1. provide a forum to reflect the thinking of informed and concerned individuals—especially Reform rabbis—on issues of consequence to the Jewish people and the Reform Movement;

2. increase awareness of developments taking place in fields of Jewish scholarship and the practical rabbinate, and to make additional contributions to these areas of study;

3. encourage creative and innovative approaches to Jewish thought and practice, based upon a thorough understanding of the traditional sources.

The views expressed in the Journal do not necessarily reflect the position of the Editorial Board or the Central Conference of American Rabbis.

The *CCAR Journal: The Reform Jewish Quarterly* (ISSN 1058-8760) is published quarterly by the Central Conference of American Rabbis, 355 Lexington Avenue, 18th Floor, New York, NY, 10017. Application to mail at periodical postage rates is pending at New York, NY and at additional mailing offices.

Subscriptions should be sent to CCAR Executive Offices, 355 Lexington Avenue, 18th Floor, New York, NY, 10017. Subscription rate as set by the Conference is $100 for a one-year subscription, $150 for a two-year subscription. Overseas subscribers should add $36 per year for postage. POSTMASTER: Please send address changes to CCAR Journal: The Reform Jewish Quarterly, c/o Central Conference of American Rabbis, 355 Lexington Avenue, 18th Floor, New York, NY, 10017.

Typesetting and publishing services provided by Publishing Synthesis, Ltd., 39 Crosby Street, New York, NY, 10013.

The *CCAR Journal: The Reform Jewish Quarterly* is indexed in the *Index to Jewish Periodicals.* Articles appearing in it are listed in the *Index of Articles on Jewish Studies* (of *Kirjath Sepher*).

ISBN: 978-0-88123-212-7

GUIDELINES FOR SUBMITTING MATERIAL

1. The *CCAR Journal* welcomes submissions that fulfill its Statement of Purpose whatever the author's background or identification. Inquiries regarding publishing in the CCAR Journal and submissions for possible publication (including poetry) should be sent to the editor-elect, Rabbi Paul Golomb, Rabbi@Vassartemple.org.

2. Other than commissioned articles, submissions to the *CCAR Journal* are sent out to a member of the editorial board for anonymous peer review. Thus submitted articles and poems should be sent to the editor with the author's name omitted. Please use MS Word format for the attachment. The message itself should contain the author's name, phone number, and e-mail address, as well as the submission's title and a 1–2 sentence bio.

3. Books for review and inquiries regarding submitting a review should be sent directly to the book review editor, Rabbi Evan Moffic, at *emoffic@gmail.com*.

4. Inquiries concerning, or submissions for, *Maayanot* (Primary Sources) should be directed to the *Maayanot* editor, Rabbi Daniel Polish, at *dpolish@optonline.net*.

5. Based on Reform Judaism's commitment to egalitarianism, we request that articles be written in gender-inclusive language.

6. The *Journal* publishes reference notes at the end of articles, but submissions are easier to review when notes come at the bottom of each page. If possible, keep this in mind when submitting an article. Notes should conform to the following style:

a. Norman Lamm, *The Shema: Spirituality and Law in Judaism* (Philadelphia: Jewish Publication Society, 1998), 101–6. **[book]**

b. Lawrence A. Hoffman, "The Liturgical Message," in *Gates of Understanding*, ed. Lawrence A.Hoffman (New York: CCAR Press, 1977), 147–48, 162–63. **[chapter in a book]**

c. Richard Levy, "The God Puzzle," *Reform Judaism* 28 (Spring 2000): 18–22. **[article in a periodical]**

d. Lamm, *Shema*, 102. **[short form for subsequent reference]**

e. Levy, "God Puzzle," 20. **[short form for subsequent reference]**

f. Ibid., 21. **[short form for subsequent reference]**

7. If Hebrew script is used, please include an English translation. If transliteration is used, follow the guidelines abbreviated below and included more fully in the **Master Style Sheet**, available on the CCAR website at *www.ccarnet.org*:

"ch" for *chet* and *chaf* "ei" for *tzeirei*

"f" for *fei* "a" for *patach* and *kamatz*

"k" for *kaf* and *kuf* "o" for *cholam* and *kamatz katan*

"tz" for *tzadi* "u" for *shuruk* and *kibbutz*

"i" for *chirik* "ai" for *patach* with *yod*

"e" for *segol*

Final "h" for final *hei*; none for final *ayin* (with exceptions based on common usage): atah, Sh'ma, <u>but</u> Moshe.

Apostrophe for *sh'va nah*: b'nei, b'rit, Sh'ma; no apostrophe for *sh'va nach*.

Hyphen for two vowels together where necessary for correct pronunciation: ne-eman, samei-ach, <u>but</u> maariv, Shavuot.

No hyphen for prefixes unless necessary for correct pronunciation: babayit, HaShem, Yom HaAtzma-ut.

Do not double consonants (with exceptions based on dictionary spelling or common usage): t'filah, chayim, <u>but</u> tikkun, Sukkot.